JOHN

Over the centuries, John's Gospel has served to introduce many to Jesus and the Christian faith. This volume makes a wonderful companion to John's Gospel. Writing for the non-specialist, Dr Cook makes solid scholarship accessible for everyone. Well-written and insightful introductions, reflections, and study questions relate the Gospel to today's reader. I warmly recommend this stimulating and engaging volume.

Dr Andreas Köstenberger
Founder of Biblical Foundations™
Author of *A Theology of John's Gospel & Letters and John* (BECNT)

JOHN

Jesus Christ is God

William F. Cook

CHRISTIAN
FOCUS

William F. Cook III has taught New Testament for twenty-four years. For the past fifteen years at The Southern Baptist Theological Seminary in Louisville, Kentucky. In addition to his teaching, Dr Cook has been the Lead Pastor at The Ninth and O Baptist Church in Louisville for over fourteen years.

Copyright © 2016 William F. Cook

ISBN 978-1-78919-717-6

10 9 8 7 6 5 4 3 2 1

Printed in 2016
by
Christian Focus Publications Ltd.,
Geanies House, Fearn, Ross-shire,
IV20 1TW, Scotland, U.K.

www.christianfocus.com

Cover design by Daniel van Straaten

Printed and bound by
Bell & Bain, Glasgow

Contents

Preface

John's Gospel is the mature reflections of the last living apostle. John the apostle wrote this book approximately fifty-five years after the resurrection of Jesus. During those years he had reflected on the words and deeds of Jesus and the result is that the pages of the Gospel contain the seasoned thinking of one of Jesus' closest friends. When John wrote, not only did he think about what Jesus said and did, but he considered what it meant for his audience. The Fourth Gospel is not a distillation of abstract theological ideas, but a powerful presentation of the most magnificent life ever lived. It is also more than the recounting of historical events. John chose each scene with the utmost care and thought and presented it in a way that accomplished his overall purpose in writing (20:30-31).

I have written this commentary for the non-specialist, including those who are only beginning their study of the Fourth Gospel. I have sought to make my exposition straightforward and unencumbered by technical issues that can bog down one's initial study of the Gospel. As I wrote I kept in mind the layperson, the ministerial student, or even a pastor that wants a clear explanation of the biblical text. Furthermore, I have sought to make comments of relevant application to help the reader feel something of the Gospel's spiritual impact. Advanced students of the Gospel will be familiar with much of this material and will find that more technical commentaries delve more deeply into disputed matters. The footnotes indicate those who have had an impact on my understanding of the Gospel.

I am very grateful for the assistance Grayson Engleman provided by reading the manuscript and offering many recommendations that greatly improved the reading of it. In addition, I am thankful for the work of my former doctoral student, Dr Jason Mackey, who tracked down numerous references for me. I have had the privilege of teaching for these past fifteen years at The Southern Baptist Theological Seminary and am indebted to Dr Al Mohler and the Trustees for the sabbatical time to work on John's Gospel. Furthermore, I express heartfelt gratitude to The Ninth and O Baptist Church for the privilege of serving as their Lead Pastor and giving me the privilege of preaching through John's Gospel.

I would be amiss, however, not to dedicate this work to my wife, Jaylynn. She has been a constant source of love and encouragement to me for the past thirty-three years and especially in the completion of this commentary. She continues to be the godliest person I have ever known and the love of my life.

WILLIAM F. COOK
January 2016

A Brief Introduction to John's Gospel

Who was John the apostle?

John was one of the twelve disciples of Jesus. His name means 'Yahweh is salvation'. He was a son of Zebedee and a brother of the apostle James. Some have speculated that their mother was Salome. This connection comes by comparing Mark 15:40; 16:1 and Matthew 27:56. If she were the sister of Mary, Jesus' mother (John 19:25), then John and James would have been Jesus' maternal first cousins; however, this is far from certain. Traditionally five books of the New Testament are attributed to John: the Fourth Gospel, three Johannine epistles and the book of Revelation.

John is not referred to often in the New Testament, but it must be remembered that we do not know very much about the exploits of any of the apostles apart from Peter and Paul. When John does appear in the biblical witness he is usually in the company of others. It is learned in the Synoptic Gospels that John and James, along with Peter and Andrew, were four of the first disciples Jesus called to follow Him (Mark 1:19-20; Matt. 4:21-22; Luke 5:1-11). John and James had worked with their father in a successful fishing business, for they had 'hired servants' to help them (Mark 1:20).

John, along with James and Peter, were Jesus' 'inner circle'. They are found with Jesus on several significant occasions: at the resuscitation of Jairus' daughter (Mark 5:37); on the Mount of Transfiguration (Matt. 17:1); and in the Garden of Gethsemane (Mark 14:33). Unfortunately in the Garden they were overwhelmed with sorrow and fell asleep. What is significant, however, is that these were the men that Jesus wanted with Him at that moment of crisis. Furthermore, during the final week of Jesus' life, John is mentioned along with Peter, James and Andrew as asking Jesus about the time of the destruction of the temple and the end of the age (Mark 13:3-4). Jesus also entrusted to John and Peter the preparations for His final meal in the upper room (Luke 22:8).

The Synoptic Gospels provide additional insight into John's personality. His only recorded words in the Synoptic Gospels reveal something of an exclusive outlook: 'Teacher, we saw someone casting out demons in your name and we tried to prevent him because he was not following us' (Mark 9:38; Luke 9:49). Jesus rebuked him for his elitist attitude. On another occasion John and James wanted to call down fire on a Samaritan village that refused to show hospitality to Jesus (Luke 9:54). While their faith in God's power is commendable, their aggressive dispositions revealed their continued need to develop more of Jesus' character. It is not surprising that Jesus called James and John the 'Sons of Thunder' (*Boanerges*, Mark 3:17).

A similar incident occurred when John and James approached Jesus about sitting on His right and left in the kingdom (Mark 10:37). Jesus responded by telling them that these privileged positions were not His to give; however, Jesus predicted that they would drink the cup (of suffering) He would drink and be baptized with the baptism (of suffering) He would experience (Mark 10:35-40; Matt. 20:20-28). Jesus' words to them came to pass as James was the first apostle to be martyred (Acts 12:2) and the early chapters of Acts describe Peter and John being arrested. Toward the end of his life John would be exiled on the island of Patmos (Rev. 1:9).

In the book of Acts, John is listed among the twelve (Acts 1:13) and when James is executed the author notes that he was John's brother (Acts 12:2). Every other reference to John in Acts finds him in the company of Peter. John and Peter are described as healing a lame man on their way to the temple to pray (Acts 3:1ff). The religious leaders arrest them for preaching about the resurrection of Jesus (Acts 4:1ff). These leaders saw them as 'uneducated and untrained men', but by this they meant they lacked formal rabbinic training; however, they did recognize them as 'having been with Jesus' (Acts 4:13). Although commanded not to preach in the name of Jesus anymore, they demonstrated bravery by refusing to be silent. The last explicit reference to John in the book of Acts was when he and Peter were sent by the Jerusalem leadership to investigate the revival in Samaria under the ministry of Philip. When Peter and John laid their hands on the Samaritans they received the Holy Spirit (Acts 8:14). The only specific reference to John in the Pauline epistles is Galatians 2:9; when Paul described John, along with Peter and James (Jesus' half-brother), as a pillar of the Jerusalem church.

The apostle John is not mentioned by name in the Fourth Gospel; however, the 'sons of Zebedee' are referred to in John 21:2. Many evangelical scholars understand the individual referred to as the 'beloved disciple' in the book to be the apostle John (13:23; 19:26; 20:2; 21:7, 20, 24). The only person called 'John' in the Gospel is John the Baptist; however, his title ('the Baptist') is never used. This omission is highly unusual. However, since John the apostle is never mentioned by name there is no need to include 'the Baptist' to differentiate him from the apostle. Furthermore, Peter is associated with the beloved disciple in three instances (13:23-24; 20:2-9; 21:20-24) and a close connection between these two has been established in the Synoptic Gospels and Acts. Therefore, while the evidence is not beyond dispute it seems reasonable to assume that the 'beloved disciple' and the apostle John should be understood as the same person.

The 'beloved disciple' is first mentioned in the Gospel as leaning back on Jesus' breast at the Last Supper and asking Jesus to identify His betrayer (13:23). The Gospel of Mark (14:17) makes clear that this meal was reserved for the twelve. The beloved disciple's nearness to Jesus at the meal and the fact he could make inquiries for the other disciples indicates his relationship with Jesus was very close. As Jesus hung on the cross the beloved disciple along with Jesus' mother stood nearby (19:25-27). Jesus entrusted His mother into this disciple's care. Presumably this was because Jesus' brothers did not yet believe in Him. This makes even more sense if perhaps John and Jesus were cousins. On the resurrection morning the beloved disciple and Peter ran to see the empty tomb (20:3-10). After examining the empty tomb John left believing that Jesus was alive, but he did not understand at that time the resurrection from the Scriptures (20:9).

The beloved disciple was present when Jesus appeared to a group of disciples at the Sea of Galilee after His resurrection. After an unsuccessful night of fishing, Jesus asked them if they had caught anything. The beloved disciple recognized that it was Jesus standing on the shore speaking to them (21:7). Later, following a discussion between Jesus and Peter about the latter's death, Peter asked Jesus about the beloved disciple's future (21:22). Apparently some misinterpreted Jesus' response ('if I want him to remain until I come, what is that to you?') to mean that the beloved disciple would not die before Jesus' second coming (21:23). When these words were written the beloved disciple in all probability was near death.

A few matters of introduction to the Gospel

Strictly speaking the book is anonymous. Scholars believe the superscription ('According to John') was added about A.D. 125 to distinguish it from the other Gospels. The traditional understanding is that the Gospel was written by the apostle John in his old age. This view goes back to Irenaeus, Bishop of Lyons, in the late second century. Irenaeus claimed to have a link to the apostle John through Polycarp, the Bishop of Smyrna martyred in 156 at the age of eighty-six. In a letter preserved by the early church historian Eusebius, Irenaeus tells a friend how, as a young man, he sat at Polycarp's feet and heard him recount conversations with the apostle John and the instruction he received from the apostle.[1] We can imagine Polycarp as a young man listening intently and soaking in the teaching of the aged apostle.[2] While certainty is not a possibility, there is a consensus among evangelical scholarship that John wrote his Gospel in the mid-80s of the first century. There is also a consensus that he wrote his Gospel in Asia Minor, likely in or near Ephesus.

---

1. Eusebius, *Ecclesiastical History* 3.23.

2. Johannine authorship will be accepted for the Fourth Gospel in this commentary. Admittedly, Johannine authorship is a debated subject in biblical scholarship. For a full discussion of the topic, consult any good New Testament Introduction or any technical commentary.

John's purpose is stated plainly in 20:30-31: 'Therefore many other signs Jesus also performed in the presence of the disciples, which are not written in this book; but these have been written so that you may believe that Jesus is the Christ, the Son of God; and that believing you may have life in his name.' The manuscripts of the Greek text of the Gospel vary slightly here, in a way that allows some scholars to hold to an evangelistic purpose for the writing of the book and others to hold to a discipleship purpose. The variation affects the tense of the verb translated as 'may believe'. Some manuscripts have the Greek aorist subjunctive, which would allow for the paraphrase, 'may come to believe.' Other manuscripts have the present subjunctive, which would allow for the paraphrase, 'may keep on believing.' The latter suggests that John's primary audience is believers; while the former suggests a focus on converting unbelievers. One wonders if this may be putting too much weight on the significance of a verb tense. It may be better to allow for the overall narrative of the Gospel to be the main factor in determining if the purpose is evangelistic or discipleship. Carson makes a strong case for an evangelistic purpose for the Gospel.[3] I think, however, it is possible that John wrote with both thoughts in mind.[4] For instance, the Gospel likely would have been read in Christian house churches in Asia Minor. As the text was read, believers' faith in Christ would be greatly strengthened and their love for Him would grow deeper. They would also be better equipped to share their faith using the stories of Jesus they heard read from the Gospel. They would have learned how Jesus dealt with different kinds of people, and this would have helped them as they evangelized family and friends. Furthermore, it is not unlikely that there would have been seekers that would gather with family and friends to learn more about Jesus. As the Gospel was read and taught undoubtedly many would come to saving faith. Today many evangelistic Bible studies begin with the Gospel

---

3. D. A. Carson, Douglas J. Moo, and Leon Morris, *An Introduction To The New Testament* (Grand Rapids: Zondervan Publishing House, 1992), 168-72.

4. Craig L. Blomberg, *Jesus and the Gospels: An Introduction and Survey*, 2nd ed. (Nashville: B & H Academic, 2009), 196.

of John and many current seekers begin their search for Jesus there as well.

As one reads the Gospel one should continually return to John's purpose statement and ask, 'How does this scene fulfill John's intention?' John accomplishes his purpose in the stories he tells, in the statements of Jesus he records (for example, the 'I am' sayings), his presentation of Jesus' signs, and the recounting of Jesus' sermons. With every story, statement, sign, and sermon John wants his readers to know that 'Jesus is the Christ'.

1

Jesus Christ is God!

(John 1:1-18)

You can say almost anything you want about Jesus today, except that He is God. Most contemporary people, like most people in Jesus' day, find that thought offensive. If one believes that Jesus is God then they must believe what He says is true. To acknowledge that Jesus is God is to affirm that all other religions are false and that Christianity alone is true. This is exactly what John teaches in his prologue. John's prologue may be the most magnificent and beautiful passage in the Bible. There is no passage of comparable length that sets forth in grander fashion the deity and majesty of Jesus Christ.

The passage begins with a stirring announcement of Jesus' deity ('and the Word was God') and concludes in like fashion ('the only begotten God'). In between these two dramatic affirmations is a stunning declaration that the eternal Word became 'flesh and dwelt among us'. It is as if the aged apostle did not think that his readers could properly comprehend his story unless they understood from the very beginning that the central figure, Jesus Christ, is God. One cannot help but stand (or fall!) in speechless wonder before the Word made flesh. Scholarly discussion on the background and structure of the passage, although important, should not distract the reader from this spectacular presentation of our glorious Savior.

There are several questions that must be answered as the passage is examined: What is the structure of the passage?

What is the cultural and philosophical background to John's use of the term 'Word' (*logos*)? What is the main point John wants to communicate to his readers? As to the structure of the passage, some scholars have suggested that the prologue is an early Christian hymn the author incorporated into the Gospel. This is possible, but in its present form the prologue is a fitting introduction to many of the Gospel's principal themes. Others understand the prologue to be in the form of a chiasm (inverted parallelism).[1] Again, while this is certainly possible, the chiastic arrangement puts the emphasis of the passage in the wrong place – on mankind's response to the Word (1:12-13). The main thought of the passage is found in the affirmation of Jesus' deity. Therefore we should understand the structure to unfold along the lines of heightened prose.[2]

John identifies Jesus as 'the Word' (*logos*). The term *logos* had a conceptual background both in Greek philosophy and Judaism.[3] In Greek philosophy, the *logos* referred not only to the spoken word, but also to the unspoken word still in the mind – reason. When applied to the universe, it referred to the rational principle that brought order and unity to the cosmos. Others point to the similarities between John's *logos* and the personification of wisdom in the book of Proverbs and later Jewish wisdom literature (Prov. 8:22-31; Wisdom of Solomon). It is more probable that John's primary conceptual background is the Old Testament. In the Old Testament, God's word is the dynamic force of His will. God created the heaven and earth by His spoken word (Gen. 1:3; Ps. 33:6). God speaks, and His will is accomplished (Isa. 55:11). John was fully aware that the term would resonate with both his Jewish and Gentile readers.

As I have already suggested, I believe the main point of the passage is to declare the deity of Jesus Christ. Jesus is God, the

---

1. Craig L. Blomberg, *Jesus and the Gospels: An Introduction and Survey*, 2nd ed. (Nashville: B & H Academic, 2009), 247.

2. D. A. Carson, *The Gospel according to John*, Pillar New Testament Commentary (Grand Rapids: William B. Eerdmans Publishing, 1991), 113.

3. See Craig A. Evans, *Word and Glory: On the Exegetical and Theological Background of John's Prologue*, Journal for the Study of the New Testament Supplement Series, vol. 89 (Sheffield, England: Sheffield Academic Press, 1993) and Carson, *John*, 114-16.

preexistent creator who took on human flesh in order to make the unseen God visible and to provide a way of salvation for those who would believe in Him. One final thought: this passage should not be seen as disconnected from the rest of the chapter. In the prologue we hear John the apostle's witness to Jesus. In 1:19-34 we will hear the testimony of John the Baptist and in 1:35-51 the testimony of some of Jesus' earliest followers.

Jesus the Word and God (1:1-5)
John makes four dramatic points concerning the Word in these opening verses. First, he affirms twice the Word's preexistence with God (1:1a, 2). John's opening comments direct his readers back to the opening lines of the Bible in Genesis ('In the beginning…'). His point is that there has never been a moment in time or in eternity past when the Word did not exist.

Second, the thought that the 'Word was with God' suggests that the Word exists in the closet possible relationship to God, but at the same time is distinct from God (1:1b-2a).[4]

Third, John confesses that the Word 'is God'. In verse 2, John repeats the thought of the Word's eternality. His assertions are remarkable. Our familiarity with this passage has dulled its impact upon us. Jesus' deity is a battleground in our pluralistic age. You can say almost anything except that 'Jesus Christ is God'. Yet, this is the very thing John declares here.

Fourth, John continues by explaining that God created all things through the agency of the Word (1:3-5). He makes his point both positively (1:3a) and negatively (1:3b). This repetition of a thought is characteristic of Johannine style. His point is that there was nothing created that the Word did not create. John next introduces two of his major themes,

---

4. Cults like the Jehovah's Witnesses assert that 1:1c should be translated, 'and the Word was a god.' Sentences, however, of this form in the Greek (two nouns joined by a form of the verb 'to be') normally placed the article before the subject of the sentence, regardless of the word order. So the translation, 'the Word was God,' is the correct translation. This rule is often called Colwell's rule after the thorough examination by the Greek grammarian E. C. Colwell in 'A Definite Rule for the Use of the Article in the Greek New Testament,' *Journal of Biblical Literature* 52 (1933): 12-21. For a contemporary discussion, see Daniel Wallace, *Greek Grammar: Beyond the Basics* (Grand Rapids: Zondervan, 1996), 266-69.

'life' and 'light'[5] (1:4). These concepts tie back to the creation account in Genesis as well. All life and light, both physical and spiritual, come from the Word.

The first hint of the incarnation is described as 'a light shining in the darkness' (1:5). The evangelist alludes to trouble on the horizon. There is debate as to whether the darkness could not 'understand' (NIV, NASB) or 'overcome' (ESV, NLT, RSV) the light. Both thoughts can be argued from the content of the Gospel. It seems slightly more probable that John intends the idea of 'to overcome'.[6] The battle between darkness and light will be a major theme in the book. Light is closely associated with Jesus throughout the Gospel (3:19; 8:12; 9:5; 12:46). John's use of the present tense of the verb 'shining' may be his way of saying that even after fifty years the light of the Word still illuminates the darkness.

Jesus the Word and John the Baptist (1:6-8)

The second movement of the prologue is a contrast between John the Baptist and the Word. In this Gospel, the Baptist is referred to merely as John. In contrast, the Synoptic Gospels refer to him as John the Baptist. The difference likely has to do with the fact that in the Fourth Gospel John the apostle is never mentioned by name, and therefore there is no need to distinguish him from John the Baptist. The contrast between John the Baptist and the Word could not be stated any more plainly: 'There came a man sent from God' (1:6a). The Word has been described in terms of deity, while John is called 'a man'. But John is not any man – he is a man sent on a mission from God (1:6b).

The purpose of John's mission is 'to testify to' or 'to bear witness to the light'.[7] The thought of John as a witness is the

---

5. 'Life' is a key theme in John. He uses the term thirty-six times in the Gospel; no other New Testament book has it more than seventeen times.

6. See Carson, *John*, 138; Leon Morris, *The Gospel according to John*, New International Commentary on the New Testament, rev. ed. (Grand Rapids: William B. Eerdmans, 1995), 76.

7. 'Witness' is another key word introduced in the prologue. The noun ('witness' or 'testimony') is used fourteen times in the Gospel. By comparison, Matthew does not use it, Mark uses it three times, and Luke uses it once. John uses the verb ('to testify' or 'to bear witness') in the Gospel thirty-three times; in contrast, Matthew and Luke use it once and Mark does not use it.

most common characteristic of him in the Fourth Gospel. He is the first in a long line of witnesses to Jesus in this Gospel (cf. 5:31ff). The goal of the Baptist's testimony was that mankind might come to believe in the Word.[8] The apostle John makes an unusual comment when he notes that John the Baptist was not the light. This has led some to think that the Gospel was written in part against a John the Baptist cult (cf. Acts 19:1-10). However, the evidence for this is slight. It is reasonable, however, to assume that man's natural inclination to lift up powerful personalities to a dangerously high level may in part be the reason for the apostle's comment. Great men of God, like John the Baptist, are never comfortable with the spotlight on them but instead desire to direct people's attention to Jesus (cf. 1:29-35).

Jesus the Word Rejected and Accepted (1:9-13)
Scholars debate whether verse 9 belongs with verses 6-8 or with verses 10-13. I understand it to relate to the latter (NASB, ESV, NIV; contra NLT). Verses 9-13 introduce the thought of the incarnation ('coming into the world') and mankind's rejection and acceptance of the light (1:10-13). John the Baptist's witness was not to an abstraction, but to a person. The reference to Jesus as 'the true light' affirms Him as the authentic light over and against every false light.

The term 'world' (*kosmos*) is used three times in verses 9 and 10 and is especially important in John's Gospel.[9] *Kosmos* is used in several different ways in the Johannine literature: the material universe as the object of creation (John 1:10); Satan's system of priorities and thought focused upon the temporal (1 John 2:15-16); humankind (and the earth) as the object of God's love and redemptive plan (John 3:16); and the mass of unbelievers who are hostile to God's plan as a result of succumbing to Satan's system of priorities and thought (John 15:18). This is all the more astonishing when we consider that the 'world' in its rebellion is the object of

---

8. John uses the verb 'to believe' ninety-eight times in the Gospel, but he never uses the noun (faith).

9. The term 'world' is used seventy-eight times in the Gospel and another twenty-three times in 1 John; by contrast, the next largest occurrence is twenty-one times in 1 Corinthians and only forty-seven times in all of Paul's writings.

God's love (3:16), and the Father sent Jesus to give His life for the world (6:51) so that He may save it (3:17; 12:47). The phrase, 'the light enlightens every man,' is likely a reference to the general revelation through nature that exists as a result of the creative work of the Word (cf. 1:1-5; Rom. 1:19-20; Acts 17:27-31).

There are two main thoughts in verses 10-13. First, the stunning assertion of the world's rejection of the Word (1:10-11); and second, that those who believe in Him experience a new birth (1:12-13). The Word came into the world that He created, and mankind failed to recognize Him (1:10). Even worse, He came to His own people (Israel) and they did not receive Him (1:11). This is startling! The world the Word created did not recognize Him, and the people that waited for Him rejected Him. As the Jewish messiah He was not what they expected, or even what they wanted. They longed for a military leader and not a dying Savior.

However, all was not lost, for those who 'received him', that is 'believed in his name', 'he gave the right to become children of God' (1:12). John makes it clear that the work of being accepted into God's family is not the result of human decision (although there is a human element involved in 'believing' and 'receiving'), but it is the result of being 'born of God' (1:13a). John will elaborate on this supernatural birth in Nicodemus' encounter with Jesus. For now this acceptance should not be understood to be the result of family relationships or human initiative, but a divine work wrought by God in a person's heart (1:13b). John makes it clear at the very beginning of the Gospel that membership in God's family is by grace alone ('he gave the right').

The incarnation of Jesus the Word (1:14-18)

The final section of the prologue sets forth the incarnation of the Word as God's climatic revelation to mankind (cf. Heb. 1:1-4). Jesus is identified specifically with the Word for the first time in 1:17; however, John's audience would have known this from the opening lines. This theologically rich passage deserves considerable reflection. However, as theologically rich as it is, the primary message is straightforward. These verses, and indeed the entire prologue, are moving toward the definitive assertion that Jesus, the Word, is God come in human flesh.

Each phrase in this paragraph is the distillation of John's fifty years of theological reflection on the incarnation. His assertion that the Word 'became flesh' suggests that the Word existed before the incarnation, a thought John had established earlier. John chose to use the term 'flesh' rather than the more natural term 'body'. The term 'flesh' does not carry for John the same theological meaning found in Paul's writings. Rather, John is making a powerful comment concerning the incarnation, that the Word became flesh with all the frailty associated with being a human being (1:14a).

The fact that the Word 'dwelt among us' means that He did not remain aloof or separate from those He created, but instead He lived among them (1:14b). Even more importantly, the word translated 'dwelt' is used in the LXX in relationship to the tabernacle, and literally can mean 'to pitch the tent'. The tabernacle was the place where God manifested His glory to His people in the days before the building of the temple (Exod. 25:8-9; 33:7ff.). John is stating that God's glory is now manifested in the person of the Word. He writes that because the Word dwelt among them they were able to see God's glory (1:14b).

John continues by confessing that the Word is 'the one and only Son' (NIV) of the Father, 'full of grace and truth' (1:14c). The word often translated 'begotten' (KJV) does not mean that the Word did not exist before He was born.[10] Rather, the idea here is that Jesus the Word is the Father's Son in a way that no one else could ever be. The phrase 'from the Father' suggests that God sent Jesus into the world.

John declares that the Word is 'full of grace and truth'. Truth is an idea that John makes much of; however, grace is used by him only in the prologue.[11] The Word is presented as the perfect balance of grace and truth; in fact, He is filled with both. The imagery harkens back to God's covenant faithfulness

---

10. The Greek word *monogenes* is best understood along the lines of being unique ('one and only'). It is used in this way in the LXX to describe Isaac over against Ishmael as sons of Abraham (Gen. 22:2, 12, 16).

11. John uses 'truth' twenty-five times and relates it closely with Jesus, who is 'the truth' (14:6).

to Israel (Exod. 34:6). The ultimate manifestation of God's covenant faithfulness is seen in the sending of His Son.

It seems odd for the evangelist to bring the Baptist back into the discussion at this point (1:15). I think that he does so for two reasons. First, what he has just said about the Word is almost too marvelous to believe, and the Baptist becomes a second witness to the apostle's comments. Second, he is preparing to openly identify the Word with Jesus, and John the Baptist was the one who came to testify concerning Him. John the Baptist's statement is another affirmation of the Word's preexistence (1:15b). John the Baptist was about six months older than Jesus, but the Word existed before the Baptist was born.

We should understand 1:16-17 to be the words of the apostle rather than the Baptist. The apostle now turns to the abundant blessings that Jesus bestows on His people. He focuses on the thought of grace ('grace upon grace'). This phrase has been understood in two primary ways. A number of evangelical scholars understand it in the sense of accumulation ('grace upon grace').[12] The thought is that of one wave of grace after another; the grace of God through Christ is inexhaustible. The phrase can also be translated as 'grace instead of grace', suggesting the thought of replacement.[13] This interpretation is that the grace of Christ replaces the grace of the law. The latter interpretation is to be favored in light of 1:17 and the thought of replacement that occurs in John 2–4. This interpretation in no way diminishes God's grace exhibited through the law, but emphasizes the greater blessings of the new covenant over the old covenant. The superiority of this gift is seen in the fact that 'the Law was given through Moses' (1:17a), but 'grace and truth were realized through Jesus Christ' (1:17b). For the first time in the prologue Jesus is mentioned specifically by name.

John began the prologue by stating plainly the deity of the Word and he closes the prologue in the same manner (1:18).

12. F. F. Bruce, *The Gospel and Epistles of John* (Grand Rapids: William B. Eerdmans Publishing, 1983), 1:43; Craig S. Keener, *The Gospel of John: A Commentary* (Peabody, MA: Hendrickson Publishing, 2003), 1:421.

13. Raymond Brown, *The Gospel according to John*, Anchor Bible Commentary (Garden City, NY: Doubleday, 1964), 1:15-16; Carson, *John*, 132.

He states that 'no one has seen God at any time', that is, in His totality or essence. God revealed Himself to His people in various ways as depicted in the Old Testament, but never in His fullness. Moses saw the back side of God's glory, but no one could look on God and live. Isaiah saw the train of His robe filling the temple. Now with the incarnation of Jesus, the invisible and glorious God has revealed Himself to mankind.

John highlights again the close relationship between Jesus and the Father ('in the bosom of the Father'). This picks up the thought in verses 1-2, that the Word was 'with God'. The intimacy of this relationship will be explained further as the Gospel unfolds in terms of the Father-Son relationship.[14] For now John is content to say that Jesus has made the invisible God visible.

Reflections

There are three thoughts that I want to consider as we conclude this marvelous passage. First, we must recognize the absolute supremacy of Jesus Christ. The twenty-first century evangelical church needs to recapture the glory and greatness of Jesus. The contemporary church has a vision of Jesus that is far too small, and it is evident in our lack of passion in worship and our hesitancy to advance the gospel to the ends of the earth. When a church catches a glimpse of Jesus' greatness, her worship intensifies and her members willingly sacrifice time, money, and life to take the gospel to the nations. This is what motivated the early Christians to lay down their lives willingly in world evangelization.

Second, the prologue hints of the battle that lay ahead for Jesus (and the church!). Man is shrouded in moral and spiritual darkness and in desperate need of the light. Jesus' ministry will be a spiritual battle. It is the war between the kingdom of God and the kingdom of darkness. It will be a battle between God's truth and the devil's lies. The victory, however, belongs to the light, for the darkness cannot overpower it. The battle Jesus inaugurated with His incarnation is carried on by the church. The church should

---

14. There is a textual variation that reads, 'the only begotten Son' (KJV), but the better reading is 'the only begotten God' (NASB, NIV).

not expect to make significant advancement into the kingdom of darkness without significant resistance by Satan and his forces. The church must cling tenaciously to God's promise that the darkness will not extinguish the light!

The third point of emphasis is the possibility of transformation. Those who believe in Jesus become children of God. The apostle will illustrate this as the Gospel unfolds. Some will choose to stay in the darkness like Nicodemus (at least for a time) and others will come into the light like the Samaritan woman.

STUDY QUESTIONS

1. How does John's opening line differ from that of the other Gospels?

2. Why do you think John begins his Gospel as he does?

3. What is John's main message in the prologue? Support your thought from the biblical text.

4. What aspect of Christ's person in this passage did you need to be reminded of most?

5. Where do you see this battle between the light and the darkness most clearly in your life?

2

The Testimony of John the Baptist
(John 1:19-34)

'Who are you?' is the question of the day for many people. Self-discovery is thought to be a necessary component of a healthy self-esteem. Some people spend much of their life seeking to discover who they are and to find their place in this world. Often Christians struggle as well to understand their gifts, abilities, and place in God's plan. The religious establishment wondered who John the Baptist thought himself to be. What does he say about himself? As the passage unfolds we discover not only who John believes himself to be, but also who he believes Jesus to be.

The author has at least two main thoughts he wants to communicate in this larger section (1:19-51). First, he clarifies the relationship between Jesus and John the Baptist (1:19-34). Second, he provides a study in the nature of conversion and true discipleship (1:35-51). This section should be seen as a literary unit because of the sequence of days (1:29, 35, 43). The apostle provides no background on John the Baptist, either in the prologue or here, implying that his readers are familiar with him. In these verses the reader learns who the Baptist was not (1:19-21), who he understood himself to be (1:22-28), and who he believed Jesus to be (1:29-34).

The delegation and John's denials: 'Who are you?' (1:19-21)
John the Baptist makes three specific denials in response to the delegation's question, 'Who are you?' He denies that he is the Messiah (1:20), Elijah (1:21a), or the prophet (1:21b).

The opening words, 'This is the testimony of John,' should be understood as the heading for what follows (1:19a). The idea of 'witness' and 'testimony' has already been associated with John in the prologue (1:6-8, 15). The impact of his ministry is seen when a delegation from Jerusalem comes to question him concerning his identity (1:19b). The Jewish people believed that God had not spoken to them prophetically since the conclusion of Malachi's ministry, but John appears to be a prophet. So the Jewish leaders ('the Jews') send a delegation (Levites, priests, and Pharisees) to question John the Baptist.[1]

John denies emphatically that he is the Messiah – *Christos*, 'anointed one' (1:20). Messianic hope in first-century Judaism took a variety of shapes. Some Jews anticipated a Messianic figure in the mold of David who would come and throw off the yoke of Roman domination (Ps. Sol. 17). Those at Qumran looked for two messianic figures – a priestly messiah and a kingly messiah (1 QS 9:11). Still others expected an eschatological prophet like Moses (Deut. 18:15-18).

They respond to his denial by asking him if he is Elijah (1:21a). Many Jews looked for a great eschatological figure like Elijah to precede the coming of the Messiah. The Jews remembered that Elijah had not died (2 Kings 2:11) and believed that the same prophet would come back to earth to announce the end time (Mal. 3:1; 4:5-6). John denies that he is Elijah. When Jesus later said the Baptist was Elijah (Matt. 11:14, 17; 17:10-13), He meant it in the sense that John fulfilled the prophecies concerning Elijah (cf. Luke 1:17), but not that he was the literal Elijah.

The delegation continued by asking John if he was the 'the prophet' (1:21b). This is a reference to the Moses-like prophet spoken of in Deuteronomy 18:15, 18. John denies that he is that prophet. In our contemporary age of self-promotion it is convicting and refreshing to find a man like John the Baptist who did not seek titles for himself.

Who is John and what is he doing? (1:22-28)
1:22-23: If John is not one of these popular eschatological figures, then who is he (1:22a)? His unwillingness to

---

1. The phrase, 'the Jews', appears seventy-one times in the Gospel in contrast to seventeen times in the Synoptics. John generally uses the term in a negative light, often referring to the religious leaders.

cooperate frustrates his inquirers. They are concerned about bringing back an answer to those who sent them (1:22b). John replies by referring to Isaiah 40:3 (1:23). He is a herald, a forerunner. Those who lived at Qumran applied the same passage to themselves. They felt that they were to prepare for the Messiah's coming by isolating themselves and studying the Scriptures (1 QS 8:13-16). John, on the other hand, did not isolate himself, but preached a message of baptism and repentance. The Synoptic authors apply Isaiah 40:3 to John's prophetic ministry, but here John applies it to himself. In its original context Isaiah refers figuratively to preparing the roads to allow Israel to return home from Babylonian exile. John saw himself as one whose ministry was to prepare the way for the Messiah to come and bring Israel out of spiritual exile and back to God.

1:24-25: The Pharisees, who are a part of the delegation from Jerusalem, probe further about his baptismal activity (1:24). What authority does he have to baptize if he is not the Messiah, Elijah, or the prophet? Scholars debate the origin of John's baptism.[2] At Qumran they practiced daily washings as a symbolic ritual depicting holiness. We know from later rabbinic writings that Gentile converts to Judaism practiced a self-administered baptism as a part of the conversion process. It is debated if such a practice was carried out at this time. However, it seems unlikely that Judaism would imitate an act that was practiced by early Christians. If this is the case, then John was calling the Jewish people to become God's people by summoning them to repentance and demonstrating that repentance through a once-for-all baptismal act.

1:26-27: John confesses that his water baptism is only anticipatory. Rather than refer to the Spirit-baptism by Jesus here, as it appears he is about to do, he points instead to the fact that there is among them 'one you do not know' (1:26). He is the most important one, so much so that John is not worthy to untie the strap of His sandals (1:27). It is commonly acknowledged that this was the task of a slave and not to be performed by someone's disciple. John's humility at this

---

2. D. S. Dockery, 'Baptism,' in *Dictionary of Jesus and the Gospels*, ed. Joel B. Green and Scott McKnight (Downers Grove, IL: InterVarsity Press, 1992): 55-58.

point is astonishing. The religious leaders think he may be an eschatological figure. The crowds are flocking to him in the Judean wilderness. But he does not consider himself worthy to loosen the strap of the Messiah's sandals.

These events are described as having taken place 'at Bethany on the other side of the Jordan' (1:28). This site should not be confused with the Bethany that is two miles outside Jerusalem. The precise location has puzzled scholars. What seems clear is that it was located east of the Jordan River.

John's witness concerning Jesus (1:29-34)

In this section we hear John's witness to Jesus. He proclaims Jesus to be 'the Lamb of God' (1:29-31), 'the one who will baptize with the Holy Spirit' (1:32-33), and 'God's Chosen One' (1:34).

Jesus is the Lamb of God (1:29-31)

John identifies Jesus as 'the Lamb of God, who takes away the sin of the world' (1:29). What did John mean when he called Jesus 'the Lamb of God'? Scholars have understood the reference in a variety of ways. Some have pointed to the Warrior Lamb of Jewish Apocalyptic thought.[3] Others relate it to the lamb provided by God for Abraham when he was ready to offer up his son of promise, Isaac, in obedience to God (Gen. 22:13). However, what Abraham was spared from doing at the last moment God will actually do in the sacrifice of His Son. Another possibility for the background is the sacrificial lamb of Isaiah 53:6.[4] The thought of sacrifice seems to be in view in the words, 'takes away the sin of the world.' John's Gospel moves in this direction with the climax of Christ's sacrificial death (6:51; 10:15; 15:13).[5] While it may not be possible to be absolutely certain of John the Baptist's

---

3. 1 Enoch 90:38; Testament of Joseph 19:8; cf. Revelation 7:17; 17:14. Carson, *John*, 150; Brown, *John*, 1:58-60; and George R. Beasley-Murray, *John*, Word Biblical Commentary, vol. 26, 2nd ed. (Nashville: Thomas Nelson Publishers, 1999), 24-25, prefer this understanding.

4. Blomberg, *Jesus and the Gospels*, 187.

5. Gary M. Burge, *John*, The NIV Application Commentary (Grand Rapids: Zondervan Publishing House, 2000), 73-74; Andreas Köstenberger, *John*, Baker Exegetical Commentary on the New Testament (Grand Rapids: Baker Academic, 2004), 66-68; and Morris, *John*, 127-31, favor the idea of sacrificial imagery.

intention, it seems more likely that it should be understood along the lines of sacrificial imagery. John continues his testimony to Jesus by acknowledging Jesus' superiority because of His preexistence (1:30; cf. 1:15).

John's description of Jesus as the Lamb of God has significant application for a world buried under the weight of the guilt of sin. Many faithful believers continue to bear the guilt of their sins that have been paid for through the death of the Lamb. Christ bore the sins of His people on the cross and we should enjoy the freedom that comes with the knowledge of sin's forgiveness. Furthermore, Christ's atoning work was for the world, that is, people of every nation and kind. No matter the sin and no matter one's background, if you belong to Christ, your sins are forgiven.

John states again Christ's preeminence (1:30). Jesus' preeminence is exemplified in His preexistence, a thought brought out in the prologue (cf. 1:15). While John the Baptist and Jesus were cousins it is clear that John did not understand fully Jesus' true identity (1:31a). John's baptismal ministry revealed the Messiah to Israel (1:31b).

Jesus is the one who will baptize with the Holy Spirit (1:32-33)
John continues by testifying that Jesus is the one who will baptize with the Holy Spirit. He referred to his own baptism of repentance earlier but waited until here to discuss Jesus' Spirit baptism. He describes the Spirit coming on Jesus at His baptism (1:32). It appears that until he baptized Jesus John did not know that Jesus was the Messiah. We know from Luke's Gospel that John and Jesus were distant relatives; however, there is no indication that they had ever met. God told John by what sign he would be able to identify the Messiah (1:33). While the Spirit would often come on people for specific tasks in Old Testament times, He would remain on Jesus. The fact that the Spirit would remain on Jesus is mentioned twice (1:32, 33).

The reference to the baptism with the Holy Spirit in 1:33 points toward Pentecost and beyond. While Jesus' early followers were baptized with the Spirit on the day of Pentecost (Acts 2:1-4), every believer is baptized in the Spirit at the moment of conversion (1 Cor. 12:13). The Baptist draws a clear contrast here between his water baptism and Jesus' Spirit baptism. John's baptism was preparatory, because it symbolized repentance.

Jesus is the Chosen One of God (1:34)
Finally, John confesses Jesus to be God's 'Chosen One' (1:34). Many manuscripts read 'the Son of God' (NASB, NIV, NRSV) in the place of 'God's Chosen One' (ESV, NJB, NLT). It is slightly more likely that the original reading was 'Chosen One'. It is less likely that a scribe would have changed 'Son of God', which is a major Christological title in John, to 'Chosen One' rather than the other way around.[6] The thought is that God chose Jesus to be Messiah and Redeemer (cf. Isa. 42:1).

Reflections
John the Baptist's life and ministry teach us several important lessons. First, John had a clear understanding of himself and the Messiah. His task was to point people to Jesus. It is easy for us to become confused as to what God has called us to do. Like John the Baptist, God has called us to point people to Jesus and not to ourselves.

Second, John's humility is a stirring challenge to the pride that resides in every heart. There is something within fallen nature that clamors for attention and recognition. Success is the breeding ground for pride. Large crowds have a way of making us forget who we are and where we come from. John never forgot he was just a voice. He refused all flattering titles. He saw himself as unworthy of untying the Lord's sandal.

Third, notice that John was a voice, not in Jerusalem, nor at the temple, but rather in the wilderness. He spoke for God in a geographical and spiritual wasteland. John's message and call to repentance resonated in people's hearts. People came from great distances to hear him because he was a Spirit-empowered spokesperson calling people back to God. When God's hand is on a pastor and congregation they will not have to use gimmicks to attract people. Today, as in John's day, people are hungry for an authentic word from God.

---

6. Brown, *John*, 1:66-67; Carson, *John*, 152; Morris, *John*, 134.

STUDY QUESTIONS

1. What roles did John deny in this passage?

2. Who did John confess Jesus to be?

3. What do you think to be the most likely background to the phrase 'Lamb of God'?

4. What can we learn from John the Baptist about humility?

3

Jesus' Early Followers Bear
Witness to Him

(John 1:35-51)

W e come now to the third section of the opening chapter
of the Gospel. In the prologue we 'hear' John the
apostle's testimony to Jesus (1:1-18) and in the next passage
John the Baptist's witness to Jesus (1:19-34). In this section
we hear the testimony of some of Jesus' earliest followers.
The titles ascribed to Jesus here are very impressive: 'Rabbi'
(1:38, 49), 'Messiah' (1:41), 'him of whom Moses in the Law
and also the Prophets wrote – Jesus of Nazareth, the son of
Joseph' (1:45), 'Son of God,' 'King of Israel' (1:49), and 'Son of
Man' (1:51). This passage also gives us insight into Johannine
discipleship. First, a disciple must follow Jesus (1:37f, 43);[1]
that is, they must 'come and see' (1:39, 46), experiencing Him
for themselves. A part of this following is to go and bring
others to Jesus (1:41, 45). Second, a disciple must know who
Jesus is, as reflected in the titles ascribed to Him throughout
this section. In addition, it should be noted that the material
in this section (as well as chapters 2:1–4:54) preceded Jesus'
encounter with the four fishermen in Mark 1:16-20. This
passage and following help us understand that prior to Jesus'
Great Galilean Ministry described in the Synoptic Gospels

---

1. 'To follow' is a key concept in the Johannine discipleship (1:43; 8:12; 10:27;
12:26; 21:19-20).

Jesus had an Early Judean ministry described only by John. The following passage describes five who followed in faith.

Andrew and an unnamed disciple: The witness of a mentor (1:35-40)

1:35-37: The evangelist continues his recounting of the opening days of Jesus' ministry – 'the next day' (1:35a; cf. 1:29). Two of John's disciples are standing with him as Jesus passes by (1:35b). The apostle describes rather graphically that the Baptist 'looked at Jesus as he walked' by and declared for a second time that he is 'the Lamb of God' (1:36; cf. 1:29). John intentionally directed his disciples' attention to Jesus as indicated by the word 'Behold'. The influence of John's witness to Jesus is seen in that the two men 'followed Jesus' (1:37). John the Baptist was doing what the prologue says he would do: 'bear witness to the light' (1:6-8).

1:38-40: The two men apparently do not inform Jesus immediately of their interest in getting to know Him. Jesus catches them off guard when He asks, 'What do you seek?' The best they can come up with is to ask Him where He is staying (1:38). They address Him as 'Rabbi'. John translates the term for his Greek-speaking readers ('which translated means Teacher').[2] At this point in the first century the title was not considered an official office as much as a deferential address to a respected teacher. Jesus invites them to spend the evening with Him since it was already late in the day, being the 'tenth hour' (4 p.m.).[3]

Only Andrew is specifically identified by name. The other may have been the apostle John, but we cannot be certain. We don't know a lot about Andrew, but he appears to have been a person serious about following God. He likely had undergone John's baptism of repentance. He is referred to as 'Simon Peter's brother', even though Peter had not yet been introduced

---

2. This is the first of six instances in which John translates an Aramaic term for his readers. The others are 'Messiah' (Christ, 1:41; 4:25), 'Cephas' (Peter, 1:42), 'Siloam' (Sent, 9:7), 'Thomas' (Didymus, Twin, 11:16; 20:24; 21:2), and 'Place of the Skull' (Golgotha, 19:17).

3. The Jewish people counted the hours of the day from dawn, while the Romans counted the hours of the day from midnight on. It is most likely that John is using Jewish reckoning of time here.

into the story. Again, at the feeding of the five thousand he is referred to as 'Simon Peter's brother' (6:8). Andrew lived in the shadow of his more famous brother; however, one gets the impression that he was a humble man and probably grateful to God that he had the opportunity to introduce his brother to Jesus. The simplicity of the encounter suggests it is an authentic historical reflection. On the other hand, in typical Johannine fashion, the author may intend the penetrating nature of the words to carry much more impact than one might expect. On numerous occasions as the Gospel unfolds it becomes clear that the crowds seek Jesus because of His miracles. For example, after the feeding of the five thousand Jesus says to the crowds, 'you do not seek me because you saw signs, but because you ate of the loaves and were filled' (6:26). Like the crowds, what do these two disciples seek? This is a salutary and penetrating question for everyone who loves Jesus. Why do we seek Him? Do we seek Him for what He can do for us, or because of who He is? In one sense there is no such thing as absolutely pure motives this side of heaven. But Jesus' question reminds us that we must beware of seeking Him for selfish reasons rather than out of a love for Him. Jesus' response is also much more significant than it appears on the surface. The invitation to 'come (e.g., 3:21; 5:40; 6:35; 7:37) and see' (e.g., 6:40; 9:39; 16:16; 17:24) is a summons to salvation. Philip uses similar language in his conversation with Nathaniel (1:46). Andrew demonstrates his 'conversion' by seeking out his brother Simon and confessing Jesus to be the Messiah.

Peter: The witness of a brother (1:41-42)
As mentioned above, Andrew's first act after his encounter with Jesus is to find his brother Simon and tell him that they have found 'the Messiah' (1:41). John adds for his readers the Greek translation 'Christ' (both Messiah and Christ mean 'anointed one'). The majority of first century Judaism understood the Messiah to be a Davidic descendant anointed by God and who would overthrow the Romans and re-establish a Jewish kingdom. Andrew is described as bringing Peter to Jesus (1:42).

Jesus gives Simon the name 'Cephas'. Cephas was an Aramaic name; Peter was the Greek equivalent meaning 'rock'.

When God changed someone's name in the Old Testament it had significant implications for their future. God changed Abram to Abraham and Jacob to Israel. In the four Gospels, Peter was anything but a rock. At best he could be described as impulsive. In Acts he became the leading figure in the early days of the Church. Jesus renamed him not because of who he was, but of who he would become by God's gracious work in his life. No one (except God) can foresee the possibilities in a person when they come to Christ. Andrew had no idea how bringing his brother to Jesus would change the world.

Philip and Nathaniel: The witness of a friend (1:43-51)
1:43-46: The day after His encounter with Peter Jesus goes into Galilee and calls Philip to follow Him (1:43). Philip is not given an introduction and it seems the evangelist expects his readers to know who he is. Jesus' command is simple and straightforward: 'Follow me.' This was not the normal way that a rabbi gathered followers in the ancient world. In Judaism a person would typically approach a rabbi about becoming a disciple rather than the other way around. Jesus speaks to Philip in terms similar to those spoken to Andrew and the unnamed disciple in the previous section (cf. 1:39). We do not know much about Philip outside John's Gospel (cf. 6:5-7; 12:21-22; 14:7-9). He was from Bethsaida, Peter and Andrew's hometown (1:44).[4]

The emphasis of the text is that Philip follows Jesus by finding Nathaniel (1:45a). Nathaniel's name is not found in the lists of the Twelve, but he is commonly thought to correspond to Bartholomew in the lists (Mark 3:18; Matt. 10:3; Luke 6:14; Acts 1:13).[5] Philip tells him that they have found the one of whom 'Moses in the Law and also the prophets wrote, Jesus of Nazareth, the son of Joseph.' Nathaniel was from the village of Cana (21:2) and shows disdain for the fact that Jesus comes from Nazareth (1:46a). We don't know exactly what Nathaniel may have been thinking when he

---

4. Bethsaida was a fishing village just northwest of Capernaum on the opposite side of the Jordan River, north of the Sea of Galilee.

5. While we cannot be certain of this correspondence, it is interesting that in the lists of the disciples in the Gospels, Philip's and Bartholomew's names are placed side by side.

said, 'Can anything good come from Nazareth?' It could be
that he knew that the Messiah was to come from Bethlehem
(cf. 7:41-42; Mic. 5:2), or the fact that Nazareth was an
insignificant village with a population of around 2,000
people. It was located a little over three miles southeast of
Sepphoris, the capital of the region. Philip simply challenges
Nathaniel to investigate for himself (1:46b). Philip's words,
'Come and see,' are very similar to what Jesus said to
Andrew and his companion (cf. 1:39a).

1:47-51: Jesus reveals His supernatural knowledge of
Nathaniel by identifying him 'as an Israelite in whom there
is no guile', even though He has never met him previously
(1:47). Jesus' point is that Nathaniel is a genuine person and
not filled with duplicity (cf. Ps. 32:2). Nathaniel is stunned
that Jesus knows him (1:48). Jesus' comment should be
understood as an example of His divine insight – that is, His
ability to know something about someone that no person
could possibly know. The same will be true when Jesus meets
the Samaritan woman (4:17-18).[6]

Nathaniel's response identifies him as another follower
of Jesus (1:49). His identification of Jesus as the 'Son of
God' (2 Sam. 7:14; Ps. 2:7) and 'King of Israel' (Zeph. 3:15;
cf. John 12:13; 18:33, 39; 19:3, 19, 21) should be understood
along messianic lines. Jesus' promise that Nathaniel will
see 'greater things' is likely pointing toward the very next
episode where Jesus turns water into wine, as well as His
comment in verse 51.

Jesus' statement is introduced by 'truly, truly' (*amen,
amen*) heightening its importance. The phrase occurs in this
double form eighty-five times in John's Gospel and never in
the Synoptic Gospels. Its usage is intended to introduce an
authoritative statement by Jesus.

Jesus' identification of Himself as the 'Son of Man' has
as its background Daniel 7:13-14. The phrase 'Son of Man'

---

6. The following is a sample list of Jesus' supernatural knowledge. He knows
that His time has not yet come (2:4), the nature of His own death (2:19; 6:51; 10,
15, 17, 18; 12:24; 15:13), the identity of His betrayer (6:70; 13:10-11), the purpose
of the blind man's and Lazarus' sicknesses (9:3, 7; 11:4), that Lazarus has died
(11:14), that Peter would deny Him three times (13:38), and that Peter would die by
martyrdom (21:18,19).

was Jesus' favorite self-designation. The title is used thirteen times in John and a total of eighty-three times in the four Gospels. In Daniel 7:13-14 the Son of Man is pictured as a heavenly figure who in the end times is entrusted by God with authority, glory, and power. Outside the Gospels the title is used in the New Testament only by Stephen (Acts 7.56) and John (Rev. 1:13; 14:14).[7] Jesus chose the term because it did not carry overt messianic overtones. His statement, 'you will see the...,' is reminiscent of Jacob's vision in Genesis 28:10-17 where there was a ladder (or stairway) extending from earth to heaven, with angels ascending and descending on it. Jesus' point is that He is the one who connects heaven and earth. The implication is that He is greater than Jacob as 'the new Israel'.

Reflections

This passage intertwines thoughts of Christology, discipleship, and evangelism. The presentation of Jesus in chapter one is stunning. By the end of the chapter, the reader is left with a magnificent understanding of Jesus' identity. In addition to helping the reader understand who Jesus is, this passage illustrates the importance of knowing Jesus and following Him if one is to consider oneself Jesus' disciple. Each one that followed Jesus recognized Him to be the long-awaited Messiah.

Furthermore, John the Baptist, Andrew, and Philip all demonstrate that following Jesus involves telling others about Him. Andrew and the unnamed disciple (John) follow Jesus as a result of John the Baptist's testimony (1:36), suggesting those in our circle of influence are people with whom we should share our faith. Andrew introduces his brother Peter to Jesus, which highlights the importance of witnessing to our family members (1:41-42). Finally, Philip exemplifies the opportunity of sharing one's faith with friends (1:46). Those who love Jesus want to introduce Him to others and the best place to begin is with those with whom we already have a

---

7. It is used in John's Gospel to describe Jesus' heavenly origin and access (3:13; 6:62), His glory (12:23; 13:31), His exaltation on the cross (3:14; 8:28; 12:34), His authority to judge (5:27), and His authority to give life (6:27, 53).

relationship. Evangelism is an important mark of faithful discipleship.

Study Questions

1. Who was the last person that you told about Jesus?

2. List some friends, co-workers, and family members that you can begin to pray for and eventually to talk to about Jesus.

3. Who led you to faith in Christ and what were the circumstances?

4. Which of Jesus' five followers in this passage do you relate to best?

4

Jesus turns Water into Wine
(John 2:1-12)

John 2 begins a major section of the Gospel that highlights Jesus' seven signs (2:1-12:50). This division of John is often called 'The Book of Signs'. Interspersed in and among these signs are discourses calling people to a faith decision. Sometimes these discourses are associated with a particular sign and at other times they stand alone. As this large section unfolds, the Jewish leadership will grow in their hostility toward Jesus. They will interrogate Him as to His identity, examine His signs, listen to His words, and ultimately find Him deserving of death (11:50).

The first unit of this major section (2:1–4:54) describes events that are typically thought to precede Jesus' Galilean Ministry described in the Synoptic Gospels. This unit begins and ends in Cana of Galilee (2:1; 4:46). Further setting off this section is the fact that the first event, Jesus turning the water into wine, is described as the 'beginning of his signs' (2:11), and the healing of the nobleman's son at the end of this section, is described as Jesus' second sign (4:54). These are the only two signs John numbers. There is some question about what is the major theme that runs through this section. Some suggest 'abundance' and others 'newness'. These two themes are not mutually exclusive and both seem to fit within this unit at different points; as the passages unfold the major themes will be highlighted.

The second chapter of John can be divided into two major episodes: the story of Jesus' turning the water into wine (2:1-12) and His cleansing of the temple (2:13-25). The turning of the water into wine is the first sign in Jesus' ministry in the Gospel and it may have been the first miracle He ever performed. In many ways this beautiful passage is simple and straightforward; however, there are a number of questions that circulate around it. What is its relationship to the preceding material? What is the meaning of the sign? Does the reference to the third day have special significance? Why did Jesus speak to His mother as He did? The most important question however is, what is John's main point in the narrating of this event? We will address these questions in the following discussion.

Some degree of symbolism can be affirmed in the story without denigrating the historical character of the event. John has chosen intentionally this event to begin his 'Book of Signs'. The keys to its interpretation are the phrases 'They have no wine' (2:3) and 'you have kept the good wine until now' (2:10). It is also significant that this first sign is performed at a wedding. The Old Testament frequently used a wedding as a symbol of the arrival of the messianic age (Isa. 54:4-8; 62:4-5). Jesus employed the same imagery in His teaching concerning the kingdom of God (Mark 2:19-20; Matt. 8:11; 22.1-14; Luke 22:16-18). The messianic age was to be characterized by abundant wine (Jer. 31:12; Hos. 14:7; Amos 9:13-14; cf. 1 Enoch 10:19; 1 Bar. 25:5). Jesus announces the arrival of the kingdom of God with these powerful eschatological metaphors. What was unexpected was that with the arrival of the Messiah the old institutions must pass away. Jesus taught that you cannot put new wine into old wineskins and you cannot put a new patch on to an old garment (Mark 2:19-22). The fact that they had run out of wine indicates the bankruptcy of pharisaical Judaism. Rituals like the six stone water jars for purification were all it had left. Jesus' ministry could not be contained in the old forms. God had kept the best until now (2:10). Paul put it like this: 'the old has gone and the new has come' (2 Cor. 5:17)!

The setting and circumstances: 'They have no wine' (2:1-3)
2:1: A wedding is a beautiful setting for Jesus to begin His public ministry. Weddings were monumental moments

in the lives of first-century Jewish people. It was a time of great festivity lasting as long as a week (cf. Judg. 14:12; Tobit 11:18). The wedding took place on 'the third day'. Scholars debate the significance of the reference to the 'third day'. Nowhere else in the Gospel does John spell out the days between events as he does beginning in 1:29 (cf. 1:35, 43) and culminating with the reference to 'the third day'. If one goes back to 1:29 ('The next day') and follows the sequence of days it is possible to count them so that the turning of the water into wine culminates Jesus' first week of ministry. Was John referring to the seven days of creation in the opening scenes and intending to communicate a new creation motif? If he was, he did not make it as clear as he could have in the counting of days. Without more help from John it is likely that the counting of the days is nothing more than a way of tying this passage to the previous section. Jesus told Nathaniel in the previous episode that he would see 'greater things' than these and this is an immediate example. The point is that just a few days after Jesus made that statement His words came to pass. The clearing of the temple in the next passage is another example of these 'greater things'. Some wonder if the reference to 'the third day' points forward to Jesus' resurrection on the third day. This seems unlikely since Jesus' resurrection in this Gospel is not referred to as happening on the third day.

2:2-3: Little is actually known of how a wedding was performed in first-century Palestine, but it was surely a festive event. The entire community would be involved. The village of Cana was not a very important place and in the New Testament is mentioned only in this Gospel (2:11; 4:46, 50; 21:2). Its exact location is unknown, but the most likely setting is west of the Sea of Galilee and approximately nine miles north of Nazareth at Khirbet Kana. The running out of wine was more than a minor social embarrassment since the family had an obligation to provide for their guests. This would have broken an unwritten code of hospitality. There is nothing to indicate that Jesus and His disciples' presence was the reason for the shortage. As to why Mary was taking matters into her own hands, we can do no more that speculate that she had some kind of role at the wedding. Informing Jesus of the shortage was probably not a request for a miracle but rather demonstrated her confidence in Jesus' resourcefulness. Since there is no mention of Joseph after Jesus' childhood it may be inferred that he was dead.

An awkward exchange: 'Do whatever he says' (2:4-5)

2:4: Jesus' response to His mother appears abrupt and harsh at first glance. However, the term 'woman' should not be interpreted in a derogatory manner. Jesus uses this same word when speaking to His mother from the cross (19:26), when addressing the Samaritan woman (4:21), and when speaking to Mary Magdalene in the garden (20:15). Interestingly in John's Gospel, Mary is never called by name; she is referred to as Jesus' mother. Jesus' words, 'Woman, what does that have to do with us?' suggest that He is communicating a change in their relationship as He inaugurates His messianic ministry. A similar situation occurs in the Synoptic Gospels when Jesus' mother and siblings want to see Him and He defines His family as those who do God's will (Mark 3:33-35).

More important theologically is Jesus' comment, 'My hour has not yet come.' The phrase is found several times throughout the Gospel (5:28; 7:6, 30; 8:20; 12:23, 27; 13:1; 16:32; 17:1). These statements present Jesus as moving toward His time of destiny. Even now, at the beginning of His ministry, He is very conscious of the coming cross. Jesus' hour arrives at the time of His passion (12:23). This is John's way of bringing out the fact that God's purpose is worked out in Jesus' death on the cross. In addition, John builds suspense in the narrative each time he mentions that Jesus' hour has not yet arrived. The reader is left to wonder what the hour is and when it will arrive. The point is that we are not to see the cross as a sad accident ending a life full of promise and hope. Instead we are to understand the cross and resurrection as the culmination of God's plan in Christ.

2:5: Mary obviously did not interpret Jesus' comments to her as an insult. Rather, she is satisfied that Jesus will do something to help the situation. Her advice to the servants, 'Whatever he tells you to do, do it,' reveals her confidence in Him and offers all believers good advice to follow.

The inauguration of the messianic age: 'You have saved the best wine until now' (2:6-10)

The actual miracle is described with stunning brevity, but the events leading up to it are given in more detail (2:6-9). The story's climax is found in the steward's words, 'you have saved the best till now' (ESV, 2:10). We should take special notice of how Jesus performs the miracle. He is not described as touching the water jars, commanding the water to become wine, nor even praying; rather, He willed it and the transformation took place.

2:6: John indicates that the water jars are for the Jewish rite of purification. The six stone jars were capable of holding twenty-thirty gallons each. Based on a twenty-five-gallon average, the combined total would have been approximately one hundred and fifty gallons. The rabbinic literature stipulated that stone jars could be used as permanent vessels for purification. The number six has been interpreted by some as indicating one short of perfection; however, when Jesus turns the water into wine He does not make another jar.

2:7-8: The fact that they have run out of wine and have only the water for ritual purification indicates the bankruptcy of Judaism in contrast to the abundant supply of the messianic age. Jesus commands them to fill the jars with water and take them to the headwaiter. John notes that they filled them to the brim. In one sense, the amount received corresponds to the amount obeyed. Could John in a subtle way be suggesting that we often receive less than the full riches of God's blessings because we fail to obey to the fullest extent?

2:9-10: The headwaiter is stunned at the quality of the wine. It was a common practice at a banquet to serve the best wine first, and then, when people's taste buds became less discriminating, to serve a cheaper wine. The exact opposite takes place here. As far as he knew, the family had saved the very best wine until now. The progression in the narrative is remarkable – from 'no wine' to 'six stone waterpots' for ritual purification, to the sparkling wine of the kingdom.

A concluding comment: 'His disciples believed in him' (2:11-12)

John noted that this was Jesus' first sign – *semeion* (2:11). The term sign emphasizes the significance of the action rather than the miracle itself (4:54; 6:14; 9:16; 11:47).[1] John wanted his readers to understand that Jesus' miracles were not simply works of wonder, but that they convey spiritual truth. The signs reveal Jesus' glory. Jesus calls them His 'works' (cf. 7:21). In the prologue the evangelist writes: 'we saw his glory,' and now he describes the first of a series of signs in which that glory was manifested. The glory was not visible to everyone who saw the miracle; therefore the glory is identified with the miraculous act itself. The servants saw the sign but not the glory; the disciples by faith perceived Jesus' glory in the sign and believed in Him. This is the first of numerous instances in which John describes individuals believing in Jesus, which was his purpose in writing (20:30-31).

The passage concludes with a reference to Jesus, His disciples, and His family going down to Capernaum. John describes them as 'going down' because Cana was in the hill country, but Capernaum was located on the shore of the Sea of Galilee. Capernaum was approximately sixteen miles northeast of Cana and became Jesus' base of operation for His Galilean ministry (Matt. 4:13).

Reflections

The events associated with the miracle at Cana teach the inauguration of the messianic age. Judaism had run its course and much of it had become burdened with Pharisaical legalism. Much of Judaism focused on outward rituals but lacked heartfelt love and devotion toward God. Just as much of first-century Judaism was spiritually bankrupt, there is a significant amount of casual Christianity today that goes through the motions of religion but lacks a passion for Jesus. The life and worship of casual Christianity lacks the joy associated with a wedding, which was a symbol in ancient

---

1. Carson, *John*, 175, describes John's use of the term 'sign' in the following: 'The New Testament uses several words to denote what we call "miracles." One of the most common, *dynameis* ("mighty works") is not found in John; another, *terata* ("wonders," "portents," "miracles") is found only when linked with *semeia* ("signs"), as in "signs and wonders"; but this combination is found only once in the Fourth Gospel (4:48). John prefers the simple word "signs": Jesus' miracles are never simply naked displays of power, still less neat conjuring tricks to impress the masses, but *signs*, *sign*ificant displays of power that point beyond themselves to the deeper realities that could be perceived with the eyes of faith' (emphasis original).

Judaism and early Christianity of the arrival of the messianic age (Isa. 54:4-8; 62:4-5), and the kingdom of God (Matt. 8:11; 22:1-14; Luke 22:16-18; Rev. 19:9). This passage should cause us to ask whether our hearts are dry and our spiritual passions weak and anemic. Do we know anything of true hunger for the Living Bread and a thirst for the Living Water? Or do we continue on performing our spiritual disciplines and carrying out our religious rituals with no sense of desire for God? While it is too much to say that the kingdom of God is all joy, like a wedding, with no suffering and sacrifice, there is something wrong when one's spiritual life always lacks the joy of a banquet. Too many believers' spiritual lives are characterized by robotically performing spiritual disciplines like prayer, Bible reading and such, but lack the powerful presence of God in their personal lives and ministries. This passage is a sober rebuke of ritual without love, of spiritual practices devoid of holiness, and of a monotonous religion that knows nothing of the joy of the Lord.

STUDY QUESTIONS

1. In what ways did Jesus' and Mary's relationship change at Cana?

2. What are rituals in the church today that may correspond to Jewish ritualism described in this passage?

3. In what way is the kingdom to be like a wedding feast? How can we take that imagery too far and in what ways do we sometimes not take it far enough?

4. Why do you think the servants who knew what had happened to the water did not see Jesus' glory and believe in Him as the disciples did?

5

Jesus Cleanses the Temple
(2:13-25)

The imagery of Jesus that we often picture in our minds is the Jesus of Renaissance art. This Jesus is somewhat gaunt and serene looking; more like a hippy at Woodstock than a first-century Palestinian. Certainly the Jesus of twenty-first century religion does not get mad. The Jesus of John's Gospel, however, is a strong, defiant, courageous preacher of righteousness who is not afraid to denounce hypocrisy and sham in one's religion. He bravely confronts His enemies and does not shy away from necessary conflict. This side of Jesus is seen quite clearly in this episode.

There are two important questions related to this passage. First, how does this clearing of the temple relate to the one described at the end of Jesus' ministry in the Synoptic Gospels? Second, what did John intend to communicate to his readers by recounting this event? The question as to how many times Jesus 'cleansed the temple' is much debated. Many scholars believe that John relocated this passage chronologically in order to highlight Jesus' coming death and resurrection. Thus, Jesus did this only once and it was near the conclusion of His ministry. While this is possible, it seems that the reference to the 'forty-six years' of building the temple (2:20) dates this event to approximately A.D. 28 and therefore too early to correspond to the clearing described in the Synoptic Gospels. Also in favor of two clearings of the temple is that at

Jesus' trial He was accused of saying that He would destroy the temple and build another not made with human hands (Mark 14:58). While Jesus is not recorded as saying anything like this in the Synoptic Gospels, it appears to be a muddled memory of what Jesus said a couple of years prior at the first clearing of the temple (2:19). Therefore it seems reasonable to assume that the passing of time caused those who made the accusations to forget exactly what Jesus said.

The second and more important question is, what did John intend to communicate to his readers by recounting this event? The emphasis here of John's theme of messianic abundance/replacement is that Jesus is the new temple. The 'old' temple was no longer necessary because the practice of animal sacrifices would end with Jesus' once-for-all sacrifice. In addition, the temple was being desecrated by the selling of animals and changing of coins (2:16). God's glory no longer resided there as it once did. Ezekiel described the glory of God leaving the temple (Ezek. 10:18); now the Shekinah glory of God was being manifested in Jesus, the new temple. John depicts Jesus as the Messiah, arriving at the temple for the first time since inaugurating His messianic ministry (Mal. 3:1).

The passage unfolds in three parts: first, Jesus' clearing of the temple (2:13-17); second, His confrontation with the religious leaders (2:18-22); and finally a concluding statement concerning spurious faith (2:23-25).

Jesus' Zeal: The Temple Cleansing (2:13-17)

The importance of the temple to Judaism cannot be overstated. The temple was not only the central shrine where atonement for sin was made, but it was considered to be God's primary dwelling place. Solomon built the first temple in 949 B.C., but the Babylonians had destroyed it (2 Kings 25). The second temple was rebuilt in 515 B.C. Herod the Great began an expansion of the temple area in 20 B.C. This temple was finally completed in A.D. 64 but was destroyed by the Romans in A.D. 70.

2:13: The setting for this episode is the Jewish Passover. This is the first of three Passovers mentioned in John's Gospel (2:13; 6:4; 11:55; cf. 12:1). The Passover Feast was one

of three annual pilgrimage festivals (Deut. 16:16). Therefore
Jesus traveled from Galilee to Judea to celebrate the feast.
Passover commemorated the deliverance of the Jewish
people from Egypt and was celebrated in the early spring
(March–April). The Festival of Unleavened Bread, marking
the beginning of wheat harvest, began the following day.
The city would have been filled with pilgrims from around
the world.

2:14-16: Jesus is repulsed and outraged that God's temple
had become a farmers' market. The selling of animals likely
began outside the temple precinct as a means of providing
a service to pilgrims, but the service eventually relocated
to the Court of the Gentiles. The term for temple (*hieron*)
denotes the area surrounding the temple, including the
Court of the Gentiles, in distinction from the temple building
proper (*naos*), from which Gentiles were excluded. The noise
and smell of the animals would have made it impossible
for a Gentile to approach God in prayer. One wonders why
Jesus reacted as He did on this occasion since He would
have seen a similar situation on earlier visits. His response
likely had to do with this being His first visit to Jerusalem
after inaugurating His messianic ministry at Cana. John
emphasized three actions by Jesus: driving out the animals,
scattering the coins on the floor, and overturning the tables
(2:14-15). Jesus' explanation for His actions was, 'Take
these things away; stop making my Father's house a place
of business' (or place of trade) (2:16, ESV). The point is that
His Father's house has become a marketplace rather than a
place of worship.

Jesus' disciples later came to understand this event as the
fulfillment of Psalm 69:9. Jesus' life was fueled by zeal for
His Father's honor (2:17). The Psalm describes how David's
zeal for God's house caused him problems with his enemies;
now one greater than David experiences the same response.[1]

---

1. Carson, *John*, 180, adds, 'With other New Testament writers, however, John
detects in the experiences of David a prophetic paradigm that anticipates what must
take place in the life of "great David's greater Son." That explains why the words
in 2:17, quoted from the LXX, change the tense to the future: *Zeal for your house
will consume me....* For John, the manner by which Jesus will be "consumed" is
doubtless his death.'

The Request for a Sign: Jesus' Death and Resurrection (2:18-22)

The religious leaders understand the response of Jesus to be a messianic act and demand that He perform a sign that demonstrates His authority to do this (2:18). The irony in Jesus' answer is that ultimately the Jews themselves were to be the means of bringing about this sign; however, they fail to recognize it when it happens. Jesus does not say that He will destroy the temple, but that they will destroy it and He will raise it (2:19). They fail to grasp that He is speaking about Himself and not the literal temple (2:19-20). John supplies a commentary to clarify the meaning for his readers (2:21). There is further irony in the fact that to put Jesus to death is to offer the one sacrifice that can truly expiate sin and end the necessity of the temple sacrifices. After Jesus' resurrection the disciples remember Jesus' words and 'they believed the Scriptures and the word Jesus had spoken' (2:22). It is interesting to note how Jesus' words are placed alongside Scripture as the object of the disciples' faith.

Jesus' Knowledge: Spurious Faith (2:23-25)

These concluding verses of the chapter describe the unsatisfactory nature of Jerusalem's response to Jesus in addition to providing a transition to the next episode. The evangelist indicates that Jesus performed numerous signs during this visit to Jerusalem that are not recorded (2:23). John depicts the crowd's response by using a play on words. To paraphrase John's thought, 'during the feast many trusted in Jesus, but he did not entrust himself' to them (2:23b-24a). This may very well indicate the spurious nature of their faith (cf. 6:66; 8:31ff). In addition, John highlights again Jesus' omniscience ('he himself knew what was in man'), which will be on display in His encounters with Nicodemus and the Samaritan woman.

Reflections

Many Christian radio and television ministries have become little more than a marketplace for religion. They spend more time trying to sell 'ministry' items and 'helps' than they do teaching the Word of God. The same is true in many Christian organizations where the leaders tend to live like Fortune 500

CEOs rather than godly servant-leaders. A similar attitude can be said of many that sit in the pews, who are more enamored with their retirement portfolios than living for God's honor. Materialism and consumerism are two of Satan's biggest traps for Western Christianity. Jesus finds this infatuation with 'things' morally and spiritually repulsive. When Jesus came to the temple during the Passover He found 'God's house' unfit for worshiping God. Christian leaders must take into account Jesus words: 'stop making my Father's house a place of business.'

In addition, when Jesus' disciples thought back on this event they saw it as a fulfillment of Psalm 69:9. Jesus was zealous and passionate for God's name and honor. The righteous indignation He expressed was His response to the trivialization of God's worship. Worship is an important thought in John's Gospel (4:19-24; 9:38). Far too many believers never feel a holy jealousy for the defamation of God's honor. Obviously it is easy for our righteous anger to become unholy, and we must be on guard against this, but true disciples should feel passionate about God being rightly worshiped and His name revered.

In summary, as one looks back over the entire chapter, several thoughts emerge. Jesus is at the center of both stories. In the first He turns the water into wine and in the second He clears God's temple. In the first He reveals His glory and in the second His zeal. In the first He alludes to His death by the reference to His 'hour' and in the second He tells the religious leaders, 'Destroy this temple, (his body) and in three days I will raise it up' (His bodily resurrection). In the first passage we see His kindness in meeting the pressing need of the moment, and in the second His judgment on materialism. In the first they believed in Him and saw His glory and in the second they eventually came to believe in the word which He spoke. Once again, we see the marvelous insight of the last living apostle, who had reflected on Jesus' words and deeds for five decades before writing this Gospel.

STUDY QUESTIONS

1. Why do you think that John included this passage in the Gospel?

2. Can you think of a contemporary application of Jesus' clearing the temple?

3. When you reflect back on the past year of your life, do you believe that you lived with an appropriate zeal for the Lord's honor? If not, what do you think has been the cause?

4. Jesus referred to His body as a temple. What did Paul write to Christians in 1 Corinthians 6:19, 20 concerning the temple?

5. What would you consider to be evidence that a person may have a spurious faith?

6

Jesus and the Rabbi
(John 3:1-21)

Life is filled with unexpected twists and turns. Sometimes things in life turn out very differently from what one would ever expect. For example, the guy voted most likely to succeed in High School turns out to be a collegiate flop, while the geekiest guy in the school marries the prettiest girl and makes a fortune starting a software company. John chapters three and four would have been just as shocking to its first readers. In chapter three one of the most well respected rabbis in Judaism is described as being in spiritual darkness, and after a conversation with Jesus, he leaves as confused as when he came. However, in chapter four, an unnamed woman of questionable reputation comes to believe that Jesus is the Messiah and then leads an entire village out to meet Him. One never knows what God will do!

Jesus' encounter with Nicodemus is one of the most famous episodes in the Gospels. It fulfills several functions in the flow of John's narrative. First, Nicodemus is an example of those to whom Jesus did not entrust Himself in the previous passage (2:25). This connection is obvious from the wording in 2:25b, 'for he himself knew what was in man' and in 3.1, 'Now there was a man of the Pharisees...' Second, this account continues the idea of newness introduced in the previous sections. In those passages Jesus is described as inaugurating a 'new age' (2:1-12) and being the 'new temple' (2:13-25). Here, Jesus explains to a leading rabbi the absolute necessity of a 'new birth'.

There are a number of important thoughts to keep in mind when reading the passage. (1) The major theme of the passage is the new birth and Jesus makes four references to it (3:3, 5, 7, 8). (2) Three times Jesus uses the phrase 'truly, truly' stressing the importance of His words (3:3, 5, 11). (3) The only two explicit references to 'the kingdom of God' in John's Gospel are in this passage (3:3, 5). (4) The first use of 'eternal life' in this Gospel is found here (3:15). (5) The verb 'to believe' is used seven times in 3:12-18. (6) John uses the term 'light' five times in 3:19-21. (7) This passage is an elaboration on John's statement in the prologue about being 'born of God' (1:13).

You can be very religious but not converted: An inquisitive rabbi (3:1-2a)

Nicodemus is a striking reminder that one can have an orthodox theology and still not be converted. The reference to Nicodemus as a ruler of the Jews indicates that he was a member of the Pharisaic sect in the Sanhedrin. He appears to express a true desire to learn more about Jesus. The fact that he came 'at night' indicates that Nicodemus came to Jesus during the night, but the reference probably carries symbolic significance regarding his spiritual condition as well (1:4; 3:19-21; 9:4; 11:10; 13:30; 19:39). John's point is that Nicodemus is living in spiritual darkness despite his esteemed position (3:2a). Later in this passage, John will contrast the differences between those who come to the light and those who love the darkness (3:19-21). Nicodemus reappears in the Gospel again at a meeting of the Sanhedrin where he shows sympathy for the cause of Jesus (7:50) and then he helps Joseph with the burial of Jesus' body (19:39).

'You must be born again' – An important theological discussion (3:2b-15)

Nicodemus makes three comments during the conversation (3:2b, 4, 9), each of which Jesus greets with a response that is longer than the previous one (3:3, 5-8, 10-15).

Nicodemus' first comment and Jesus' reply (3:2b-3)
Nicodemus begins politely enough by acknowledging Jesus' signs as an indication that He comes from God (3:2b). The use

of the pronoun 'we' by Nicodemus indicates that his inquiry is not only for himself and that the actions of Jesus had led to a lot of discussion.

Jesus brushes aside Nicodemus' niceties and gets to the heart of the issue. His use of 'truly, truly' underscores the importance of the matter. Jesus declares to Nicodemus that a person must be born again if he is to see the kingdom of God. The term translated 'born again' can also be translated 'born from above'. It is likely that John chose this word to communicate this dual aspect. The point is that this is something only God can do ('from above') and it results in a dramatic transformation ('born again'). Jesus demands that Nicodemus be remade by the power of God. No matter one's religious pedigree or training, each person must be born of God if they are to enter His kingdom.

Nicodemus' second comment and Jesus' reply (3:4-7)
Nicodemus misunderstands Jesus' point about being 'born again' (3:4a). He interprets Jesus' words literally. Misunderstanding is a common theme in the Gospel (2:19-21; 4:10-15, 31-34). These 'misunderstandings' provide Jesus with the opportunity to expand and deepen His teaching.

Jesus responds to Nicodemus' bewilderment by telling him unless one is 'born of water and the Spirit he cannot enter the kingdom of God' (3:5). Jesus' use of 'truly, truly' stresses the importance of His point. The phrase 'born of water and the Spirit' is parallel to being 'born again', but expands on the concept. Jesus is making a reference to Ezekiel 36:25-27 (cf. Titus 3:5). In the Ezekiel passage God promises, 'I will sprinkle clean water on you, and you shall be clean.... And I will give you a new heart.... And I will put my Spirit within you.' Jesus is referring to the spiritual cleansing that takes place in regeneration.[1]

---

1. Three other interpretations of this phrase are: (1) some understand it to be a reference to Christian baptism; however, this practice does not begin until after Pentecost. (2) Others interpret it as referring to John's baptism of repentance, but why would Nicodemus have found that so difficult to comprehend? (3) Another suggestion is that it is a contrast between physical birth ('with water') and spiritual birth ('born of the Spirit'). This would seem to go along with what Jesus said in verse 6; however, the use of water as a reference to physical birth (amniotic fluid or semen) is rare in ancient literature.

Water is a key metaphor in John's Gospel. Along with the reference here about 'water and spirit' Jesus turns water into wine (2:1-11), offers the Samaritan woman 'living water' (4:7-14), heals a lame man by a pool of water (5:1-7), walks on the water (6:16-21), says, 'if any man thirsts let come to me and drink, and out of his innermost being shall flow rivers of living water' (7:37-39), has a blind man wash mud from his eyes in a pool of water (9:6-7), washes the disciples' feet (13:1-11), and after He was pierced on the cross 'blood and water came out of his side' (19:34).

Jesus tells Nicodemus that while people become members of an earthly family by natural birth, they only become members of God's family by a spiritual birth (3:6-7). Jesus is emphatic about the point that there is no other way than that of rebirth ('you must be born again'). The word 'must' is a key term in the book and suggests the thought of divine necessity.[2] 'You' is plural and refers to Nicodemus and those he represents. What was true of Nicodemus is true of everyone; you must be born again if you are to know God.

Jesus explains further that one cannot control the work of the Spirit any more than one can control the wind (3:8). The Spirit's sovereign and hidden work in a person's heart is evidenced by the effects in that person's life, just as you can see evidence of the wind blowing through the trees. There is a word-play with the words 'wind' and 'spirit', for they translate the same Greek (*pneuma*) and Hebrew (*ruach*) words.

Nicodemus' third comment and Jesus' reply (3:9-15)
3:9-10: Jesus' message is still imperceptible to Nicodemus. After a brief question expressing his incredulity he fades into the background and disappears from sight until later in the book (3:9). Jesus' response suggests that Nicodemus, as Israel's teacher, should have understood these things (3:10). These truths can be found in Old Testament passages such as Deuteronomy 30:6, Jeremiah 31:33 and Ezekiel 36:25-27. Nicodemus' experience is proof that religious knowledge does not necessarily bring true spiritual insight.

---

2. The word is used of the necessity of the crucifixion (3:14; 12:34), of the resurrection (20:9), of things Jesus did in the execution of His ministry (4.4; 9:4; 10:16), and of John the Baptist's eclipse before Jesus (3:30).

3:11-12: The importance of these words is indicated by the use of 'truly, truly' (3:11). There is some debate over how to interpret Jesus' use of the pronoun 'we'. It can be understood as a reference to Jesus and the disciples, but more likely it refers to Jesus and the Father (cf. 1:18; 7:16f; 8:26, 28; 12:49; 14:24). This twofold witness (Jesus and the Father) confirms Jesus' words as fact. Beginning with verse 12 the idea of faith is referred to seven times in the next six verses. The 'earthly things' that Nicodemus will not believe refer to the previous discussion concerning the new birth, which is not very difficult to grasp (3:12). However, if Nicodemus refuses to believe these elementary teachings, how will he ever be able to believe the rest of what Jesus says?[3]

3:13-15: Nicodemus' inability to understand is evidence that he does not have saving faith. The key to grasping Jesus' meaning is faith in a crucified Son. Jesus explains that there is a great distance between this world and heaven (3:13; cf., 1:51; 3:31; 6:38, 42). He bridged that distance, validating His divine stature by defeating death and returning to heaven (cf. 16:5-11). Jesus points to the events recorded in Numbers 21.8-9 to illustrate His statement (3:14). When the Israelites were wandering in the wilderness God sent a plague of serpents to punish them for their rebellious attitudes. If they obeyed God's command to look at the 'lifted up' bronze serpent after being bitten they would be healed. The idea of Jesus being 'lifted up' in John's Gospel refers to His death, resurrection and exaltation. This is the first of three 'lifted up' sayings in the Gospel (8:28; 12:32). The purpose of the lifting up of the Son of Man is that those who believe, that is, those who look to Him in faith, will 'in him' have eternal life (3:15). This harkens back to the Prologue where John writes that 'in him was life and that life was the Light of men' (1:4). This is the first reference to 'eternal life' in the Gospel. It refers to a life lived in fellowship with God that begins now and lasts throughout eternity. Eternal life is the life of God, which resides in Christ ('in him was life') and is given to all believers. John uses the word 'eternal' seventeen times in

---

3. 'You' is plural (in Gk.) in the second usage in verse 11 and in all four uses in verse 12, including Nicodemus and his fellow members in the Sanhedrin.

the book. Interestingly enough, the Father, Son, or Spirit are never described as having it.

You must make a choice: Faith or Unbelief (3:16-18)

There is some debate as to where Jesus' words end and comments by the evangelist begin. Most scholars understand these verses to be John's interpretation and reflections on Jesus' encounter with Nicodemus. The Nicodemus episode is a picture of the battle between light and darkness. At the heart of the passage is the thought of how God's gift of eternal life is to be appropriated. Eternal life is the result of faith in the Son of God (3:15, 16, 18), while disbelief results in judgment and condemnation (3:18, 19, 36). This sums up the two worldviews characteristic of John's Gospel; one is either attracted to or repulsed by the light (3:19-21). The theological significance of the passage can be seen in the important terms that permeate it: love, light, darkness, judgment, world, believe, and eternal life.

3:16: This may be the best-known and most beloved verse in the Bible. It establishes the depth of God's love for the world. The word 'for' connects this verse to verse 15 and explains what happened to make eternal life a possibility. This is John's first use of the word 'love' (*agapao*), a verb used thirty-six times in the Gospel, more than twice the number in any other book of the New Testament with the exception of 1 John (thirty-one uses). John uses the verb *phileo* (also meaning love) more than anyone else in the New Testament, though the figures are smaller. He uses it thirteen of the twenty-five times it is found in the New Testament. It is interesting that John uses both verbs more than twice as much as any other New Testament author. Clearly the concept mattered much to him and he rightly became known as 'The Apostle of Love'. John refers to Jesus as God's 'only begotten' Son. The thought is that Jesus is God's unique Son in that His essential nature is the same as the Father's.

Jesus' death is a revelation of the Father's love. Its purpose is brought out both negatively and positively. Negatively, those who do not believe will perish (what John means by this terrible reality is not spelled out); positively, those who believe will have eternal life. One should notice that eternal life is a present reality. John knows of no other state. As many have noted, this verse is the gospel in a nutshell. Whenever we question God's love for us all we need to do is to go back to John 3:16 and be reminded that God loved us so much that He gave His one and only Son to die in our place. God truly and deeply loves His children.

3:17: John again contrasts a negative thought with a positive one (3:17). In the previous verse the coming of Jesus is described as God's gift ('he gave') and in this verse Jesus is described as God's emissary ('sent the Son into the world'). God did not send His Son into the world 'to judge the world but that the world might be saved through him.' God's motivation for sending His Son was love (3:16) and salvation (3:17). How do we reconcile the thought that God did not send the Son into the world to judge the world (3:17) with the thought in 9:39 that Jesus came into the world for judgment? We must see that the offer of salvation implies judgment. Salvation and judgment are in one sense two sides of the same coin. The fact of salvation for all who believe implies judgment on all who refuse to believe. The concept of judgment here parallels the earlier reference to condemn. John's main point here, however, is that Jesus' primary purpose in coming was salvation and not judgment.[4] Salvation was central to His mission. It is interesting to notice that the word 'world' appears three times in this verse. The 'world' is mankind in opposition to God and under the dominion of Satan, yet it is the object of God's love (3:16) and the focus of Christ's mission (3:17).

3:18: John presents a contrast that highlights only two categories (3:18). Those who believe in Christ are not judged and those who do not believe in Him are judged already. This is another example of John's realized eschatological perspective. Judgment is not only off in the future but is a present reality. The basis of their judgment is their refusal to trust in Christ. Faith in Jesus is the decisive issue.

---

4. The concept of 'judgment' is important in John's Gospel. He uses the verb nineteen times and the noun form twelve times. While we must be careful not to make too much from the number of occurrences, it does show his interest in the doctrine of divine judgment.

A Cosmic Conflict: Light and Darkness (3:19-21)

John explains in these verses why some believe and some do not. This refusal to trust in Christ is part of a cosmic battle between light and darkness. John uses the term 'light' five times in these three verses. Those who put their faith in Jesus and practice the truth are described as being 'in the light', while those who refuse to come to the Light are described as 'loving the darkness', 'hating the light' and 'refusing to come to the light' so their wickedness may not be exposed. Therefore the difference between the believer and the unbeliever lies in their different attitudes toward the Light. Light exposes and reveals who we really are. Those who believe will come to the light, but those who refuse to believe 'hate(s) the light'. Hate is a very strong term and John uses it twelve times. Their refusal to believe is a moral issue more than intellectual one. They love darkness and hate light. John could not have chosen stronger words to describe the spiritual battle that goes on in a person.

John wants his readers to understand that what was going on with Nicodemus was more significant than just an intellectual battle between two rabbis. Nicodemus is caught up in a cosmic conflict between truth and error, light and darkness, eternal life and judgment. Nicodemus ventured briefly into the light and did not like what he saw, so for the time being he returned to the darkness. These concluding verses remind us that our world is a bloody battlefield in the war of all wars between God's kingdom and the kingdom of darkness, between God's truth and Satan's lies. The stakes are people's eternal destiny. God's truth, however, is a powerful weapon that illuminates the darkness and confronts people with the gospel of saving grace.

Reflections

Jesus' encounter with Nicodemus is an arresting reminder of the necessity of grace. A person can know much about the Bible and the things of God but still be devoid of His grace. It is not as simple as catechizing our children and studying the Bible with them (as necessary as that is). There is a war going on between the light and the darkness and spiritual truth without accompanying grace will not save a person. Fortunately, 'the Light shines in the darkness and the darkness cannot overpower it' (1:5). Praise the Lord!

This story also reminds us that evangelism is not just about passing on a gospel witness, but it is an assault against the evil one. Outside of Christ people are in spiritual darkness. Outside of Christ they love the darkness and they hate the Light. They fear that the Light will expose them for who they truly are. Yet God's truth and intercessory prayer are powerful weapons in a believer's arsenal.

We learn as well that salvation results in a dramatic transformation that is comparable to a new birth. This is something only God can do ('born from above') and results in a dramatic inward transformation ('born again'). The outward manifestations of this inner transformation are seen more quickly in some than in others, but those truly converted are changed nonetheless. The new birth is the result of the Spirit's work in a person's life.

Study Questions

1. Why do you think John included the encounter between Jesus and Nicodemus?

2. Paraphrase John 3:16 in your own words.

3. What do verses 19-21 teach you about spiritual darkness (see also John 1:5; 9:4; 11:10; 13:30; 19:39)?

4. Why do you think Jesus chose Numbers 21:8-9 to illustrate what he was saying in 3:13-15?

7

Jesus is Greater than John the Baptist
(John 3:22-36)

In October 1975, my dad gave me tickets to the watch 'the fight of the century' – 'The Thrilla in Manila'. It was the third and final fight between Muhammad Ali and Joe Frazier for the Heavyweight Boxing Championship of the World. If I had known at the time that I would eventually live in Louisville, Kentucky, I might have cheered for Muhammad Ali rather than for Joe Frazier on that night. However, I didn't like Ali's brash talk about being the greatest, but on that night he proved himself to be the greatest boxer in the world. While Ali might still be considered the greatest fighter to have ever strapped on the gloves, his cocky disposition turned off many people. This longing for greatness illustrates a reality we see every day – success is the breeding ground for pride. What is true in the sports world is no less true in the realm of ministry and service to King Jesus. It is not uncommon for those whom God has used to lose focus on pointing people to Jesus and begin to make ministry about themselves.

About two thousand years ago John the Baptist exhibited a disposition quite different from Muhammad Ali. John attracted large crowds to the Judean wilderness. As we see in chapter one, some wondered if he might not be the Messiah or a great eschatological figure. Yet John deflected attention from himself and pointed people to Jesus. On the banks of the Jordan River John the Baptist revealed how truly great he was by acknowledging the superior role of Jesus. The major point of this passage is that Jesus is superior to John the Baptist because Jesus is 'from above' and John is 'from below'. In the process, we learn something about what true humility looks like.

This passage can be divided into two sections. In the opening section the Baptist helps his followers understand why Jesus' ministry must increase and his must decrease (3:22-30). In the following section, John the apostle reflects on why Jesus is superior to John the Baptist (3:31-36).

John the Baptist embraces his inferior role to Jesus (3:22-30)
The evangelist indicates that both Jesus and the Baptist's ministries overlapped for a time. The events in John's Gospel up to this point still precede Jesus' Galilean Ministry described in the Synoptic Gospels (cf. John 2:24; Mark 1:14; 6:14-29; Matt. 14:1-12; Luke 3:19-20). John's Baptist's final words in the Fourth Gospel appear in this passage, 'He must increase, but I must decrease.'

A misplaced focus (3:22-26)
For a period of time Jesus and John carried on simultaneous baptismal ministries, although later the evangelist notes that Jesus Himself did not baptize (3:22-23; 4:2). John was baptizing in Aenon ('spring') near Salim ('peace'). This site is probably located four miles southeast of Shechem in Samaria (3:23).[1] The Dead Sea Scrolls indicate that ceremonial washing and purification were subjects of deep interest among religious sects (2:25). Earlier, at the wedding at Cana, reference was made to the concept of purification (cf. 2:6).

Oddly enough, the ensuing discussion has to do more with the success of Jesus' ministry and less to do with purification and baptism (3:26). From John's response one wonders if the theological issue was merely a cover-up for envy at Jesus' growing popularity. It is not unlikely that John's disciples felt badly for their mentor. The crowds were dwindling and his influence seemed to be waning. This is the kind of sinful battle that often rages in the heart of a pastor when he sees

---

1. See Brown, *John*, 1:151.

the growing attendance at another church, while his church's attendance is stagnant or declining. When the standards of worldly success creep into a minister's heart he begins to measure success by 'nickels and noses'. He develops the compulsion to be known as the pastor of the biggest and best church in town. Ultimately there develops a culture around the pastor or leader of an unrelenting drive for more. It is easy even for those who love Jesus to fall into this trap as illustrated by Jesus' disciples on several occasions (Mark 9:30-37; 10:35-45).

The thoughts of a humble servant (3:27-30)
John the Baptist did not have room for competitive rivalries. He responds to the thought of Jesus' growing popularity with a series of powerful statements. First, God's providence determines ministerial success (3:27). These words are true of Jesus and John (and of everyone!). Jesus' and John's ministries were the result of divine providence, so there was no place for envy or jealousy. The verb translated 'to give' is used seventy-six times in the Gospel, especially with regard to the things the Father gives the Son. This wrong kind of talk can be heard at pastors' conferences where ministerial 'groupies' divide up and fight over their favorite preachers. Instead of being jealous over the successful ministry of others, we should rejoice in what God is doing through them.

Second, John reminds them emphatically in 3:28 that he had told them he was not the Messiah but his forerunner ('I am not the Christ'). He illustrates his relationship to Jesus by comparing it to being like the best man at a wedding (3:29). Jesus is the bridegroom and John is the bridegroom's friend who 'rejoices greatly at the bridegroom's voice'. John's joy is full because of the privilege of serving the bridegroom. Many of Jesus' followers become cynical and embittered when they fail to receive the attention and accolades they think they deserve. This is one reason why many of God's servants have lost their joy in serving. They began with fullness of joy for the privilege of serving their Savior, but somewhere along the way something happened. They forgot that they are here to serve the bridegroom. When we long for the glory that belongs only to God we will find ourselves frustrated, disappointed, and angry that we do not get the public recognition we think we deserve. John was full of joy because he was fulfilling his intended role (3:29). He rejoiced in Jesus' success.

Third, John tells his followers, 'He must increase, but I must decrease' (3:30). These are the Baptist's final words in John's Gospel. John reaffirms for the last recorded time his subordinate position. These words sound strange to those Christian leaders that yearn for a celebrity status in the evangelical world. Yet, these are the words of someone that Jesus described as the greatest man ever born (Matt. 11:11). They should be the prayer of every believer, and especially of every gospel minister. It is not easy to see another's influence grow and ours wane; it is even harder to rejoice in the fact, but John did. John realized that his service was not about himself, but that he served One greater than himself, and as a result he was filled with joy.

Theological reflections from an aging apostle (3:31-36)

John elaborates further on why Jesus is greater than John the Baptist. The simple straightforward explanation of the previous verses now expands into more abstract statements.[2] The author, from decades-long reflections on Jesus' superiority, sets forth three reasons for the greatness of Jesus: His heavenly origin (3:31), His heavenly testimony (3:32-34), and His heavenly authority (3:35, 36).

Jesus is superior because of his heavenly origin (3:31)

Jesus is superior to John because He comes from heaven ('the one who comes from above'). The phrase, 'the one who is of the earth,' applies here especially to John the Baptist. Jesus' heavenly origin is an important thought for the apostle as seen in the fact that he repeats it twice in this verse and once earlier in the chapter, with a slight variation in the wording (3:13). This is one way John reveals that Jesus is the Christ, the Son of God. The words 'above all' establish Jesus' absolute supremacy to all things and to all people. Clearly, this is something that could not be said of John the Baptist.

---

2. Although this section can be construed in a general fashion, the contrast John has in mind is primarily between Jesus and John the Baptist.

Jesus is superior because of his heavenly testimony (3:32-34)
John's second point is that Jesus' heavenly origin makes Him uniquely qualified to reveal the Father and to speak for Him (3:32a). However, despite Jesus' heavenly origin many reject His testimony (3:32b), but those who accept His witness 'confirm' God's truthfulness (3:33). They do not make the message true, but they acknowledge it is true. John adds that the Father has given Jesus the Spirit 'without measure' (3:34).[3]

Jesus is superior because of His heavenly authority (3:35-36)
The final reason for Jesus' superiority to the Baptist is based on the fact that the Father loves the Son and has given Him all authority (3:35). The mutual love of the Father and the Son means much in this Gospel. It is stated explicitly twice in the Gospel that the Father loves the Son, but it is implied throughout. The Greek word used here of the Father's love is *agapao*, but in 5:20 it is *phileo*. This variation suggests that a significant distinction should not be made between these two words in John. The idea that God has placed absolute authority into the hands of the Son is affirmed elsewhere in the New Testament (cf. Heb. 1:2, 3, 13; Col. 1:16-18).

This final verse brings this chapter to a fitting conclusion (3:36). As in 3:19-21, there are only two responses a person can make to Jesus: unbelief (loving darkness) or belief (coming to the light). John contrasts those who believe and those who do not obey. Those who believe have eternal life. Those who disobey the Son not only do not 'see life', but God's wrath 'abides' on them. The opposite of belief here is not unbelief, but disobedience. This is the only occurrence of 'wrath' in John's Gospel (cf. Rom. 1:18-25). Even as God's wrath is a present reality ('abides') for the disobedient, so eternal life is the present experience of those who trust in the Son; that is, they enjoy the benefits of eternal life now.

---

3. Gary Burge, *The Anointed Community: The Holy Spirit in the Johannine Tradition* (Grand Rapidsj: Eerdmans, 1987), 55, understands Jesus as the subject and the thought to be that He dispenses the Spirit without limit. However, this does not seem to make as much sense in this context where God is both the sender and the giver.

Reflections

We see in these verses another example of John the Baptist's true greatness. It seems that those who are truly great never fully understand their significance. He refuses to get baited into a comparison of his ministry with Jesus' ministry. Some of his disciples were not quite so wise. There seems to be a sinful tendency in the human heart that longs for recognition. We indulge it at our own peril. The Baptist had a grasp of who he was and who Jesus is. Gospel ministers must deal ruthlessly with the insatiable longing for human acclaim.

Furthermore, we see the keen insights of the elderly John as he reflected on this situation. After decades of meditating on the person of Christ, he grasps something of the significance of Jesus' heavenly origin. It is interesting to see the Trinitarian nature in his thinking. He describes the close relationship between the Father and Son, as well as the role of the Spirit in Jesus' ministry (3:34)

Finally, a truth that runs through this chapter is that every person's destiny is determined by their personal response to the Son. It is evident from the concluding verse in this section that saving faith is demonstrated by a lifestyle characterized by obedience. On the other hand, if one confesses that they know Jesus, but their lifestyle is characterized by disobedience, it is unlikely that they have saving faith (cf. Gal. 5:19-21; 1 Cor. 6:9-11; Eph. 5:6-8). Many in the church believe that because they prayed the 'sinner's prayer', or walked down an aisle, they are saved. Yet, they live without any desire for God and their lives completely contradict their confession. We need to harken to the words of John the Baptist, 'Bring forth fruit in keeping with repentance' (Luke 3:8).

STUDY QUESTIONS

1. What were John the Baptist's three responses to the thought that Jesus' ministry was surpassing his own?

2. Why do we find it so hard to rejoice in God's blessings on others?

3. Can you think of other places in the New Testament where Jesus relationship to His people is compared to a marriage relationship?

4. What were the three points that John the apostle made concerning Jesus' superiority to John the Baptist?

5. What similarities do you find in John 3:19-21 and 3:36?

8

Jesus and the Samaritan Woman
(John 4:1-30)

The story of Jesus' encounter with the Samaritan woman is one of the most touching and beloved stories in the Bible. The story reminds us that Jesus came to save sinners. While we may never say it, many believers have a tendency to write people off as being too far gone to be a recipient of God's grace. If we were to think this about anyone we would likely have thought it about the Samaritan woman. You get the very real sense that she lived with great shame and felt terribly alone. She has been married five times and the man she woke up beside on the morning of the day she met Jesus was not her husband. Surely, if anyone has slipped too far into the dark it was this woman.[1] Yet, the Light shines in the darkness and the darkness cannot overpower it! This story gives hope to every person who loves someone that seems beyond the reach of God. Never give up hope in Jesus' power to save.

John has intentionally placed this story in close proximity to Jesus' encounter with Nicodemus so that the reader can contrast the two. Nicodemus is Jewish, well-educated,

---

1. In order to be fair to the woman, it must be admitted that we cannot know how many times she had been divorced and how many times she had been widowed. Furthermore, it is impossible to know if she was at fault each time she was divorced. Nevertheless, the sense of the passage is that she has lived an immoral life to some degree.

religious, moral and male. This woman is a Samaritan, probably illiterate, religiously compromised, immoral, and female. Another difference is that Nicodemus is named but this woman's name is never given, even though she obviously had one. The reader will be quite shocked as the story unfolds to discover that, unlike Nicodemus, this unnamed woman comes to believe in Jesus as the Messiah.

While the story is used often as an example of how to evangelize (and there certainly are a number of implications that can be gleaned from this passage), this is not John's primary intention. This passage fits into the overall narrative of 2:1–4:54 by illustrating that the messianic age cannot be confined to the old forms of Judaism and that the new age brings with it a new universal offer of the gospel.[2] This principle will be further illustrated in the chapter as the local Samaritan village confesses Jesus to be 'the Savior of the World' (4:42) and when Jesus heals the royal official's son (4:46-54).

After the initial encounter is described (4:1-6) the story develops around two key topics: living water (4:7-15) and true worship (4:16-26). As their conversation unfolds the woman demonstrates a growing understanding of Jesus' identity: 'Sir' (4:11, 15), 'Prophet' (4:19), 'Christ' (4:25, 29), and 'Savior of the World' (4:42). The story concludes with the woman leaving behind an empty water jar and returning to the village to tell others about Jesus.

A divine appointment (4:1-6)
4:1-3: Jesus departs from Judea for Galilee because He is concerned that the Pharisees may begin to investigate Him because of His growing baptismal ministry (4:1-3). The evangelist inserts the parenthetical thought that Jesus was not baptizing but His disciples (4:2). The route many faithful Jewish people sometimes took from Judea into Galilee was by crossing the Jordan into Perea and then traveling north to cross the Jordan again into the valley of lower Galilee. Yet, it was not uncommon for Jewish people to travel the shorter

---

2. Blomberg, *Jesus and the Gospels*, 265.

route through Samaria.[3] For the modern reader, the word 'Samaritan' may not carry negative overtones (i.e., 'the good Samaritan'), but this was certainly not the case among Jews in Jesus' day. The animosity between Jews and Samaritans had existed for centuries and was still very intense at the time (cf. 2 Kings 17; Ezra 4:1-5; Neh. 4:1-23; 6:1-19).[4]

4:4-6: Jesus 'had' to go through Samaria because God had made an appointment for Him at Jacob's well. Although the exact location of Sychar remains unknown the location of Jacob's well is well attested.[5] John comments that it was at the sixth hour (noon) when Jesus encounters the woman. Two things may be going on here. First, John may be contrasting the fact that Nicodemus approached Jesus under the cover of darkness, while the Samaritan woman encountered Him under the noonday sun. Second, a woman normally would not draw water during the hottest part of the day, so she may have been something of an outcast because of her lifestyle. John's observation that Jesus was tired highlights His true humanity (4:6). Unlike Jesus, we often miss appointments God makes for us. Our smart phones and iPods keep us from noticing people. We assume that people are not interested in hearing a good word about Jesus. Yet we have no idea what God may be doing in someone's life. No one would have ever dreamed that God was about to do something so wonderful in this woman's life – no one except Jesus.

Jesus' offer of 'Living Water' (4:7-15)
4:7-9: Jesus initiates the conversation by requesting a drink of water (4:7). John describes the disciples having gone into the village to buy food, explaining why Jesus was alone when the woman arrived (4:8). While it seems odd that Jews, who preferred not to travel through Samaria, would buy food in

---

3. Morris, *John*, 226, n16, notes that Josephus makes the point that although there existed great antipathy between Jews and Samaritans, Jews passing from Judea to Galilee or back nevertheless preferred the shorter route through Samaria (*Ant.* 20.118).

4. When the Assyrians conquered Israel in 722 B.C., they left a remnant of Israelites there and imported hundreds of pagans. The resulting intermarriage produced a racially mixed race that became the Samaritans.

5. Carson, *John*, 216, locates the encounter near the modern town of Askar, which is just east of Mount Gerizim and Mount Ebal.

a Samaritan village, it must be remembered that Galileans were not as scrupulous as Judeans, and unless they carried a large supply of food with them they had to buy provisions somewhere. The Samaritan woman is shocked that Jesus, a Jewish man, would speak to her (4:9a). John adds a note for his readers to explain the woman's comment (4:9b). Jesus broke several taboos in speaking to her. First, as mentioned earlier, Jews and Samaritans felt disdain toward one another and would not speak to one another. Second, for a Jewish man to speak to a woman that he did not know was considered inappropriate. Third, Jesus knew that this woman had lived an immoral life and He had never committed a sin.

4:10-12: Jesus quickly moves the conversation to spiritual matters (4:10). If only she knew who He really was she would be asking Him, not for physical water, but living water.[6] She 'misunderstands' Jesus and thinks that He is speaking of the water in the well, to which He has no access – the well is over 100 feet deep (4:11). She wryly asks Jesus if He is greater than 'our father Jacob' who dug the well (4:12). The irony is yes, Jesus is greater than Jacob!

4:13-14: Jesus clarifies His meaning by contrasting the water in the well with the living water that He offers (4:13-14). Those who drink the water from the well will thirst again (4:13), but those who drink the 'living water' will never thirst again (4:14). The all-encompassing nature of Jesus' words is impressive: everyone who drinks from the water in the well will thirst again. No matter how many times a person returns to the well, and no matter how much they drink, they will thirst again. But the water that Jesus offers quenches the deepest thirst of the human soul. This gift of living water is the eternal life that results from the Holy Spirit's ministry (4:14; 7:38-39). Jesus draws on familiar Old Testament imagery (cf. Jer. 2:13; Isa. 12:3; Zech. 14:8).

The life Jesus gives is no stagnant thing – it is abundant, vibrant ('springing up'), and satisfying (cf. 10:10). The contrast could not be greater – if you want to thirst again drink from Jacob's well, but if you want your thirst satisfied drink the

---

6. Living water referred to water that was flowing rather than the stagnant water of a cistern or well.

living water Jesus offers. Most people spend their entire lives seeking that one person or thing that will quench their thirsty soul. Often they seek for it with the many good things life has to offer – family, friends, career, but none of those things were ever intended to fill the longing of the human heart that can only be filled by God. This woman had sought to fill it with relationships with men, but none satisfied. Her heart was dry and parched and she must have felt lonely and ashamed.

4:15: While it is impossible to know if her request for the living water is sarcastic or sincere ('Sir, give me this water'), it is likely that we should interpret her response somewhat positively in contrast to Nicodemus' 'How can this be?' (3:9). Even though she does not grasp the full import of Jesus' words, she likes what she's hearing.

Jesus' invitation to true worship (4:16-24)
The topic changes at this point in their conversation from 'living water' to 'true worship'. The word 'worship' is used eight times and 'worshipers' is used twice in 4:20-24. Jesus turns the spotlight on to the woman's life. When the light enters the world it exposes the darkness. Nicodemus withdrew from the light. Surprisingly she does not flee but chooses to remain in the light even as she attempts to redirect the conversation away from herself.

4:16-18: Jesus' request that she call her husband is another example of His omniscience (4:16). The knowledge John attributes to Jesus is part of the way in which he demonstrates that Jesus is the divine Christ. While her answer may be technically true, Jesus knows that she is living with a man out of wedlock (4:17-18). As Jesus describes her past it must have been very painful for her, but she had to have her sin exposed by the light.

4:19-20: She recognizes Jesus' prophetic powers and seeks to introduce a topic of religious controversy in order to divert attention from herself (4:19). The proper place of worship had long been a source of debate between Jews and Samaritans (4:20). Mount Gerizim, which towered over the well, was the Samaritans' holy place. Abraham and Jacob built altars in the general vicinity (Gen. 12:7; 33:20) and Moses blessed the people from there (Deut. 11:29; 27:12). The Samaritans built a temple on Mount Gerizim (ca. 400 B.C.) that the Jews later destroyed (ca.128 B.C.).

4:21-22: Jesus encourages her to believe Him when He tells her that the debate over the proper place to worship the Father is coming to an end. Now is a time of transition and soon ('an hour is coming') it will not be important where a person worships (4:21). The Samaritans' worship of God was defective because they rejected much of God's Word. The Samaritan Bible was limited to the Pentateuch and therefore eliminated much of God's revelation (4:22a). Out of all the nations of the world God chose the Jewish people to be the means by which He would shine the light of salvation (4:22b). The Messiah was Jewish and the Jewish people had a more complete revelation of God than did the Samaritans.

4:23-24: There is a change in redemptive history taking place ('an hour is coming, and now is') so that true worship will not be relegated to a particular place. God is seeking (4:23b) true worshipers that will worship Him 'in spirit and truth' (4:23a). Exactly what Jesus means by 'spirit and truth' is debated.[7] It likely carries the idea that worship 'in spirit' is worship that arises from the deepest recesses of a person's being, and in light of the previous discussions about the Spirit, it is the result of the Spirit's work in a believer's heart. To worship 'in truth' carries the thoughts that it is genuine and authentic, but it is also true to who God is as revealed in Scripture. God is more interested in the worshiper than the location of worship. God is seeking people who will worship Him in this way. Jesus repeats the thought that the kind of worship that God desires is worship in spirit and truth but adds the thought that 'God is spirit' (4:24). Because God is spirit and not confined to a body, He is everywhere present and this helps explain why worship is not confined to a specific locale. John communicates again the thought of divine necessity with his use of 'must'.

Lessons from an empty water jar (4:25-30)
4:25-26: The woman responds that one day the Messiah would clear up the disagreement related to the place of

---

7. One Greek preposition governs both words ('in spirit and truth') and makes them a single concept.

worship. The Samaritans understood the Messiah to fulfill the role of a teacher. Jesus tells her plainly that He is the long-awaited Messiah. This is the only occasion before His trial that Jesus directly acknowledges His Messiahship. Jesus felt free to declare Himself to be the Messiah in this setting because the Samaritans did not expect the Messiah to be a political-military figure.

4:27-30: The disciples return just as Jesus and the woman are finishing their conversation. They are shocked to see Him speaking to a Samaritan woman for reasons discussed above. It may be that the reason they did not ask Him why he was breaking contemporary morals by speaking to her was because they knew Jesus' tendency to do the unexpected. John notes that she left her water jar and returned to the city (4:28-29). While she may have exaggerated slightly the extent of her conversation ('Come see a man who told me all the things that I had done') she was convinced that He was no ordinary man. Her invitation to the crowd is similar to what we heard spoken by Jesus to Andrew (1:39) and by Philip to Nathaniel (1:46).

Reflections
Several insights come to mind from this story. First, Jesus is truly amazing. He is comfortable with people from various backgrounds. In chapter 1 He interacts with men much like Himself – Galileans, hardworking, and spiritually open as demonstrated by their being followers of John the Baptist. In chapter 2 we find Him at a wedding. He did not isolate himself or hide Himself away but went to the places where people were gathered. In chapter 3 He speaks comfortably with Nicodemus, a well-educated, well to do rabbi. Now we discover in chapter 4 Jesus interacting with someone from another race, religion, and lifestyle (immoral). The more like Jesus we become the more comfortable we are with people from all walks of life. We know that no matter who a person is, or what they have done, they need living water. Life becomes less about us and more about Jesus and His mission.

Second, the life Jesus gives is dynamic and vibrant. It's not like the stagnant water of a well, but the energetic and exciting water from a flowing stream. This life results from the Spirit working in a believer's heart and producing a longing to worship God 'in spirit and truth'. The idea of living water is not far removed from a believer's life in the kingdom being like a wedding. Obviously there is much heartache and pain in this life, but the life Jesus gives is not static or stagnant. There is far too much soberness in the church and not nearly enough godly joy.

Third, it is difficult to know what, if anything, should be made of John's reference to the water jar the woman left behind (4:28). It may be nothing more than an interesting piece of eyewitness testimony, or it may simply demonstrate her haste to tell the town's people about Jesus. However, Brown understands it to have symbolic significance.[8] If Brown is correct, and I think he is, at this point then John intended his readers to see the jar as symbolizing the woman's life. She went day after day to the well of human relationships longing to have her thirst quenched by finding the right husband. Over time she gave up on marriage and lived with a man out of wedlock, but still her thirst remained. After taking a drink of the living water offered by Jesus her life is changed dramatically. She went to the well in the heat of the day to avoid contact with other women. Now she returns to the city and shares about her encounter with Jesus, and the men of the village go to see for themselves. If this is how the incident is to be understood then Jesus is presented as the one that can satisfy mankind's deepest longings.

STUDY QUESTIONS

1. Why do you think John located this story where he did? Did John have more than just chronological considerations in mind?

2. While the story is not about evangelistic strategies there does seem to be implications about approaching people with the gospel that can be learned by Jesus' example. What are some that you see in this passage?

3. Why do you think this woman responded more positively to Jesus than Nicodemus?

---

8. Brown, *John*, 1:173.

4. Is there someone in your life that you may have given up on? How does this story give you fresh hope for their salvation?

9

Jesus the Missionary
(John 4:31-54)

We come now to the final scenes of this larger section that begins in 2:1 and concludes in 4:54. Jesus uses His encounter with the Samaritan woman to teach His disciples about true food (4:31-38). He encourages them to have a missional mindset that transcends strictly Jewish boundaries. He illustrates this for them in the conversion of a Samaritan village (4:39-45) and the salvation of a Gentile official and his household (4:46-54). The Samaritan woman demonstrates the power of one's story. Her simple invitation, 'Come and see a man that told me all the things that I had done' results in a gospel harvest (4:29). In a similar way, a father's willingness to take Jesus at His word culminates in the salvation of an entire household (4:53).

True Nourishment: Jesus instructs the disciples on the importance of missional living (4:31-38)
4:31-34: As the villagers make their way out to speak to Jesus His disciples urge Him to eat, but He has food to eat they know nothing about (4:31-32). They wonder if anyone has given Him something to eat (4:33). Their misunderstanding of Jesus' statement provides Him with the opportunity to speak to them about true food, which is sowing gospel seeds for the harvesting of souls (4:34-38). Just as food strengthens one's physical body, doing the Father's will gives spiritual

strength and vitality (4:34). Jesus makes much of doing God's will in the Fourth Gospel (cf. 5:30; 6:38; 8.26; 9:4; 10:37-38; 12:49-50; 14:31; 15:10; 17:4). The pronouns 'I' and 'you' emphasize the differences in thinking between Jesus and the disciples. Equally important for Jesus is accomplishing the work the Father sent Him to do (cf. 5:36; 17:4; 19:28, 30). Jesus' final words from the cross in this Gospel are, 'It is finished' (19:30). Jesus prayed to the Father, 'I glorified you on earth, having accomplished the work you gave me to do' (17:4). The next several verses should be interpreted as an aspect of the work Jesus came to do and the work He leaves behind for His followers (4:35-38).

4:35: Jesus' statement 'Do you not say, "There are yet four months, and then comes the harvest"?' is likely a proverbial thought that the harvest cannot be rushed; however, these fields are ready whether the disciples realize it or not. Jesus turns their attention from the agricultural harvest imagery to the spiritual harvest by pointing out the crowd coming from the village. The Lord of the harvest is at work (Matt. 9:37-38)!

4:36-38: The disciples must be involved in the work because the issues at stake are eternal (4:36a). The work of harvesting souls for the kingdom is not to be done in a spirit of competition, but the important point is that we play a part in the process. Each person has a task, 'one sows and another reaps,' and one role does not supersede another (4:36b). When a sinner comes to faith in Christ, whether we were the one who planted the seed or the one who got to 'pick the fruit', both laborers can rejoice because a sinner has received life eternal (4:37).

As to who the 'others' are here ('others have labored and you have entered into their labor') it is difficult to be certain (4:38). The reference may refer to the work of Old Testament prophets including John the Baptist. However, in the present context, it may be best to understand the comment as a reference to Jesus' ministry to the Samaritan woman and her testimony to the town's people. Many believers fail to experience the full joy of the Lord because of their failure to be a gospel witness – either sowing gospel seed or getting the privilege of 'picking the gospel fruit'. The evangelistic stakes are high – eternal life hangs in the balance for the unredeemed.

When a person shares their faith it does for one's spiritual life what eating a good meal does for a hungry person. It provides a renewed energy and vitality that is lacking in the lives of those who seldom share their faith.

The fruit of the woman's testimony: Don't underestimate your story (4:39-42)

John's first illustration of the principle that Jesus taught is the arrival of the men from the village who heard about Jesus from the Samaritan woman (4:39). He emphasizes the Samaritans' faith by repeating the verb three times in these verses (4:39, 41, 42). The point is that the woman's testimony bore fruit to eternal life. Later Jesus will tell the disciples, 'You did not choose me but I chose you, and appointed you that you would go and bear fruit' (15:16). This is exactly what the Samaritan woman did. She was an unlikely candidate to introduce the Messiah to anybody, but her simple testimony causes the villagers to 'come and see' for themselves. Although they came out to see Jesus because of the woman's testimony, after hearing Jesus for themselves they believe him to be 'the Savior of the world' (4:42). Jesus remained two more days and many more Samaritans came to trust in Him. This is one of only two references in the New Testament that specifically identify Jesus as the 'Savior of the world' (cf. 1 John 4:14). How wonderful that the only time in the Gospels where this title is used of Jesus it is by Samaritans, which gives some insight into the purpose of this passage.

Jesus is the giver of life: The healing of the royal official's son (4:43-54)

The story of the healing of the royal official's son is the second illustration of the power of the gospel. The story presents Jesus as the giver of life (cf. 1:4). John has already recounted Jesus bringing the gospel to a respected Jewish teacher (3:1-21), then to an outcast Samaritan woman and her village (4:1-42). Now He goes one step further from 'official Judaism' by healing the son of a Gentile official who worked for the Roman government (4:46-54).

The healing of the royal official's son completes the Cana-to-Cana cycle (2:1–4:53). It begins and ends with Jesus performing a sign (2:11; 4:54) The Johannine account here underscores one very important point: that Jesus' word is powerful and effectual. The very hour of healing is the very hour when Jesus tells the father that his son lives. As a result of the events the father and his family put their faith in Jesus, which is the author's ultimate aim for the book (20:30-31). This combination of miracle and belief is what distinguishes the Johannine signs. Jesus' powerful works are intended to evoke a response and to reveal His identity. Jesus' miracles are signs intended to elicit faith.

The setting: Jesus returns to Galilee (4:43-45)
Jesus returns to Galilee (4:43) where He spent most of His life and ministry.[1] He grew up in Nazareth, about 3.5 miles from Sepphoris, the Gentile administrative center of Galilee. Soon after Jesus began His public ministry He relocated his base of operation to Capernaum, a thriving fishing village on the Sea of Galilee. While the Synoptic Gospels focus on Jesus' Galilean ministry, John's Gospel focuses primarily on Jesus' Judean ministry with fewer references to episodes in Galilee. It is approximately fifty miles by road from Sychar to Cana (4:46), a journey of two to three days by foot.

A father's desperate plea: 'Heal my dying son!' (4:46-47)
God can use life's desperate moments to reach a person for eternity as illustrated by this pagan father's desperate plea for the life of his son. The father travels from Capernaum to Cana to beg Jesus to heal his son, 'for he was at the point of death'. This is the first of three references to the seriousness of the boy's condition (4:47, 49, 51). The journey from Capernaum to Cana is about sixteen miles.

The Savior's powerful word: 'Your son lives' (4:48-50)
Jesus' response seems harsh, but He is confronting a mentality that sees Him simply as a miracle worker. His statement, 'unless you see signs and wonders you will not believe,' is a challenge not only to the royal official ('Jesus said to him') but

---

1. At first glance, 4:43-44 appear to contradict one another. While the Galileans welcome Jesus, it is based on their amazement of His miracles (cf. 2:23-25), not on true faith. Jesus sharply criticized their desire for signs and wonders.

also to the Galilean people – 'you' is plural (4:48). They were in danger of becoming so enthralled with Jesus' miraculous power that they failed to see that His miracles were intended as signs to point them to faith in Him (cf. 6:2, 26, 30).

The father pleads with Jesus to accompany him to his home before his son dies. Jesus speaks a word ('Go; your son lives') that requires the father to exercise faith. The father demonstrates his faith by immediately returning home (4:50). He learned that Christ's word is as good as His presence.

The subsequent events: 'The whole household believed' (4:51-54)
Cana is in the Galilean hills and Capernaum is below sea level on the shore of the Sea of Galilee. As the official travels back to Capernaum he encounters his servants along the way who report that his son had been healed at 1:00 p.m. on the previous day, the very time that Jesus pronounced him healed. The father left Cana after Jesus pronounced his son's healing and apparently spent the night along the way before completing his journey the following day (4:51-52). As a result of the healing the father and his household believed in Jesus (4:53; cf. 20:30-31). John concludes the story by noting that this was the second sign Jesus performed in Cana (4:54; cf. 2:11).

Reflections
We see Jesus in this chapter taking the gospel out of strictly Jewish confines to the Samaritans (4:1-42) and to a Gentile (4:43-54; cf.10:16; 11:51-52). The church in Acts followed the same pattern (cf. 8:4-40; 10:1-11:30). These passages teach that Jesus is the 'Savior of the world'. What was true in the ministry of Jesus and the early church is to be equally true today. We must see ourselves as spiritual farmers sowing gospel seed among the nations. Churches are not to see themselves in competition with other churches. We are to work together and rejoice together in the gospel harvest. Much of the contemporary church is anemic because of her failure to understand the importance of obeying this evangelistic call.

Jesus' signs were intended to lead people to faith in Him. John recounts the story of the royal official so that his readers will trust in Jesus. The meaning of this particular sign is that

Jesus is the giver of new life. Three times it is noted that the boy was seriously ill and at the point of death (4:46, 47, 49). Furthermore, John mentions three times that the boy lives (4:50, 51, 53). In addition, the word 'believe' is used three times (4:48, 50, 53). It is likely that John wanted his readers to understand this miracle as more than an act of physical healing, though it was that, for he also wanted to demonstrate Jesus as the giver of life – physical and spiritual. This truth is evidenced by the fact that the man and his household were saved by placing faith in Jesus. Outside of Christ people are spiritually dead. While they are alive physically their hearts are hard and their ears are deaf to spiritual truth. Their only hope is the transformation that the gospel brings. Jesus is the giver of new life.

It is obvious that the concept of 'life' meant much to John. He wrote his Gospel so that his readers might have life (20:31). The term itself occurs thirty-six times in the Gospel (thirteen times in the Johannine epistles and seventeen times in Revelation). John uses the verb 'to live' seventeen times in the Gospel. In the prologue he declared that in Jesus 'was life and that life was the light of men' (1:4). Jesus came that His followers might have abundant life (10:10). John has made it clear that the life Jesus offers must be appropriated by faith (3:16; 11:25-26). While we must be careful not to denigrate the historicity of the event, because it really did happen, it is proper to ask why John recorded it. For John, the miracle was more than a sheer display of Jesus' divine power, for it also teaches the principle that life eternal is appropriated by faith. Apart from faith in Jesus we are like the dying son. Faith is accepting Jesus' word and acting on it, as the father did.

This is not the only time in the Gospel that John uses a sign to point to our desperate need of Jesus. In chapter 9 we see that the healing of a blind man teaches what it means when Jesus takes one from spiritual darkness to spiritual light. In chapter 11 we learn what it means that Jesus is 'the resurrection and the life' in the resurrection of Lazarus from the dead. As the elderly apostle thought back over a period of about fifty years he came to understand more and more clearly how Jesus' miracles were signs that taught magnificent truths about Him. The frustration Jesus experienced was that people often got so caught up in His miracles that they missed the signs (2:23-25; 4:48).

Study Questions

1. What do you think was John's main point in describing Jesus' teaching to the disciples about true food in 4:31-38?

2. We all have a mission field as believers (John 17:18; 20:21). Who is your mission field?

3. Why do you think that churches find it so hard to rejoice in the growth of other churches?

4. What do you think John's main point was in telling the story of the royal official?

10

Jesus Heals the Lame Man
(John 5:1-30)

John 5 begins a new section of the Gospel. This phase of Jesus' ministry is characterized by escalating conflict. John is interested in selecting typical events and discourses to illustrate the Jewish people's response to Jesus. Chapters 5–10 are often referred to as the Festival Cycle. John intends to show Jesus as fulfilling and/or surpassing elements in these festivals. The festivals are the Sabbath (5:1-47), Passover (6:1-71), Tabernacles (7:1-10:21), and Dedication (10:22-42).[1]

A forensic motif is noticeable in these chapters as well. Jesus' trial, which begins formally in chapter 18, in one sense begins here, as interrogators from Jerusalem approach Him examining His case. In virtually every chapter in this larger section 'the Jews' play the role of interrogator. They assess Jesus' testimony, weigh the evidence, and make a judgment. This interesting literary format places the reader in the thought-provoking position of being forced to evaluate the evidence. By 10:42, the majority of the witnesses and the evidence are in and the jury must deliberate.

Chapter 5 can be divided into three major units. The first is a description of Jesus healing a lame man on the Sabbath (5:1-18). The second section is known as the Divine-Son discourse. Here

---

1. For a helpful discussion of the background to these Jewish Festivals, see Gary M. Burge, *Jesus and the Jewish Festivals: Uncover the Ancient Culture, Discover Hidden Meanings* (Grand Rapids: Zondervan, 2012).

Jesus sets forth His equality with the Father and His dependence upon Him (5:19-30). In the third section, Jesus calls a series of witnesses to affirm the truthfulness of His self-testimony. This section concludes with Jesus' explanation of why the religious leadership is unable to believe in Him (5:31-47).

The question of Jesus' identity is as controversial now as it was during His earthly ministry. The 'Jesus question' continues to divide religious scholars and seekers alike. Some scholars believe Jesus to have been a political revolutionary, or a wise teacher, but that His claims to divinity were invented by His followers. Others think that Jesus was an eschatological prophet, and still others that He was more akin to a Cynic sage. This is not the place to recount the Quest for the Historical Jesus but instead to notice that the Jesus question was as controversial in His day as it is in our own. More interesting than whom scholars understand Jesus to be, is coming to grips with who Jesus believed Himself to be. In this passage Jesus gives us a glimpse into His self-understanding. The results were as controversial then as they are now.

The Power of Jesus: Healing the Lame Man (5:1-9)

5:1: We can only imagine the pathetic scene of a multitude of crippled and sick people gathered around a pool of water thinking that the water had curative powers. It's hard to imagine the intense longing and anguish of waiting for the water to be stirred and then the race to be the first one into the pool and to be healed (5:7). Despite the probable gathering of a large number of people Jesus focuses His attention on one man – a man that did not even know who Jesus was. The man likely became a cripple as the result of some kind of sinful activity (5:14). He demonstrates no faith in Jesus and in the end reports Jesus to the religious leaders as the One who encouraged him to break the Sabbath tradition (5:15). He is a very different person than the blind man healed in chapter 9.

5:2-9: John establishes the setting in the opening verses (5:1-2).[2] This is Jesus' second trip to Jerusalem in John's Gospel (cf. 2:13). The evangelist does not indicate which feast brought Jesus to Jerusalem on this occasion. The crucial point

---

2. 'After this' indicates an indefinite period of time (cf. 6:1).

is that the healing took place on the Sabbath. The Sabbath was considered a weekly festival and it was governed by strict rules. By healing on the Sabbath Jesus broke one of the rabbinic rules governing the day. In addition, Jesus' command for the man to carry his pallet broke another Sabbath rule. The day's importance in this section is seen in the repetition of 'the Sabbath' (5:9, 10, 16, 18).

The miracle took place by the 'pool of Bethesda' (5:2). The site is normally identified as one of the twin pools near the present day St. Anne's Church. Apparently the pool was thought to have healing properties and the infirm were placed near it. Later copyists, to explain why people waited by the pool in large numbers, inserted 5:3b-4.[3] Jesus nowhere addresses the supposed healing powers of the water. The man had been in this condition for thirty-eight years, which is longer than many people in the ancient world lived (5:5). He is described as being 'ill', but in light of verse 7 we should understand the man to be lame or even paralyzed. It is hard for us to imagine what it was like for a person to languish in this condition in the ancient world. The lack of hygiene and health care would have filled him with hopelessness and despair. We should understand Jesus' knowledge of the man's situation as another example of his divine insight (5:6a; cf. 1:48; 4:18). Jesus' question picks up on the man's sense of hopelessness (5:6b). The people believed that if a person was placed into the water before anyone else after the water had been stirred (by an angel?) he would be healed (5:7). Jesus commanded that the man pick up his pallet and walk, and the man was healed instantly (5:8-9a). John adds the thought that this happened on the Sabbath to prepare the reader for the following debate (5:9b).

The Danger of Legalism: Legalism blinds us to God's goodness (5:10-18)

The first open hostility toward Jesus in John's Gospel is in this passage; however, it was foreshadowed in the prologue

---

3. Most scholars do not believe that this passage was part of John's original text but that it was added by a later scribe and represents an ancient tradition that provided helpful background information. For further discussions, see Bruce M. Metzger, *A Textual Commentary on the Greek New Testament* (London/New York: United Bible Societies, 1975), 209.

(1:5, 11).[4] These verses fall into three sections: The healed man and the Jews (5:10-13), Jesus and the man (5:14-16), and Jesus' defense of His actions by appealing to His relationship with the Father (5:17-18).

5:10-13: The issue of the Sabbath comes to the forefront. The Jewish leadership confronts the man about carrying his pallet on the Sabbath (5:10). It was not the Law of Moses that was broken by the man carrying his pallet, but rather the tradition of the elders. As mentioned above, the tradition of the elders distinguished thirty-nine categories of work that might not be done on the Sabbath. The thirty-ninth was the carrying of a load from one dwelling to another (*Mishnah, Sabbat* 7:2). The man suggests that the Jesus is responsible for his actions, but he did not know where Jesus was because He had slipped away into the crowd (5:11-13).

5:14-16: Jesus later finds the man in the temple. Possibly the man went there to offer praise to God for his healing. Jesus' words imply that the man's condition had been the result of sin; however, clearly Jesus did not equate all illness with personal sin (5:14; cf. 9:2). The 'nothing worse' is undefined but likely refers to eternal punishment (cf. 5:26-29). Surprisingly, after this encounter, he reports Jesus to the authorities, possibly insulted by Jesus' comment (5:15). The healed man's statement about Jesus to the religious leaders ('the one who had made him well') brings Jesus into direct conflict with the religious establishment. The Jews were completely unconcerned with the fact that this man was healed. They were consumed with adherence to their Sabbath traditions. Instead of praising God for the man's healing they begin to persecute Jesus (5:16). They were blinded by tunnel vision. It was the Jews who were disobeying Scripture rather than Jesus (cf. Lev. 19:18). We should pray that God would guard us from the same kind of narrow thinking. Their legalism hardened their hearts toward those in need and prevented them from seeing God at work among them.

5:17-18: Jesus defends His actions by appealing to His relationship with His Father. 'My Father' is working on the

---

4. See the following for the rising hostility toward Jesus: 7:1, 19-20, 25-26, 30, 32, 44, 45; 8:37, 40, 59; 11:8, 53, 57.

Sabbath and so must the Son (5:17).[5] First-century Judaism referred to God as 'our Father' but very seldom, if ever, as 'my' Father. Jesus is stating that His relationship with God is beyond anything they know. The religious leaders understand Jesus to be claiming equality with God (5:18b). We need to remember that at that time the one true God was so highly venerated that His name was not even pronounced by Jews. Jesus' claim is blasphemous to them. In essence, Jesus claims authority to determine appropriate and inappropriate activity on the Sabbath. The reference that they were trying to kill Jesus shows how seriously they took this kind of God-talk (5:18). This is the first mention of their intention in the Gospel. The next section provides Jesus' explanation of His words and actions.

Sometimes we are not as different from the religious leaders as we might think. Whenever we equate our 'sacred' traditions – musical style, the order of worship, or a particular ministry program with Scripture – we are following the example of Jesus' opponents here. The kind of narrow thinking that equates tradition with Scripture blinds us to seeing God's work among His people.

The identity of Jesus: 'Who does he think he is?' (5:19-30)
The claims Jesus makes concerning Himself in this passage are astounding. There may be no more forceful presentation by Jesus in this Gospel concerning His relationship to the Father – one of equality and dependence. The theological importance of the discourse can be seen in the formal, systematic and extended proclamation of His unity with the Father. This is the sort of comment that caused the Jewish leaders to decide to kill Jesus (5:18).

Jesus acknowledges their accusations by affirming His equality to God. His response falls into three parts: (1) Jesus establishes His dependence and equality with the

---

5. Jewish scribes agreed that God continually upheld the universe without breaking the Sabbath. What is even more telling is that Jews made exceptions to the rule prohibiting work on the Sabbath, most notably when circumcision occurred on the Sabbath (cf. 7:23). Jesus' point in chapter 7 will be that if God is above Sabbath regulations, and they can circumcise a baby boy on the Sabbath, then He is above their traditions as well.

Father (5:19-30). (2) He brings forth witnesses that attest to His relationship with the Father (5:31-47). (3) Finally, Jesus brings His own indictment against the Jews (5:41-47). In this study we will examine the first point and reserve the final two points for the next study.

Jesus is the giver of life and judgment now (5:19-25)
Jesus answers His detractors, not by backing off or softening His claims, but by making them more explicit. He attributes to Himself actions that in the past have been ascribed only to God: the giving of life and final judgment. In verses 19-25 He deals with the giving of life and judgment now (realized eschatology) and in verses 26-30 life and judgment in the future (final eschatology). The passage is bracketed with statements concerning Jesus' dependence on the Father (5:19, 30).

The importance of Jesus' comments is noted by the use of 'truly, truly' (5:19, 24, 25).[6] Jesus then sets forth two actions attributed to God and claims that He exercises them as well (5:21-22). In the Old Testament God alone raises the dead (Deut. 32:39; 1 Sam. 2:6; 2 Kings 5:7) and executes judgment (Gen. 18:25; Judg. 11:27), but now these tasks also belong to Jesus. The purpose of Jesus performing these tasks is that He may be honored as God is honored (5:23). Jesus' statements in verses 22 and 23 are in effect claims to deity. Furthermore, His words here are an excellent example of His realized eschatology. The one who hears His words and believes has eternal life (a present reality) and will not come into future judgment. That Jesus is talking about being raised from present spiritual death to spiritual life is seen in His words, 'an hour is coming and now is, when the dead will hear the voice of the Son of God, and those who hear will live' (5:25).[7] Just as Jesus called Lazarus from physical death to physical life, He calls the spiritually dead to spiritual life. Once again,

---

6. In John, only Jesus is referred to as 'Son' (*huios*); His followers are referred to as 'children' (*teknon*). In 5:19, Jesus 'sees' what the Father is doing, and in verse 20, the Father shows Him everything he is doing.

7. This is one of only three times in the Fourth Gospel where Jesus refers to himself as 'Son of God' (10:36, 11:4) which is striking in light of John's expressed purpose (20:31).

we see how closely John associates 'life' with the Son (cf. 1:4; 10:10; 11:25-26; 20:31).

Jesus is the giver of life and judgment at the end (5:26-30)
Jesus delineates the same two divine prerogatives in verses 26-30 – except now these two tasks will be performed in the future. He explains in verse 26 ('For') why He is able to speak to dead people and grant them life. God granted Him the authority of final judgment because He is the 'Son of Man' (5:27). That Jesus is speaking of the resurrection at the end is seen in the contrast of His words in verses 28 and 25. Verse 28 says, 'an hour is coming,' but, unlike verse 25, does not say 'and now is' as Jesus points forward to the general resurrection of the dead. He must have seen the shock on their faces as He tells them He will call forth the dead at the final resurrection (5:28; cf. Dan. 12:2). So while verses 24-25 refer to a spiritual resurrection from spiritual death that takes place in the present, verses 28-30 are speaking of a future bodily resurrection from the dead. This section of the discourse concludes in words very much like those with which it began. Jesus states plainly His subordination to the Father. Earlier, He stated He does only what He sees the Father doing (5:19b), and here He states He does nothing except what He hears the Father telling Him to do (5:30).

Reflections
Who do you believe Jesus to be? In this passage He makes seven dramatic claims about Himself and His relationship to the Father: (1) The Son can do nothing without the Father (5:19, 30). (2) The Father loves the Son and reveals everything to Him (5:20). (3) The power to bestow life itself is shared by the Father and the Son (5:21). (4) God has given all judgment over to the Son (5:22). (5) The Father and the Son share equal honor (5:23). (6) Belief in the words of the Son results in eternal life (5:24). (7) The consummation of the age will be by and through the Son (5:25-30). When Jesus' teaching in this passage is considered as a whole there can be no other conclusion but that He is making a claim to deity. Therefore, if Jesus Christ is God, then He is worthy of all our trust, worship, and obedience. If He is not, then all that He says about Himself must be rejected as the foolish ramblings of an egomaniac.

These verses make clear once again that a person's eternal destiny is determined by their attitude to Jesus Christ. The moment one trusts in Christ they begin to experience, in part, the benefits of eternal life. They move from death to life and from darkness to light. This is something only God can do in a person.

STUDY QUESTIONS

1. Why do you think John recounts the story of the healing of the lame man?

2. Why do you think Jesus asks the lame man, 'Do you want to get well?' (5:6)?

3. Which one of Jesus' claims about Himself in 5:19-30 gives you the most hope? Why?

4. How do you think an unsaved friend might respond to Jesus' claim to deity in this passage?

5. Write out a prayer of praise to God that reflects your thoughts about Jesus in 5:19-30.

11

The Danger of Religion
without Conversion
(John 5:31-47)

When I speak with people about their salvation, often they tell me that they know they are saved because they were raised going to church. When I begin to press the gospel on them I find that they know all the right answers, but their lives contradict their profession. They love the things of this world and find little time for the things that really matter. The religious leadership in Jerusalem was well educated in the Scriptures, yet their hearts longed for the approval of man rather than the approval of God. They were more concerned about their traditions than the clear teaching of Scripture. Their persecution of Jesus demonstrated their failure to understand the true intent of the Scriptures. In this passage, Jesus continues His argument from 5:19-30 in a manner reminiscent of a courtroom. However, Jesus turns the table on His opponents, as He takes control of the proceedings by calling a series of witnesses to verify His claims and then condemning His opponents. The courtroom language prominent throughout the passage is evidenced by terms like 'testimony,' 'testify,' and 'accuse' (5:31, 31, 32, 32, 33, 34, 36, 36, 36, 37, 39, 45, 45). The significance of what is at stake is seen in the repeated use of 'believe' in the concluding section of the passage (5:38; 44, 46, 46, 47, 47).

Jesus calls witnesses to substantiate his claims (5:31-40)
Jesus understands that according to the Old Testament a person's testimony by itself is not legally binding (5:31; cf. Deut. 19:15; Num. 35:30). While it is not perfectly clear who Jesus means in verse 32, it is most likely a reference to the Father (5:32).

The witness of John the Baptist (5:33-35)
Jesus points to John the Baptist's testimony next (5:33; cf. 1:19-28). The masses believed John to be a prophet from God. The religious leaders sent representatives to question him about his identity and he pointed them to Jesus (1:7, 15, 19, 32; 3:26-30). Jesus tells them that His purpose in saying these things is that He desires them to be saved (5:34). What a beautiful thought! Jesus desires the salvation of those desiring to kill Him. Jesus, the Light of the world, gives the Baptist a high commendation calling him a lamp 'that was burning and was shining' (5:35).[1] The use of the past tense verbs may indicate that John the Baptist is now dead or imprisoned.

The witness of Jesus' works (5:36)
Jesus' works are an even greater testimony to His identity than John's testimony. His works are the miracles the Father has given Him to do. Nicodemus had said earlier, 'No one could do the works you do unless God is with him' (3:2). Jesus always seemed to keep in the forefront of His mind that He was on a mission from heaven.

The witness of the Father (5:37-38)
Jesus says again that the Father 'sent him' (5:37a) and He will mention it again in 5:38b. The Father's testimony to Jesus is likely a reference to Jesus' miracles, words, and the testimony of Scripture (5:38a). Jesus makes three devastating indictments against them: they have never seen God, or heard His voice, nor does His word abide in them. This explains why they do not believe in Jesus. What is disheartening is that

---

1. This may be an allusion to Psalm 132:17-18, which promised that God had 'prepared a lamp for [his] anointed' one and would 'clothe his enemies with shame'.

they failed to recognize that to see Jesus is to see the Father (cf. 1:18; 14:9) and to hear Jesus is to hear God, for He speaks the words of God.

The witness of the Scriptures (5:39-40)
Although the Jewish leaders studied Scripture in minute detail they failed to recognize the One to whom Scripture bears supreme testimony.[2] This explains why many biblical scholars that are skilled in ancient languages and have a vast knowledge of Scripture reject its teaching about Jesus. What a frightening thought that one can know the Bible but not the God of the Bible! 'To come' to Jesus is another way of saying to believe in Him (5:39). Jesus stresses their stubborn disposition and refusal to believe what the Scriptures teach about Him (5:40). The language is reminiscent of what John said about those in darkness refusing to come to the light (cf. 3:19-21). Their 'lostness' is the result of their sinful choice to reject Scripture's testimony concerning Jesus.

Jesus' indictment of the Jews (5:41-47)
5:41-43: Jesus now provides an analysis and prophetic critique of their rejection of Him. The problem is not intellectual, but rather a longing for self-glory. Jesus turns the table on His opponents and now indicts them for their failure to receive God's abundant testimony to Him. He cuts right to the heart of the matter when He tells them that the reason they do not believe the testimonies concerning Him is because they long for the approval of others (5:44). Jesus, on the other hand, does not receive glory from men because He knows what is in man (5:41; cf. 2:23-25). He knows that they do not love God because they love man's approval more than God's approval (5:42).[3] If they loved God they would have welcomed Jesus since He came in God's name, as God's representative and with divine authority (5:43a). They have demonstrated a

---

2. The verb 'search' can be understood as an imperative ('search the Scriptures') or an indicative ('you are searching the Scriptures'). Most interpreters prefer the indicative.

3. The reference to the 'love of God' can be interpreted as a reference to God's love for them (subjective genitive) or theirs for God (objective genitive). I think the latter more likely, but our love for God is in response to His love for us (1 John 4:19).

willingness to receive messianic pretenders who came in their own names, but they refuse to receive Jesus who comes in God's name (5:43b).

5:44: How troubling that the religious leaders and their followers so willingly receive glory from one another and do not seek the glory that comes from God. This is the reason that they are unable to believe, not because they don't understand Jesus' message but because of their longing for human recognition and approval. Before we condemn the religious leaders too quickly, we must recognize the same battles in our own hearts. Many of us have an overwhelming desire to be associated with people of prominence and to make sure that we receive the recognition for what we do in Jesus' name. Many believers who began to follow Jesus with the purest of motives find this sinful tendency for human acclaim to be too strong to fight. Ultimately, it is a failure to desire that Jesus receive the honor for the good things He does through us. Furthermore, we see this same mindset in evangelicalism in the rock-star status we ascribe to certain leaders. May the Holy Spirit enable us to live with a consciousness that 'every good and perfect gift is from above' and all the glory and praise should go to the One True and Living God.

5:45-47: The very Scriptures (Mosaic) that they thought they believed so devoutly would be the Scriptures that condemn them. The evidence that they do not believe what Moses wrote is that they do not believe in Jesus, because Moses wrote about Him (5:46; cf. Luke 24:25-27, 44). Jesus may have been thinking specifically of such passages as Genesis 49:10, Exodus 12:21, Leviticus 16:5, Numbers 24:17, and Deuteronomy 18:15-18 among many others. If they will not believe what Moses wrote they will not believe Jesus' words (5:47). Jesus draws a close connection here between saving faith and acceptance of what Scripture teaches. How frightening it is to consider that a person can spend a lifetime studying the Scriptures and fail to understand their true intent and thereby miss the salvation to which they point in Jesus Christ.

Reflections

I want us to reflect on some final thoughts on Jesus, the religious leaders, and us. First, we should notice Jesus' courage. Rather than backing down when His enemies accuse Him of blasphemy, He instead becomes more aggressive. He takes over the conversation to the point that it becomes a monologue. He calls witnesses to substantiate His claims. Then He condemns His opponents for not loving God. The weak anemic Jesus that we often see in Renaissance art is not anything like the courageous picture of Jesus presented by John.

Second, we are reminded again of God's desire for mankind's salvation (5:34). Jesus' purpose in speaking to them as He does is so they will be saved. Jesus takes no pleasure in their unconverted condition. Luke brings this out by focusing on Jesus' weeping over Jerusalem at the triumphal entry (Luke 19:41-44). We should pray that we would have a heart for people that desires to see even our 'enemies' saved.

Third, we see the danger of religion without conversion (5:39-47). Although the leaders knew the Scripture with their minds it had not captured their hearts (5:38-40; 45-47). They had an intellectual grasp of the Word, but the Word had not captured them. What a terrible thing to know the Scripture as well as they did but to be blind to its true meaning. It is obvious that their traditions, like the Sabbath rules, mattered more to them than the clear teaching of the Bible. We see too much of this in evangelicalism today. Churches fight over nonessential matters because those things matter more to them than the clear teaching of the gospel. The religious establishment was also more concerned with the approval of men than with the approval of God (5:42-45). They yearned for recognition and acclaim. Jesus condemned them for this a number of times during His ministry. The sin of pride is resident in the heart of all of us. Unfortunately, it grows stronger in the hearts of those who feed it.

STUDY QUESTIONS

1. Why do you think Jesus called witnesses to confirm what He was teaching about Himself?

2. In what way are Jesus' works a more substantial witness to His identity than John the Baptist?

3. What can we learn from the fact that the religious leadership knew the Scriptures so well but failed to grasp the true intent of their teaching about Jesus?

4. Why do you think we have a tendency to long for the praise of others more than praise from God?

12

Jesus Feeds the Multitudes and Walks on the Water
(John 6:1-21)

Jesus' miracles in John's Gospel are sometimes referred to as 'hard miracles'. He turns 175 gallons of water into wine, heals a boy from a distance, and heals a man who has not walked in over three decades. If those miracles are not spectacular enough, the miracles in John 6 are breathtaking. Jesus feeds thousands of people with a few pieces of bread and a couple of small fish and a few hours later He walks on the Sea of Galilee during a violent storm. As we have seen before, God does His best work when life's circumstances seem the most hopeless.

We come now to the second major festival in this section (chapters 5–10). The Passover Feast looms large in the background of this chapter. The reference to the Passover in 6:4 is as much a theological note as it is a chronological marker. The feeding of the five thousand is the only miracle Jesus performs that is recounted in all four Gospels, but only John mentions that it takes place near Passover. The Jewish Passover commemorates Israel's exodus from Egypt. The imagery of the bread, water, and references to Moses in the passage suggest that John is communicating the thought that Jesus is greater than Moses, and is leading His people to a new exodus. The feeding recalls the Old Testament miracle of manna when Israel was in the wilderness (Exod. 16:1-36). However, the bread that Jesus provides ('I am the bread of life') is superior to the bread provided through Moses in the wilderness. Those who ate the manna in the wilderness died, but those who eat the bread Jesus provides (He is the bread) will live forever. Furthermore, while Moses led the exodus generation through the Red Sea walking on dry ground, Jesus will walk on the stormy sea and proclaim Himself to be the divine 'I am' (cf. Exod. 3:14). These thoughts will become clearer as the passage unfolds.[1]

John 6 contains four scenes. First, Jesus feeds the multitude (6:1-15). Second, He walks on the surface of the stormy lake and declares Himself to be the divine 'I am' (6:16-21). Third, in response to a request by the masses for more demonstrations of power Jesus gives what is known as the Bread of Life Discourse (6:22-59). Finally, John describes various responses to the discourse (6:60-71). These stories are intended to help the reader better understand who Jesus is and deepen our faith in Him (cf. 20:30-31). One shouldn't let their familiarity with these stories rob them of the wonderful truths taught in them.

Jesus feeds thousands (6:1-15)

The feeding of the five thousand made a deep impression on the early church, for it is the only miracle except the resurrection described in all four Gospels. This should not be a complete surprise, however, since most of Jesus' ministry in John's Gospel takes place in and around Jerusalem, while the Synoptic Gospels focus on Jesus' Galilean ministry. John includes several details that are unique to his account: the reference to the Passover, the focus on Philip and Andrew, the fact that the bread was made from barley, and Jesus' comment that nothing be lost.

---

1. Some scholars question the ordering of these chapters. Chapter 5 concludes with Jesus in Jerusalem debating the religious leaders, while in chapter 6 Jesus is in Galilee without describing any transition. Some believe that the order of chapters 5 and 6 should be reversed. They suggest that this would make more sense since the healing of the royal official's son in Cana would be followed by other events in Galilee. At least two points argue against this rearrangement. First, it demonstrates a failure to understand that it is likely that several weeks separated the events between chapter 5 and 6. Second, there is no textual evidence to support the reversal of the two chapters.

A hopeless situation: A hungry multitude (6:1-9)

This opening section can be broken down into three smaller units: John establishes the setting (6:1-4), recounts Jesus' question to Philip (6:5-7), and describes Andrew's encounter with a boy (6:8-9). The fact that this event is a Johannine sign suggests that this is to be understood as more than just a sheer display of supernatural power. The miraculous feeding reveals Jesus' power to meet human need, and mankind's greatest need is spiritual life. Bread was a staple of life in first-century Israel and in the next discourse Jesus reveals Himself as 'the Bread of Life' (6:35, 41, 48, 50, 51). Those who ate the manna Moses provided died, but those who eat the bread Jesus gives them will never die. Just as those who drink of the living water will never thirst (cf. 4:13-14), those who eat the living bread will never hunger (cf. 6:35).

6:1-4: 'After this' (cf. 5:1; 7:1) refers again to an indefinite period of time and ties the feeding to the preceding events. Only John among the Gospel writers refers to the Sea of Galilee as the Sea of Tiberias (6:1). It is likely that it came to be known as the Sea of Tiberias after Jesus' day as a result of the city of the same name built by Herod Antipas. John indicates that the crowds followed Jesus because of His miracles (6:2). This is John's first reference to large crowds following Jesus. This is not surprising since he describes so little of Jesus' Galilean ministry. The feeding takes place on a mountainside near Passover (6:3-4). Passover was celebrated in the spring (March-April). John mentions three Passovers during Jesus' ministry (2:13; 6:4; 13:1). Since this is the second of the three Passovers, this one takes place one year after the temple cleansing (2:13ff) and one year before Jesus' crucifixion (13:1ff).

6:5-7: When Jesus sees the crowds approaching He asks Philip where they can buy bread to feed the multitude (6:5).[2] Philip is the logical person to ask because he is from the nearby

---

2. There are several parallels between this event and the exodus from Egypt. The Israelites had to secure both food and water after leaving Egypt and the first Passover (Exod. 15:22–16:3). Moses asked a similar question to Jesus' question, 'Where can I get meat to give all these people?' (Num. 11:13). Other parallels to the feeding of the five thousand and Numbers 11 are: the grumbling (Num. 11:1; John 6:41, 43); the description of the manna (Num. 11:7-9; John 6:31); the connection to the eating of meat and Jesus' flesh (Num. 11:13; John 6:51); and the extravagant provision (Num. 11:22; John 6:7-9).

village of Bethsaida (cf. 1:44). John notes that Jesus is testing Philip because Jesus knows what He intends to do (6:6). Philip fails the test by seeing only the problem but not the solution (6:7). Two hundred denarii were equal to about eight months' wages for a common laborer, but even that would not be enough for each one to receive more than a little. Mark's Gospel elaborates that the disciples' approach was simply to send the crowds away hungry (Mark 6:35-36). John wants to teach his readers that what seems impossible for man is possible with Jesus, a lesson that Philip was slow to learn!

6:8-9: At this point Andrew steps forward with a boy who apparently offers to help by giving his lunch.[3] Andrew is described again as 'Simon Peter's brother' (cf. 1:40). He makes the same mistake as Philip by assuming what is and is not possible for Jesus. Perhaps John wants the readers to contrast the disciples with the boy. The disciples look at the situation and decide that they do not have enough to feed everyone, so they do nothing. The boy, on the other hand, has only enough for himself, but he gives everything and Jesus uses it to feed everybody with plenty remaining. John mentions that the bread is barley, which was the grain of the poor. The fish were probably very small. Before we are too hard on the disciples we should realize that we are not that much different from them. We see the need, evaluate our resources, determine that we don't have the resources necessary to meet the need, and so we do nothing. Often Jesus wants us to give all that we have and trust Him to use our meager resources to do more than we could imagine. When it is done this way Jesus gets the glory because it is evident that He does it.

Jesus takes control: The multiplication of the bread and fish (6:10-15)

6:10-13: At this point Jesus takes control, much like the head of a family, or the host at a banquet (6:10). The fact that there is much grass confirms it is springtime before the summer heat turned it brown. John indicates that there are five thousand men present. The number of people including women and

---

3. The Greek word translated 'boy' (NIV) does not necessarily refer to a child; for the word is used of Joseph at seventeen years of age in the LXX (cf. Gen. 37:30).

children would have been much greater. John describes the miracle itself with great reserve (6:10-11). The people were instructed to sit down. The Synoptic Gospels indicate that the people were placed in groups of hundreds and fifties. Jesus takes the bread, gives thanks, and distributes it. He does the same with the fish (6:11). One difference with the sign-miracle at Cana and this miracle is that Jesus is described here as praying. John stresses the abundant supply left over (6:12). Not only was there enough for everyone to eat to their fill, but Jesus instructs them to collect the leftovers and they gather twelve basketfuls (6:12-13). The fact that there were twelve basketfuls left over meant that there was one for each of the disciples.

We are so familiar with this story that we are not as overwhelmed by it as we should be. Jesus fed thousands of people with five barley loaves and two fish. This incredible sign should cause us to be amazed with Jesus' greatness and power, and to trust Him more. The sheer quantity of the provision, in comparison to the insufficiency of what the boy gives, is incredible.

6:14-15: The crowd responds by declaring Jesus to be 'the prophet who is to come into the world' (6:14). This is a reference to the Moses-like prophet referred to in Deuteronomy 18:15-18. Jesus perceives that they want to make Him their king, even if they had to do it by force. He quickly quenches the dangerous talk by withdrawing alone to the mountain (6:15). Jesus resists the allure of a kingdom without a cross.

Jesus walks on the water (6:16-21)

Great tests sometimes come after great victories. The disciples have just witnessed one of the most spectacular demonstrations of power in the history of the world. Their confidence in Jesus must have been sky high. Nothing can stop them now! Yet immediately after the feeding of the multitude, they find themselves fearing for their lives in the midst of a storm.

As darkness begins to fall that evening the disciples set off across the lake to Capernaum (6:16-17a).[4] Jesus walking

---

4. The Sea of Galilee is fed from the Jordan River to the north and flows out again into the Jordan River to the south. Its current size is approximately seven miles wide and thirteen miles long.

on the water is described in three of the four Gospels – Luke alone omits it. John's description is very compressed when compared to the parallels (Matt.14:22-33; Mark 6:45-52). John mentions that it was dark and Jesus had not yet joined them (6:17b). It is possible that John intends to indicate more than just physical darkness (cf. 3:2; 13:30). The thought would then be that the storm had a demonic aspect to it. It seems more likely, however, that his reference is simply chronological here.

As the disciples row toward Capernaum a strong wind causes the sea to become rough (6:18). The Sea of Galilee is situated in a basin and is susceptible to sudden storms. It is approximately 600 feet below sea level and surrounded by high hills. After rowing about three or four miles they see Jesus approaching them on the water and they are frightened (6:19). Mark says that they were frightened because they thought Him to be a ghost (Mark. 6:19). Jesus calms their fears by identifying Himself with the words, 'It is I (*ego eimi*); do not be afraid.'[5] In light of John's use of the expression 'I am' elsewhere in the Gospel, as well as the exodus imagery of the chapter, it is likely that he intends to recall the name God revealed to Moses in the wilderness (Exod. 3:14). If this is the case then this miracle is intended to identify Jesus as the divine 'I am'. This miracle is not specifically said to be a sign and as a result some scholars don't understand it to be one of the seven signs, although they do understand it to be a miracle.[6]

Jesus walking on the sea is a powerful demonstration of His sovereignty over the world He created (cf. 1:1-5). The Old Testament teaches that God alone rules over the seas.

> When the waters saw you, O God,
> when the waters saw you, they were afraid;
> indeed, the deep trembled.
> The clouds poured out water;
> the skies gave forth thunder;
> your arrows flashed on every side.

---

5. Some commentators understand Jesus' words here to be nothing more than a means of identifying himself: 'It's me.'

6. See Köstenberger, *John*, 204.

> The crash of your thunder was in the whirlwind;
> your lightnings lighted up the world;
> the earth trembled and shook.
> Your way was through the sea,
> your path through the great waters;
> yet your footprints were unseen.
> You led your people like a flock
> by the hand of Moses and Aaron
> (Ps. 77:16-20).

> Then they cried to the LORD in their trouble,
> and he delivered them from their distress.
> He made the storm be still,
> and the waves of the sea were hushed.
> Then they were glad that the waters were quiet,
> and he brought them to their desired haven
> (Ps. 107:28-30).

It should be noted again that while Moses parted the Red Sea and walked through on dry land, Jesus is greater than Moses in that He walked on the Sea of Galilee. The fact that the boat immediately arrives at land after Jesus enters can be understood as another miracle, or simply as a reference to the boat making it to land very quickly after the storm ceased. If it is considered a miracle, it is a likely allusion to Psalm 107:23-32. Yet, if it is a miracle, John does not make much of it (6:21).

Reflections
The passage contains several lessons. First, God puts His people in situations that test their faith in order to develop in them even greater faith. These tests can be like pop quizzes that happen in unexpected moments during the everyday occurrences of life. At other times they are more like major exams that come in the form of life's greatest storms. We forget that God is more concerned about conforming us into Jesus' image in preparation for eternity than in making our lives easy and comfortable in the present world.

Second, our impossibilities are the platform on which God does His greatest works. It's in moments like these in this passage when we recognize that we don't have the necessary resources to do what needs to be done. Just as Jesus questioned Philip about where to buy bread, knowing that Philip would see the impossibility of the situation, in the same way He places us in similar situations so that we learn to look to Him. We can limit what God will do by assuming what is and is not possible. We look at our resources, whatever they may be, and say, 'It can't be done.' We must learn that God will not work if we give nothing, but when we give him everything, even though it is not enough, He can use it in a greater way than we could ever imagine.

Third, the two miracles are reminiscent of miracles associated with Israel's exodus from Egypt. The feeding of the five thousand reminds us of the provisions of manna in the wilderness and the walking on the water is reminiscent of the parting of the Red Sea. John presents Jesus as greater than Moses. This theme will be picked up in the following discourse.

STUDY QUESTIONS

1. What connections do you see between the feeding of the multitudes and Jesus walking on the water with the Passover and exodus stories in the Old Testament?

2. What do you believe John's main point to be in the feeding narrative?

3. What do you believe John's main point to be in Jesus walking on the water?

4. What implications do you see in each of these narratives for your own life?

13

The Bread of Life Discourse
(John 6:22-71)

This passage is related closely to the feeding of the five thousand. The themes of Passover and Exodus imagery (manna and grumbling) continue to dominate. John made it clear in the sign-miracle of the feeding that Jesus is able to meet people's physical needs in a miraculous way. The discourse draws out the spiritual implications of the sign. John's primary point in this passage is to communicate that Jesus, and Jesus alone, satisfies the spiritual hunger of those who put their faith in Him. As the discussion unfolds Jesus turns the crowd's attention away from their fixation on the manna given in the wilderness, and points out that the God who supplied the needs of His people in the wilderness is still at work.

Jesus describes Himself as 'the bread of life'. The saying is repeated with slight variations: 'I am the bread of life' (6:35, 48); 'I am the bread that came down from heaven' (6:41; cf. 6:33, 38, 50, 58); 'I am the living bread that came down from heaven' (6:51). In typical Johannine style we should understand all these slightly different sayings as meaning much the same thing. The repetition brings out the force and the importance of the saying.

It must be remembered that in the ancient world bread was a crucial element of the normal diet. People did not have the variety of food choices available today. In the Old Testament bread could stand for prosperity (Deut. 8:9; Prov. 12:11) and the lack of it for adversity (Lam. 1:11). There are places in the Old Testament where it is referred to as the 'staff of bread', that is, that which supports the whole of life (Lev. 26:26; Ps. 105:16; Ezek. 4:16). Therefore, Jesus is not speaking of something peripheral, but of what is essential to the eternal.

There is an interesting correspondence between the two kinds of food in chapter 6 and the two kinds of water in 4:10-15. The 'living water' corresponds to the food that endures to 'eternal life' (6:27). Those who drink the water from the well will thirst again, and those who eat regular food will get hungry again. However, those who drink the 'living water will never thirst' (4:14), and those who eat the heavenly bread will live forever (6:51). Jesus satisfies mankind's thirst and hunger for God. What was true in the first century is equally true in the twenty-first century.

There are several other themes woven throughout the discourse: Jesus uses 'truly, truly' several times indicating the significance of His words (6:26, 32, 47, 53); He makes repeated references to being the source of life (6:35, 40, 47, 48, 50, 51); the importance of faith (6:35, 40, 47, 51); and the thought of a future bodily resurrection – 'raise up on the last day' (6:39, 40, 44, 54).

Seeking Jesus for the wrong reasons (6:22-29)

6:22-24: The crowd was perplexed as to where Jesus could have gone. They knew that the disciples departed without Him and that He retreated to the mountain (6:22). A small fleet of boats arrives from Tiberias, possibly having heard reports of the miraculous feeding on the day before (6:23). Tiberias was a large city on the western shore of the Sea of Galilee. Herod Antipas built the city in honor of the Roman emperor, Tiberius. The city was built upon an old cemetery, and thus was considered unclean by many Jews until the second century when it became the center of Palestinian rabbinic Judaism. The multitude begin their search for Jesus at Capernaum. Capernaum is located on the northwest shore of the Sea of Galilee. Tiberias is several miles to the south.

6:25-27: From this point on the discussion moves forward by questions and comments from the crowd (6:25, 28, 30, 34,

41, 52). Jesus' response is a serious one, preceded as it is by 'Truly, truly.' He ignores their initial question and challenges their motives for seeking Him (6:25-26). He knows they are seeking Him because they 'ate of the loaves and were filled'. He warns them not to be so concerned about working for physical food that they miss the eternal life that the Son of Man gives (6:27). He is the one upon whom God has placed His seal. An ancient seal was made of wax, clay, or of soft metal. A seal indicated either ownership or authentication of an item or a document; the second sense is probably in view here.

6:28-29: The multitude picks up on the word 'work' (6:28). They were familiar with the idea of working for one's salvation. Jesus answers their question in terms of faith. He tells them that the one 'work' which God requires is that they 'believe in him whom he has sent', which oddly enough is not a work at all (6:29; cf. Eph. 2:8-9). Belief in the Son is the one indispensable thing that God requires. Jesus' statement reveals again that both the Father and Son desire for sinners to be saved.

'I am the bread of life' (6:30-40)
6:30-34: The crowd responds to Jesus' invitation to believe by requesting that He prove Himself by performing another miracle (6:30). Some in the crowd must not have been present at the feeding. They point to the manna their forefathers ate in the wilderness (6:31; cf. Pss. 78:23-24; 105:40; Exod. 16:4, 15).[1] They imply that Moses proved himself by providing the manna and that during the messianic age God would one day again provide manna (6:31). Jesus uses 'truly, truly' to stress the importance of the thought that God, not Moses, provided the manna and that God ('My Father') gives them the bread from heaven as well (6:32). The bread from heaven, which is Jesus, is superior because it 'gives life to the world' (6:33). This is the first of six references in this context to Jesus coming down from heaven (cf. 6:38, 41, 50-51, 58). Their response ('give us this bread') is

---

1. The manna was called 'bread from heaven' (Exod. 16:4; Ps. 78:23-25). It is described as white like coriander seed and tasted like wafers made with honey (Exod. 16:31). This daily gift lasted for the forty years of wilderness wanderings (Exod. 16:34-35).

similar to that of the Samaritan woman (6:34; cf. 4:15). Their misunderstanding gives Jesus the opportunity to move the discussion forward.

6:35: Jesus now declares, 'I am the bread of life' (6:35a; cf. 41, 48, 51).[2] The terminology (*ego eimi*) causes His audience to think of God's name in Exodus 3:14. In addition, He promises that 'he who comes to me will not hunger, and he who believes in me will never thirst' (6:35b; cf. 4:10-13). Jesus' point is that He nourishes and satisfies the soul's longing for God. The manna they yearn for can satisfy bodily hunger for a time, but it cannot meet their greatest need – a right relationship with God. Augustine put it this way: 'Thou hast made us for thyself, and our hearts are restless until they find their rest in thee.'

6:36-40: At this point Jesus draws a strong contrast (6:36). Even though they have seen His miracles they don't believe in Him. The reason that they don't believe is because they have not been given to Jesus by the Father (6:37a). Jesus emphasizes God's initiative in salvation here and throughout the Gospel (6:37b, 44; 10:29; 17:6; 18:9). Everyone the Father gives to Jesus comes (believes) to Him and He will not cast them out. True believers persevere because of Christ's firm hold on them. One of the reasons that Christ came down from heaven was to do His Father's will by caring for His people (6:38-39a). The expression 'raised on the last day' is prominent throughout this section (6:39b; 6:40b, 44, 54). As mentioned earlier, while John's primary eschatological emphasis is a realized eschatology, He clearly believes in a future consummation of Christ's kingdom. It is God's will, not only that no one He gives to the Son will be lost (6:39), but that 'everyone who beholds the Son and believes in him will have eternal life' (6:40).

Stop longing for what won't satisfy (6:41-51)
6:41-42: The people grumble because they do not like what they hear. Their grumbling is reminiscent of Israel's

---

2. This is the first of the seven famous 'I am' (*ego eimi*) statements in John. In the others Jesus claims to be 'the light of the world' (8:12; 9:5); 'the door' of the sheep (10:7, 9); the 'good shepherd' (10:11, 14); 'the resurrection and the life' (11:25); 'the way, the truth and the life' (14:6); and 'the true vine' (15:1). Jesus also made several absolute 'I am' statements (6:20; 8:24, 28; 18:5) alluding to God's statement to Moses in Exodus 3:14.

murmurings in the wilderness (cf. Exod. 16:8-9; Num. 11:4-23; 14:27). Just as they complained against Moses, the first giver of bread, so they complain against Jesus, the true bread from heaven. They find it inconceivable that Jesus thought He came from heaven.

6:43-47: Jesus responds to their grumbling in four ways. First, He rebukes them and explains that their problem is that God is not at work in them (4:43-44a). The word 'draws' suggests something of a process. When the Father begins to work in a person's heart He lovingly draws them to Jesus. Jesus then adds that those God draws He will raise from the dead on the last day (6:44b). Jesus wants His disciples never to forget that this life is not all that there is. Second, Jesus states again the truth of God's initiative in salvation by referring to Isaiah 54:13 (6:45). Those who accept the Father's teaching will 'come' (believe) to Jesus. Those who are 'taught by God' applies to those who actually believe in Jesus. Third, only the Son has 'seen the Father', because He comes from Him (6:46; cf. 1:18). Fourth, since Jesus comes from the Father, they should believe His words. His use of 'truly, truly' heightens the importance of believing if one is to receive eternal life (6:47; cf. 51, 58).

6:48-50: Jesus then contrasts the living bread with the manna for which they long (6:48-51). He declares again, 'I am the bread of life' (6:48). The contrast between the manna for which they long, and the bread from heaven, could not be any greater. Those who ate the manna died, but those who eat the bread from heaven will not die (6:49-50). Jesus does not mean that they will not die physically (they most certainly will), but that they will not die eternally. Why would one long for what leads to death, when one can have that which brings eternal life? Jesus came from heaven (He is the bread) for the purpose of bringing people to salvation. We should never think that it does not matter to God whether people are saved or lost. It matters so much that He sent His Son from heaven so that people could be saved. Since it matters that much to God, it should matter much to us as well.

6:51: Jesus concludes this portion of the discourse by declaring that He is 'the living bread' (6:51). Then He adds a new thought: the bread that He will give for the life of the world is His own flesh. In other words, to provide life for others, He will give His life. The use of the word 'flesh' highlights the physicality of His death. He will die a real physical death. Jesus' death will be voluntary ('I will give') and substitutionary 'for' the world.[3] The substitutionary nature of Jesus' death is remarkable in the fact that it is for the 'world'. Jesus dies for those who are held in bondage to Satan and live in opposition to God's rule in their lives.

Eating Jesus' flesh and drinking His blood: The necessity of faith (6:52-58)

The crowds argue among themselves, 'How can this man give us *his* flesh to eat?' (6:52). Jesus uses 'truly, truly' for the fourth time in the discourse. The words, 'unless you eat the flesh of the Son of Man and drink his blood,' are the most disputed words in the passage (6:53, 54, 56, 57, 58). Some understand His response as teaching about the Lord's Supper. However, there are several arguments that can be made against this interpretation. First, there is nothing in the immediate context that would indicate that Jesus' audience would have understood His words in this way. Second, it must be remembered that when Jesus spoke these words He had not yet instituted the Lord's Supper. Third, the terminology of the Lord's Supper consistently relates the bread to Jesus' body and not to His flesh. Fourth, on this interpretation, verses 51, 53-54, and 56-58 would seem to require that the Lord's Supper itself imparts salvation; however, throughout the passage faith is highlighted as the means of receiving salvation (6:35, 40, 47, 51).[4] It is better to understand Jesus as referring to the same ideas as are brought out earlier in the discourse: to personally receiving Him. The results of eating and drinking are eternal life and being raised up on the last

---

3. The preposition 'for' (*huper*) expresses another key Johannine theme (10:11, 15; 11:50-52; 13:37; 15:13; 17:19; 18:14), that is, Jesus' substitutionary sacrifice for others. See Leon Morris, *The Apostolic Preaching of the Cross* (Grand Rapids: Eerdmans, 1965), 62-64.

4. A mediating position that has much to commend it is that the primary thought in the discourse is the spiritual realities of faith and total commitment to Jesus, but it is not improbable that the early church would have seen some insight into the meaning of the Lord's Supper. For such a reading, see Morris, *John*, 3:11-15 and Carson, *John*, 296-98.

day (6:54). These are the same results as those described as 'coming' and 'believing' (cf. 6:35, 39, 40, 44, 54).

Therefore, Jesus uses this graphic language to describe the total commitment of His followers to Him. The biblical authors often use images of eating and drinking in reference to spiritual realities. Jeremiah said, 'Your words were found, and I ate them' (Jer. 15:16). The Psalmist wrote, 'As the deer pants for the water brook, so my soul pants after you, O God' (Ps. 42:1). Jesus said, 'Blessed are those who hunger and thirst for righteousness, for they shall be satisfied' (Matt. 5:6).

The benefits of eating Christ's flesh and drinking His blood are unimaginably great: eternal life and being raised from the dead (6:54b; 58), mutual indwelling with Christ (6:56), and life here and now (6:57). Abiding is a major theme in this Gospel. The amazing thought introduced here is the mutual indwelling of Christ and the believer. John will expand on this idea later in the Gospel. Jesus concludes the discourse by repeating its main thought in a slightly different way. He is on a mission sent from the Father and those who believe in Him (eat the bread from heaven) will live, unlike those who ate the manna in the wilderness and died (6:57-58). At some point during the discussion there is a change of location (6:59; cf. 6:25).

Reactions to Jesus' Discourse: Desertion, Faith, and Deception (6:60-71)

Many of Jesus' followers find these words too much to bear and abandon Him (6:60-66). Yet Peter affirms the Twelve's faith in Jesus despite the bewildering spectacle of so many abandoning Him (6:67-69). Nevertheless, for the first time in the Gospel, Judas is identified as the one who will betray Jesus (6:70-71).

Desertion: Spurious faith (6:60-66)
Many of Jesus' followers find His teaching so difficult to accept that they abandon Him (6:60; cf. 6:41). It is not that the teachings are too hard to understand; instead they are too difficult for them to believe. How could their eternal destiny be dependent on their receiving Him and His teaching? These

seemed to be the words of an egomaniac. Jesus is aware of their resistance to His teaching (6:61). He makes reference to an even more difficult thought: if they will not believe these words, how will they believe when the Son of Man is resurrected and ascended (6:62)? The reason they could not believe was because they had not received life from the Spirit and they were of the 'flesh' (6:63). Jesus knew those who did not believe, as well as the one who would betray Him (6:64). As a result of His words many of His followers abandoned Him (6:64).

Faith: Only Jesus (6:67-69)
The Twelve had witnessed Jesus feed the multitudes and, on the previous day, walk on the water. They had listened to Jesus' difficult teaching regarding what it takes to receive the life He offers. Now Jesus challenges them to make a choice (6:67). The fourth Gospel does not record Peter's great Caesarea Philippi confession of faith found in the Synoptics; however, Peter's confession here plays a similar role. This is a truly amazing statement of faith on Peter's part. The disciples saw Jesus resist an attempt to make Him king. Now they watch as many followers reject His teaching. Yet Peter has come to the settled understanding that what Jesus says is true, even if he does not fully grasp all of it. While Peter will later deny Jesus, here he demonstrates his love and commitment to Him, despite the abandonment by others.

Deception: The heart of a traitor (6:70-71)
The chapter concludes on a foreboding note. Jesus predicts that one of His closest followers will betray Him and become an instrument of the devil (6:70). One day Judas' name will become synonymous with that of a traitor. The reference that he was a devil means that he would oppose Christ as Satan does, and later he will be described as being possessed by the devil himself. If one of Jesus' closest followers will betray Him, we should never be shocked in our day to see those who appear to be disciples of Jesus abandon Him. Judas saw Jesus' signs, heard His sermons, traveled with Him for a couple of years, got to know Him in a way that few others did, and yet in the end betrayed Him.

Reflections

Jesus alone satisfies the human heart. In a society that has experimented to the point of saturation with every form of physical, material, and spiritual painkiller to fill the inner emptiness, Jesus' invitation comes with a wonderful relevance: 'He who comes to me will not hunger and he who believes in me will never thirst.'

There are many modern Galileans in the church wanting Jesus to prove Himself to them again. Jesus warned the crowd, 'Don't waste your life.' They were longing and working for that which would perish, but Jesus offered to give them that which is eternal (6:27). They were more interested in what Jesus could do for them than in who Jesus was (6:26). We can identify with this crowd in the fact that we find ourselves regularly seeking Jesus for what He can do for us rather than seeking Him for who He is. It is the difference of seeking His hand rather than His face. The better we come to know Jesus, the less interested we are in His gifts and the more we are consumed with His person.

Study Questions

1. What is the most important truth we learn about Jesus in the Bread of Life Discourse?

2. What does this passage teach about God's initiative in salvation (give specific verses)?

3. What does this passage teach about our need to respond in order to be saved (give specific verses)?

4. What do you think Jesus meant when He said that we must eat His flesh and drink His blood?

5. What do you think the original audience thought when Jesus made the above statement?

6. What are the three responses to Jesus' teaching in this passage?

14

'Come to Me and Drink'
(John 7:1-52)

The atmosphere around Jesus is becoming increasingly tense. Chapter 6 concludes with the defection of many of His followers. Chapter 7 opens with the unbelief of His brothers. Numerous times in chapters 7 and 8 hostile comments are made about Jesus (7:1, 13, 19, 25, 30, 32, 44; 8:6, 40, 59). The debate over His identity becomes more intense (7:11-13, 15, 20, 25, 31, 35, 40-43, 45-52). Who is He? Does He meet the qualifications to be Messiah?

Chapter 7 is the third account in John's Gospel of Jesus during a Jewish festival: Sabbath (ch. 5), Passover (ch. 6), and now the Festival of Tabernacles (Booths or Ingathering) (7:1–10:21). Jesus again uses elements from the feast to reveal His true identity. It was one of three Jewish pilgrimage festivals, with Passover and Pentecost (Exod. 23:14-17; Deut. 16:16). This festival took place in the fall (September-October), about six months after Passover (cf. 6:4) and about two months before the Feast of Dedication (December; cf. 10:22). The people lived in leafy shelters (booths) throughout the festival to commemorate God's faithfulness during the wilderness wanderings (Lev. 23:42-43). It was a time of celebration and thanksgiving for the harvest (Lev. 23:39-41; Deut. 16:13-15; cf. Exod. 23:16; 34:22). There were also elements that anticipated the blessings of the messianic age (Ezek. 47:1-12; Zech. 14:8). Many considered it the most popular of the Jewish festivals, possibly because it came at the end of the harvest and a change to cooler temperatures after months of drought and heat. Jesus uses two images from the feast to highlight His fulfillment of it: the water-pouring ceremony (7:37-39) and the lighting of giant candelabras (8:12).

Each day at dawn priests, accompanied by the festival crowds, went in procession from the temple to the pool of Siloam. An appointed priest filled a golden pitcher with water and carried it back to the temple. As they returned to the temple they sang Isaiah 12 with its central chorus, 'With joy you will draw waters from the well of salvation.' The priests went around the altar, and the temple choir sang the *Hallel* (Psalms 113–118) supported at appropriate times by the shouts, 'Give thanks to the Lord!' and 'O Lord, save us!' The priest who had drawn the water poured the daily drink offering of wine into one bowl and then the water from Siloam into another. The whole procedure had in mind both God's gift of water in the desert when Israel was in danger of dying of thirst (Exod. 17:1-6) and the prophecy of a river of living water flowing from the Jerusalem temple in the kingdom of God (Ezek. 47:1-12; Zech. 14:8). These passages of Scripture were all read at various points during the festival.

Jesus waited until the climax of the feast to make His dramatic proclamation (7:37-38). When the crowds were at their largest He invited anyone who thirsts to come to Him and drink. His words are reminiscent of Isaiah 55:1: 'everyone who thirsts come to the waters.'[1] The feast brought together images of God's salvation past, present, and future. It is stated in the Rabbinic tractate Sukkah 5:1: 'He who has not seen the joy of the water-drawing has not seen joy in his lifetime.' Jesus fulfills Tabernacles!

This chapter can be divided into three sections: (1) the events preceding the feast and Jesus' secret arrival (7:1-13); (2) the events during 'the middle of the feast' that focus on Jesus' identity and teaching (7:14-36); and (3) the events on 'the last, the great day of the feast' (7:37-52). Tying this section together are questions asked of Jesus (7:2-4, 15, 20, 25-26, 35),

---

1. Beasley-Murray, *John*, 113.

the reactions of the crowd to Jesus' comments (7:3-5, 12, 30-31, 40-44, 45-53), and repeated thoughts of wanting to arrest or kill Him (7:19, 20, 25, 30, 44).

Before the feast (7:1-13)
Jesus had not returned to Jerusalem since the healing of the blind man in chapter 5. He now makes His third trip to Jerusalem, this time for the Feast of Tabernacles.

A prophet without honor (7:1-5)
'After these things' refers again to an indefinite period of time. The events in this chapter take place about six months after the feeding miracle in chapter six. Jesus has not returned to Jerusalem because the religious leadership want to kill Him (7:1; cf. 5:18). His brothers encourage Him to go to Jerusalem and perform miracles to gather more disciples. They likely knew of the mass defection that took place earlier (7:2-4; cf. 6:60-66). John informs the reader that the brothers were in reality taunting Him because they did not believe in Him (7:5). It must have been painful to Jesus that His family did not believe in Him (cf. 1:11). This would likely have brought comfort to John's readers as many of them were rejected by family and friends for following Jesus. Many contemporary followers of Jesus know this reality all too well.

'The time has not yet come' (7:6-13)
7:6-9: Jesus will not go up publicly as His brothers are encouraging Him to do, but He will go up privately later (7:6, 8). John's Gospel repeatedly stresses that Jesus had a sense of divine timing (cf. 2:4). Unlike His brothers, who did not live with the intimacy with God that He experienced, Jesus would be sensitive to God's timing. His comment about the world's hatred seems odd at this point. However, the 'world' (the religious leaders) hates Him and wants to kill Him because He bears witness to its evil (7:7).
    7:10-13: Jesus remains behind for a few days after His brothers leave and then ventures to Jerusalem in secret (7:10). Even though He had not yet made a public appearance, He was the topic of conversation and debate (7:11-12). The crowds are divided over Him. Some are grumbling about Him. The

term translated 'grumbling' is reminiscent of the Jews in their wilderness wanderings (cf. 6:41; Exod. 17:3; Num. 11:1). The atmosphere in Jerusalem is tense as debate over Him escalates. The people fear the religious leadership and therefore do not speak openly about Jesus (7:13).

'In the midst of the feast' (7:14-36)
In the midst of this highly charged atmosphere the man both loved and despised bursts on to the scene. The section follows the common pattern of questions from the crowd and Jesus' detailed responses. They are not discourses in the technical sense but dialogues dominated by Jesus. Three questions are posed about Jesus in this section concerning: (1) His teaching ('How has this man become learned?') (7:14-24); (2) His origin ('we know where this man is from') (7:25-27); and (3) His intentions ('Where does this man intend to go that we cannot find him?') (7:28-36).

Jesus' teaching and authority come from God (7:14-18)
Jesus begins teaching at the temple at some point toward the middle of the week (7:14). The crowds are astonished by His teaching because they knew that He lacked formal rabbinic training (7:15). Although the question is not necessarily put to Jesus, He confesses that His teaching comes from God (7:16). This is the reason His teaching is so impressive although He lacks formal training. They would be able to understand the truth of His teaching if they were willing to obey it. One's willingness to obey the truth has more to do with understanding the truth than one's intellectual capacity (7:17). Jesus' acknowledgment that He speaks for God is evidence that He is not seeking self-glory but is seeking God's glory (7:18).

Evidence of Jesus' authority (7:19-24)
Jesus returns to the healing of the lame man on the Sabbath, which took place on His previous visit to Jerusalem (5:1-9). He accuses the crowd of transgressing the Law of Moses by attempting to kill Him (7:19). Some in the crowd are pilgrims and unaware of the religious leaders' plot and suggest He is demon possessed (7:20; cf. 8:48-52; 10:20-21).[2] Jesus does not

---

2. Other false accusations include: breaking the Sabbath (5:16, 18; 9:16),

directly respond to the accusation but points out their hypocrisy. Instead, He argues from the lesser to the greater. The Jews argue that it is appropriate to circumcise a male child on the eighth day, even if it falls on the Sabbath. Since circumcision is permitted on the Sabbath, how much more should the healing of an entire person be permitted on the Sabbath (7:23)? Their reasoning demonstrates a superficial judgment for condemning Him for doing good on the Sabbath (7:24).

The origins of the Messiah (7:25-36)
7:25-27: Jesus' identity now becomes the subject of discussion. Apparently, at this point others join the crowd who are aware of the leaders' desire to kill Him (7:25). They surmise that the leaders' failure to seize Him indicates they have changed their mind about whether or not He is the Messiah (7:26). Some doubt that Jesus can be the Messiah because they know where He is from. There appears to have been some debate among first-century Judaism as to whether the Messiah would suddenly appear out of obscurity or not (7:27). Some rabbis taught that the Messiah would be wholly unknown until He set out to procure salvation for Israel. Still others were sure about the Messiah's birthplace (cf. 7:42).

7:28-31: Jesus' words demonstrate the irony of the situation. They think they know where He is from but in reality He has come on a mission from His Father (7:28). The fact that Jesus cries out (1:15; 7:37; 12:44) underlines the significance of the point He makes here. While they so confidently assert that they know His origins, Jesus states that they do not know God (7:29). The response to Jesus is varied (7:30-31). Some are so angry that they tried to seize Him but they are unable to do so because His 'hour had not yet come' (7:30; cf. 8:59; 12:23, 37; 13:1; 17:1). Even amidst all the tension, many in the crowd believe in Him because of His signs (7:31). The division is evident.

The response of the Jewish leadership (7:32-36)
The religious leaders, aware that some are beginning to believe in Jesus, feel the need to act. 'The chief priests and the

---

blasphemy (5:18; 8:59; 10:31, 33, 39; 19:7), deceiving the people (7:12, 47), being a Samaritan (8:48), being insane (10:20), and being accursed (18:30).

Pharisees' send the temple police to arrest Him (7:32). John builds suspense by noting that the temple guards are being sent in verse 32, but they are not mentioned again until they return empty-handed in verse 45. The temple guards were responsible for maintaining order within the temple precincts. This section closes with Jesus making another comment about His return to the Father (7:33). The crowds misunderstand Jesus' statement and think He is going to Greek-speaking Jewish people scattered outside of Israel (7:35-36).

'On the last day' (7:37-52)

Jesus' invitation to the thirsty (7:37-39)
7:37-38: This passage contains one of the most debated issues in the Gospel: who is the source of the living water in verse 38? There are two primary interpretations: the source of the living water comes from the believer or from Christ. The debate centers on whether or not one places a stop at the end of the Greek text of 7:37 and separates it from the phrase beginning at 7:38. Thus it would read: 'If anyone is thirsty, let him come to Me and drink. He who believes in Me, as the Scripture said, "From his [believer's] innermost being will flow rivers of living water"' (NASB). The other interpretation moves the full stop into 7:38 and results in the reading: 'Let the thirsty who believe come and drink. As the Scripture says, "Rivers of living water will flow from his [Christ's] heart"' (NLT). The phrase 'anyone who believes' can belong to either clause, so the question is whether the believer or Christ is the source from which the Spirit flows (the 'river of living water').[3]

Those who hold to the Christological position point to the context as the major support for their position. Jesus is the fulfillment of the water-pouring ceremony and the entire context of chapters 5–10 is Christological in nature. They suggest that it would be a strange interpretation if He were making the believer, rather than Himself, the source of the

---

3. The position that the believer is the source of the living water is held by Morris, *John*, 374-78; Carson, *John*, 321-28; Köstenberger, *John*, 240; the NASB, and the NIV. The Christological position is held by Bruce, *Gospel & Epistles*, 1:182; Burge, *John*, 185; Brown, *John*, 1:321; and Beasley-Murray, *John*, 113-17.

Holy Spirit in light of 14:26 and 16:7, where Christ sends the Spirit on His mission. On the other hand, Carson points out that it would be strange for Jesus to say, 'from his heart,' if He were referring to Himself. The most straightforward reading seems to favor the latter interpretation because of Jesus' use of the third person singular pronoun ('him'). It is debated as well as to what specific Scripture reference Jesus had in mind (7:38). In light of the festival it is not improbable that He was thinking of Isaiah 12:3 and Zechariah 14:8.

The importance of Jesus' words in these verses is seen in that He spoke them on the last day of the feast when the crowds were at their largest. The fact that He 'cries out' indicates He wants as many as possible to hear. The invitation is universal in nature ('if anyone thirsts ... whoever believes in me') and therefore not restricted to a certain type of person (7:37b-38a). The only condition is that one must be thirsty (7:37b). All true spiritual advances begin with a thirst for God. Jesus uses a very powerful image here, especially for a people living in the arid land of the Middle East. They knew what it was to be thirsty and they understood how important water was for daily life. One of the tragedies of our age is that we twist our thirst for God into a thirst for other things – relationships, power, possessions, etc. We sense that something is lacking but we try and quench that thirst in a thousand different ways. Jeremiah put it this way: 'for my people have committed two evils: they have forsaken me, the fountain of living waters, and hewed out cisterns for themselves, broken cisterns that can hold no water' (Jer. 2:13).

7:39: John explains that this living water is nothing less than the Holy Spirit. This is the first use of the verb form 'glorify' referring to the glorification of Jesus (cf. 8:54; 12:28; 13:32; 14:13; 15:8; 16:14; 17:1, 4, 5, 10; 21:19). The reference refers to Jesus' death, resurrection, and exaltation. John thinks of the cross in terms of glory and not shame. Jesus' death, resurrection, and exaltation are the prelude to the Spirit's ministry.

The division among the crowd (7:40-44)
The crowd is divided over Jesus' identity. Some think that He is the Moses-like prophet (7:40; cf. Deut. 18:15). There

was a similar thought expressed at the feeding of the five thousand (cf. 6:14). While some wonder if Jesus may be the Christ, others reject this idea because He comes from Galilee (7:41-43). This division among the people over Jesus' identity will continue (cf. 9:16; 10:19). Even though some were ready to have Him arrested no one laid his hand on Him. John's readers know that this would not take place until Jesus' hour had come (7:44).

The consternation of the religious leaders (7:45-52)
John leaves the crowds for a moment and returns to the 'chief priests and the Pharisees'. The evangelist has built suspense in the text by describing the religious leaders dispatching the temple guard earlier (cf. 7:32). He describes the outcome here. It seems they heard Jesus speak and were moved by His words (7:45-46).The leadership is furious and point to the fact that none of them has believed in Jesus but only the ignorant crowd who are easily deceived (7:50). Nicodemus, however, points to the fact that it is the leadership who have broken the law (7:51). He has not been heard from since his encounter with Jesus described in chapter 3. It has been approximately eighteen months since that night. The leadership's response is swift and harsh. Their comment about no prophet coming from Galilee reveals their failure to remember Jonah (2 Kings 14:25) and Elijah (1 Kings 17:1).

Chapter 7 has reported opposition to Jesus from His family, from many of the common people, and from the religious leaders. Yet it also showed that a growing number are convinced by His deeds and claims. The leadership is increasingly frustrated in their inability to handle this 'Jesus problem'. The antagonism Jesus faced in this chapter becomes more intense in the next.

Reflections
Jesus' words in 7:37-39 are extremely important. The importance of the message is seen in the fact that Jesus waited until the last day of the feast and the crowd was at its largest. He 'cries out' so He can be heard by as many as possible. The universal nature of the invitation is astonishing ('anyone … whoever'). No one is left out because of ethnicity or social

standing. The only condition is that one be thirsty and willing to drink. As mentioned earlier, all true spiritual advances begin with a thirst for God (Ps. 42:1; Isa. 55:1; Jer. 12:13; Matt. 5:6). To drink of Jesus is to trust Him for salvation. Those who believe in Him find their soul's thirst satisfied. However, the paradox of love is that after we come to know Christ our thirsty soul on the one hand is satisfied, but on the other hand longs for more of Jesus. If the 'rivers of living water' flow from within the believer then John is describing the outworking of the Spirit-filled life. Jesus ministers to others through His Spirit-filled people. We must ask ourselves before we move on to the next passage, 'Are we thirsty?' Have we gone to Christ in faith and found our soul's satisfied in Him, and is He using us as channels of blessings to others?

STUDY QUESTIONS

1. How does this chapter fit into John's purpose as stated in 20:30-31?

2. Why do you think Jesus' brothers found it difficult to believe in Him? Do you know someone whose family rejected them because of their faith in Christ?

3. What is it that caused the crowds to grumble about Jesus (7:10-13)?

4. Make a list of statements made about Jesus in this chapter. Do you find a unifying theme?

15

'Go and Sin No More'
(John 7:53–8:11)

As marginal notes in most modern translations indicate, John 7:53-8:11 is absent from many important Greek manuscripts.[1] Many of the manuscripts that do include it contain scribal notations indicating doubt about the authenticity of the passage. While many scholars understand the story is likely to be a historical event, they do not think that it was written by the apostle John.[2] Since there is considerable

---

1. The evidence against the authenticity of the passage is significant: The story is not found in any Greek manuscripts of John before the fifth century. All the earliest church fathers omit this passage when commenting on John's Gospel and go from John 7:52 to John 8:12. No Eastern Church father refers to the passage before the tenth century when commenting on John's Gospel. When the story starts to appear in manuscript copies of the Gospel, it shows up in three different places: after 7:36; 7:44; and 21:25. In one manuscript of Luke's Gospel it appears after 21:38. The style and vocabulary are considerably different than any other portion of the Gospel. For these and further details see Bruce Metzger, *Textual Commentary*, 219-22. Carson writes (*John*, 333), 'Despite the best efforts ... to prove that this narrative was originally part of John's Gospel, the evidence is against [them], and modern English versions are right to rule it off from the rest of the text (*NIV*) or to relegate it to a footnote (*RSV*).' Köstenberger writes (*John*, 246): 'This represents overwhelming evidence that the section is non-Johannine.' Morris states (*John*, 882): 'The textual evidence makes it impossible to hold that this section is an authentic part of the Gospel.' Defending its originality is Zane Hodges, 'The Woman Taken in Adultery (John 7:53-8:11): The Text,' *Bibliotheca Sacra* 136 (1979): 318-32. This position has not found wide acceptance among New Testament scholarship.

2. A helpful study outlining the justification for this position is Gary M. Burge, 'A Specific Problem in the New Testament Text and Canon: The Woman Caught in Adultery (John 7:53-8:11),' *Journal of the Evangelical Theological Society* 27/2 (1984): 141-48.

probability that John did not write it, there is reason to avoid according canonical authority to the incident. In the comments below we will treat the verses as if they accurately describe an actual event, without thereby implying either Johannine authorship or canonical authority to the passage.

The Setting (7:53–8:2)

The scene suddenly shifts from the confrontation between Nicodemus and the Sanhedrin (7:45-52) to an early morning setting in which Jesus is addressing a large crowd in the Temple precinct (7:53–8:1). Jesus takes the normal teaching position of sitting as He speaks (8:2).

The Hypocritical Trap (8:3-6)

Without warning the Pharisees and the scribes bring before Jesus a woman caught in the act of adultery (8:3). Their duplicity is seen in three ways. First, the Old Testament law on which they base their charges requires both parties to be punished (8:5; cf. Lev. 20.10; Deut. 22.22). The male partner is conspicuously absent (8:6). One has to wonder if the woman was set up in order to trap Jesus. Second, adultery charges were very rare in Judaism because the law carefully stipulated the need for overwhelming evidence. Third, the Romans deprived the Jews of the death penalty. The one exception to this was if a Gentile was found in the Temple areas reserved for Jews alone.

The leaders use the woman as a pawn. They want to play off Jesus' well-known compassion for 'sinners' against the demands of the law. Their strategy seemed full-proof. If Jesus suggests that the woman be treated with mercy, then He can be accused of breaking the law. If He upholds the Law and called for her to be stoned, He would violate Roman law. Jesus responds by kneeling down and scribbling in the sand. While numerous suggestions have been made as to what Jesus wrote, no one can know for certain.

Jesus' response (8:7-11)

Jesus calls their bluff and calls on those without sin to begin the stoning (8:7). He then kneels down again and writes in the sand. Beginning with the oldest (and presumably the wisest) the accusers slip away (8:9). Jesus' wisdom turned the table on the hypocrites who brought the woman to Him. At last only Jesus and the woman remain (8:10). Jesus does not excuse her sin nor overlook it. He calls on her to make a decisive break with her lifestyle. His words are similar to what He told the lame man earlier, 'Behold, you have become well; do not sin anymore so that nothing worse happens to you' (5:14). She must make a change in behavior if she is to escape God's judgment. Jesus extends mercy to her while at the same time calling her to account for her sin. We are left to wonder if the woman responded positively or not to Christ's graciousness.

Reflections
Despite the doubt of the authenticity of the passage it illustrates truths found elsewhere in the Gospel. Jesus' heart for sinners to repent and turn to God is clearly evident in this passage and throughout John's Gospel. As mentioned earlier, Jesus' words to the woman sound very much like His admonition to the lame man to sin no more. Jesus' compassion should not be misunderstood as His excusing sin. While He did not condemn her, He did make it clear that her lifestyle was sinful and called her to turn away from it.

While we are left in the dark as to how the woman responded to Christ's words, many people throughout the ages who have been trapped in sin have found this story to give them hope. After reading it they have called out to God for forgiveness and grace and have found a new life in Christ Jesus. While the authenticity of the passage is debated, the story illustrates the message of the gospel: in Christ new life is possible. On the other hand, we are reminded by the religious leaders that living according to the law without God's grace in the heart leads to hypocrisy and condemnation.

16

'I am the Light of the world'
(John 8:12-30)

If 7:53–8:11 is not considered an original part of John's Gospel, then the next words Jesus speaks at the feast following 7:52 are original: 'I am the Light of the world.' This is the second of Jesus' seven 'I am' statements. While the phraseology appears simple the concept is rich and multifaceted. The prologue set the stage for the importance of light imagery.[1] John wrote, 'In him was life, and the life was the Light of men. The Light shines in the darkness, and the darkness did not overpower it' (John 1:4-5). The imagery of light conjures up thoughts from the Old Testament. God's first creation was light: 'Then God said, "Let there be light"; and there was light. God saw that the light was good; and God separated the light from the darkness' (Gen. 1:3-4). At the Exodus, God's presence was symbolized in the pillar of fire by night and the cloud by day (Exod. 13:21-22; 14:24; Ps. 78:14). Light was a symbol of salvation: 'The Lord is my light and my salvation' (Ps. 27:1; cf. Ps. 44:3; Isa. 60:19-20). It was symbolic of God's word: 'Your word is a lamp to my feet and a light for my path' (Ps. 119:105). Israel was called to be a 'light to the Gentiles' (Isa. 49:6). Isaiah and Zechariah

---

1. The word appears six times as a noun and once as a verb in the prologue (1:4, 5, 7, 8 [2x], 9 [2x]). Of the seventy-three occurrences of 'light' in the New Testament, twenty-three are in John's Gospel.

predicted that light would shine forth perpetually from the temple in the eschaton (Isa. 60:14-22; Zech. 14:5-7).

This rich symbolism enhanced the importance of light at the Feast of Tabernacles. To miss this imagery behind Jesus' 'I am' statement is to miss the richness of what He is saying about Himself. The festival background focused particularly on the pillar of fire that guided Israel during their wilderness wanderings and the eschatological hope of the messianic age.

> Toward the end of the feast of Tabernacles, people went down into the court of the women... Golden lamps were there, and four golden bowls were on each of them, and four ladders were by each, four young men from the priestly group of youths had jugs of oil in their hands and poured oil from them into individual bowls. Wicks were made from the discarded trousers of the priests and from their girdles. There was no court in Jerusalem that was not bright from the light of the place of the drawing water. Men of piety and known for their good work danced before them with torches in their hands and sang before them songs and praises. And the Levites stood with zithers and harps and cymbals and trumpets and other musical instruments without number... [2]

What a sight it must have been to see God's people dancing, singing, celebrating, and remembering His faithfulness to them. It is unclear if the lamps were lit every night, or if they remained unlit on the final night of the feast. If this is so, it reminded the people that they had not yet experienced their full salvation. In light of the fact that John presents Jesus as speaking these words on the last day of the feast (John 7:37), Jesus is declaring Himself as the one who provides that salvation.

As mentioned earlier, the lighted candelabras recalled the pillar of cloud by day and the fire by night that was with the Israelites in the wilderness as signs of God's presence. It saved them from the threatened destruction from the Egyptian army (Exod. 14:19-25) and led them through the wilderness to the Promised Land. So, in three successive chapters we find Exodus and wilderness imagery. In John 6 Jesus is the manna from heaven [The Bread of Life]; in John 7

---

2. Mishnah, *Sukkah 5:1-4.*

the water from the rock [The Living Water]; and in John 8 the pillar of fire [The Light of the World]. Therefore, when Jesus proclaims, 'I am the Light of the world,' He is appropriating again the symbolism of the festival to show the fulfillment of the history and hope of God's people in His life and ministry. As Israel followed the light from the land of Egyptian slavery through the wilderness to the Promised Land, so believers follow Jesus as 'the Light of life'. Jesus fulfills Tabernacles!

The discourse-dialogue in chapter 8 can be broken down into three sections. In the first section, the Pharisees respond to Jesus' 'I am the light of the world' statement by accusing Him again of giving self-testimony. The section concludes with a comment that Jesus 'was not arrested, because his time had not yet come' (8:12-20). In the second, Jesus warns the people that if they do not believe in Him they will 'die in their sins'. John concludes this section with a statement that many believed in Him (8:21-30). The third section is the longest and records the most volatile exchange between Jesus and His opponents thus far in the Gospel (8:31-59). The language is vitriolic as Jesus accuses His opponents of being children of the devil, while they accuse Him of being a Samaritan and demon-possessed. The chapter culminates with the people picking up stones to throw at Jesus. The final section will be explored in the next study.

'I am the light of the world' (8:12-20)
Verses 12-20 unfold in a threefold exchange between Jesus and the Pharisees. The Pharisees' comments are relatively brief compared to Jesus' words. In verse 13 they challenge Jesus' self-testimony and in verse 19 they question Him about His Father.

8:12: This section begins with Jesus making a dramatic declaration ('I am the Light of the world'), followed by a soteriological promise, stated first negatively and then positively (8:12). As we have seen many times in this Gospel, people are faced with one of two choices: to follow Jesus and have 'the light of life', or to not follow Him and 'walk in the darkness' (cf. 3:19-21; 11:9; 12:35-36). To 'follow' Jesus is the language of discipleship (1:37-38, 40, 43), which in John's Gospel involves believing in Jesus (20:30-31).

8:13-18: The Pharisees immediately challenge the validity of Jesus' self-testimony (8:13; cf. 5:31). When they questioned Him earlier on this issue He responded by "calling" a series of witnesses to substantiate His claims (cf. 5:31-40). This time He responds by appealing to His origin and destiny to validate His self-testimony (8:14). Jesus can testify concerning Himself because He comes from God and He is 'going' back to God. The term 'going' (*hypago*) is used often in this Gospel to refer to Jesus' departure from this world through His death, resurrection, and exaltation (cf. 7:33; 8:21; 13:3, 33, 36; 14:28; 16:5, 10). Jesus will add a second witness to affirm His teaching concerning Himself in 8:18.

Their problem is that since they base their judgment solely on what is visible ('according to the flesh') they do not recognize His divine origin (8:15a; cf. 7:24). Jesus' comment that He 'judges no one' (8:15b) appears to contradict His earlier statement where He says He does judge (cf. 5:30). This contradiction seems heightened by what Jesus says in 8:16 ('But even if I do judge'). So, does Jesus judge or not? The answer is yes and no. No, He does not judge like the Pharisees' judge, 'according to the flesh.' Furthermore, the Father sent Jesus for salvation, not judgment (3:16), but Jesus' ministry has an intrinsic eschatological dimension to it. His coming forces people to make a decision, because for those who reject the salvation He offers He becomes the God-appointed judge. In an ironic twist, Jesus answers the Pharisees' charges of self-testimony by offering Himself and God as the two-fold witness necessary to substantiate His claim (8:17-18).

8:19-20: The Pharisees want to know the location of His Father if His Father is going to bear witness to Him. Their question reveals their ignorance concerning Jesus' relationship to God. John mentions that Jesus spoke these words in the area near the temple treasury, which was located adjacent to the Court of the Women. The section concludes in a manner reminiscent of 7:30. As much as they wanted to arrest Jesus, His life was governed by God's timing, not man's (8:20).

Jesus' origin and nature (8:21-30)
This new section is marked out by the use of 'again' (cf. v. 20). Jesus' words here replay the theme of departure in

8:14 (8:21-22, 28). This passage also has similarities to 7:33-34, but is more serious in tone. Jesus warns His audience that they will 'die in their sin' if they refuse to believe in Him. Two verbal interchanges between Jesus and His opponents take place in these verses. In each case Jesus makes a statement about His origin or nature that His hearers misunderstand. Notice the emphatic pronouns throughout this section.

The first exchange: 'You will die in your sins' (8:21-24)
8:21-22: The consequence of Jesus' departure is that the crowd would not be able to follow Him because they will 'die in their sin' (cf. 7:33-34). What it means for one to die in their sin is not elaborated on, and makes the thought even more dreadful. John uses the verb 'to die' more often than anyone else in the New Testament (twenty-eight times). Yet John does not have a morbid interest in death. Rather, there is a serious choice that has to be made between life and death. To refuse life is to choose death. John desires that his readers choose life (20:31). The singular use of 'sin' suggests that Jesus is not speaking about individual sinful acts, but the single and decisive sin of rejecting God's Son (cf. 1:29; 8:24; 9:41; 15:22-24; 16:9).[3] The Jews misunderstand Jesus' words about His departure as in 7:25-30 (8:22). Here, however, they wonder if Jesus is talking about suicide. The irony is that Jesus would indeed lay down His life for His sheep, but He will do so of His own accord (10:17-18; 15:13).

8:23-24: The reason that they misunderstand Jesus is because they are of this world, but He is not (8:23). Later Jesus tells His disciples that they are not of this world (cf. 15:19; 17:6, 14, 16). Jesus reiterates His warning about dying in sins from 8:21 (8:24). The change from the singular to the plural is not a significant change and reminds the Jews that the sin of rejecting Jesus manifests itself in individual sinful acts. The only escape from dying in their sins is to believe that Jesus is the divine 'I am' (cf. Ex. 3:14). Jesus makes the stakes for believing of ultimate importance. If one is to move from death to life, one must recognize Jesus as the incarnate Logos of God (cf. 1:1; 8:19; 10:30).

---

3. Brown, *John*, 1:350.

The second exchange: 'Who are you?' (8:25-30)

8:25-27: Their question ('Who are you?') shows a complete misunderstanding of Jesus' words (8:25a). Unwittingly they are asking the fundamental question of the gospel ('Who is Jesus?'). Jesus' rejoinder reminds them to consider what He has been telling them from the beginning of His ministry – 'I am God incarnate!' (8:25b). Since Jesus is from God, His words, including His present words of judgment, are divinely inspired (8:26). John explains that the crowd fails to understand this crucial theological reality (8:27).

8:28-29: Jesus' final words in this portion of the discourse have to do with His being 'lifted up'. This is the second of three references to the 'lifting up' of the Son of Man in the Gospel (3:14; 12:32-34). It refers to His crucifixion, resurrection, and exaltation. The other two 'lifted up' sayings are in the passive voice, suggesting God's agency in the act. Here, Jesus places responsibility on His opponents ('When you lift up the Son of Man'). The irony is that in their 'lifting up' of Jesus to kill Him, they are at the same time exalting Him. The 'lifting up' is also a moment of judgment because it confronts His opponents with the truth of His identity ('then you will know that I am *he*'); giving the 'lifting up' saying revelatory significance. Furthermore, the lifting up confirms what Jesus has been saying all along concerning His relationship to God (5:28b; cf. 5:19, 30; 7:16).

It is debated whether verse 28 should be understood as a prophecy of judgment (i.e., it will be too late for the Jews) or a promise of hope (i.e., they will realize the truth). The answer may lie in the use of the future tense verb, 'you will know.' Jesus' comment might be a both/and rather than either/or statement. On the one hand, Jesus told Pilate that the one who handed Him over to him is guilty of a greater sin. Those who called for Jesus' crucifixion acknowledged that they had no king but Caesar. On the other hand, while this may not be a promise that all Jews will be saved, at Pentecost there were 3,000 conversions (Acts 2:41). Furthermore, Paul teaches that a significant number of Jewish people will be saved shortly before Christ's return (Rom. 11:25-32).

One wonders how Jesus could speak with such confidence and peace about His own brutal death. The reason is because

He will not die alone: as He carries out God's will, God will not abandon Him (8:29). John concludes by noting the fact that many believed in Jesus (8:30). This stands in contrast to the conclusion of the previous section where they wanted to 'seize him' (8:20).

Reflections

Once again Jesus makes a remarkable claim about Himself: 'I am the Light of the world.' The promise to those who believe in Him is equally remarkable: 'Whoever follows me will not walk in darkness, but will have the light of life.' The fact that Jesus is the Light of the world implies once again that the world is shrouded in moral and spiritual darkness. Left to ourselves we cannot overcome the darkness. Jesus, however, is the light that illuminates the darkness and allows people to see their true spiritual condition. The light must be responded to either positively or negatively. Those who follow Jesus in faith and discipleship are promised 'the light of life'. The promise Jesus makes is tremendous; they will not walk in darkness. Jesus uses the emphatic double negative to make the point that the one who follows Him will not walk in the darkness. Jesus' disciple is delivered from spiritual darkness. On the positive side the believer will have 'the light of life'. The light Jesus promises is the source of all true life.

The passage also highlights the differences between Jesus and His opponents. Jesus condemns His enemies as unable to make anything but human judgments, as not having a relationship with God, destined to die in their sins, and being worldly. Jesus, on the other hand, stands with the Father and has the Father as a witness to His true identity, has been sent from above by the Father, and has come as the redeemer sent from heaven. One wonders if all hope is lost for the Jewish people, but all is not lost. The answer is the cross (8:27-29). After they have crucified Him many will come to realize who He truly is.

STUDY QUESTIONS

1. State in one or two sentences what you think is the main point John wants to make in this passage.

2. Why do you think the imagery of light is such a powerful religious symbol?

3. How does this passage help you develop your understanding of Jesus' work of redemption?

4. How do 7:33; 8:21; 13:3, 33, 36; 14:28; 16:5, 10 help inform your understanding of John 8:13-18?

5. Make a list of what you learn about Jesus in John 8:12-30.

17

'Greater than Abraham'

(John 8:31-59)

Jesus is involved in the harshest polemic in the Gospel from this point through to the end of the chapter.[1] Jesus makes clear the fundamental difference between Him and His opponents – God is His Father and His opponents' father is the devil. As the debate unfolds it becomes more and more tense and the situation ever more volatile. The truth of Jesus' testimony (8:32, 40, 45-46, 51), and the falsehood of those who oppose Him, is the focus of the debate (8:44-45). The repeated references to Abraham are the only such references in the Gospel (8:33, 37, 39-40, 52-53, 56, 58). In verses 31-38 the issue is the Jews' relationship to Abraham and in verses 48-59 Jesus' relationship to Abraham. This debate concerning one's relationship to Abraham is determined ultimately by one's relationship to God. The passage can be divided into three sections: (1) The Jews are physical descendants from Abraham but not spiritual descendants (8:31-38); (2) The Jews are not children of God (8:39-47); (3) Jesus is greater than Abraham (8:48-59).

Slaves of Sin (8:31-38)
8:31-32: Jesus speaks to those 'who had believed him' (8:31a). The harsh nature of the debate that follows calls into question

---

1. While the entire chapter is set forth as a trial in which Jesus judges His audience, it is especially evident in this section. See Jerome H Neyrey, 'Jesus the Judge: Forensic Process in John 8:21-59,' *Biblica* 68 (1987): 509-42.

the reality of their faith. Their actions reveal that they are not true believers (cf. 2:23-25; 6:60-66). Jesus calls them to 'abide' in His word; that is, to continue believing and obeying it. His point is that continued trust and obedience is one test of true discipleship. Three things are true about those who 'abide' in His word: (1) they prove to be true disciples; (2) they will know the truth; (3) they will experience true spiritual freedom (8:32, 40, 44, 45, 46).

8:33: Jesus' comment about freedom hits a nerve with the crowd (8:33). They appeal to the fact that they are Abraham's descendants and thus have never been slaves. Their appeal to being Abraham's descendants becomes a central feature of the debate (8:37, 39-40, 47, 53, 57). Jesus speaks of freedom as the result of knowing the truth, but they deny they have ever been enslaved and make no reference to the importance of truth. One wonders what they were thinking when they said they 'have never yet been enslaved to anyone'. It could be that they were referring to the fact that as Abraham's descendants they were already spiritually free. Another possibility is that they are making a comment on their own history. If this is the case, it shows a complete misunderstanding of their present situation with the Romans as well as significant portions of their more distant past. If this latter thought is their point they demonstrate that they are so determined to distance themselves from Jesus that they deny their own history. An example of this attitude is when they tell Pilate that they have no king but Caesar (cf. 19:15).

8:34-38: Jesus addresses their two points of protest: freedom (8:34) and descent from Abraham (8:35-38). He corrects their misunderstanding concerning freedom and slavery (8:34). The solemnity of His words are evidenced by 'truly, truly'. He makes it clear that He is not talking about political freedom, but spiritual freedom. A person is not free merely because of their religious heritage. Everyone (without exception) whose life is characterized by sin is sin's slave (8:34; cf. Rom. 6:16-18).[2] To be a slave to sin is to be unable to escape its controlling power. If the Jews are not God's children (as Jesus claims) two results follow: their tenure

---

2. The present participle refers to a continual state of sin rather than specific acts.

there is limited and they have another father (8:35). Jesus repeats the promise of freedom but substitutes the word 'Son' for 'truth' (8:36). While they are physically descended from Abraham their desire to kill Him reveals that His word has no place in their hearts (8:37). Jesus concludes this section by contrasting Himself and His relationship to His Father with His opponents and their relationship to their father (8:38).

Children of the Devil (8:39-47)

8:39-41a: Their claim, 'Abraham is our father,' functions as a transition (8:39a). It is a slight shift to claim to be Abraham's descendants (8:33, 37) to having Abraham as father. The noun 'father' appears frequently in 8:39-47 (vv. 39, 41, 42, 44 [3x]), and it is always used in relationship to the Jews' father, never Jesus' Father. Jesus rebuffs their claim to being Abraham's offspring by focusing on their actions (8:39b-41a). The fact that they are seeking to kill one who told them the truth confirms that they are not Abraham's children. Jesus' declaration in verse 41a ('You are doing the deeds of your father') prepares the reader for the assertion that they are children of the devil (cf. 8:44).

8:41b-47: The Jews understand the implication of Jesus' statement and respond in two ways: first, they accuse Jesus of being a child of fornication (likely having to do with rumors about His conception); and second, they shift from claiming to be children of Abraham to being children of God (8:41b). Jesus responds by pointing out the fact that their actions discredit their claim. In fact, their actions reveal that they have another father, the devil! One's relationship to God is determined by one's relationship to Jesus because Jesus comes from God (8:42; cf. 5:43; 7:28) and is sent by God (cf. 5:24, 30; 7:16, 29, 33; 8:16, 18, 29). Their inability to understand what Jesus is saying to them proves that they are not God's children (8:43). The discussion of paternity reaches its painful conclusion with Jesus' assertion that the crowd are neither Abraham's nor God's children but the devil's children (8:44a). This infuriates the crowd. Once again, Jesus states that a person stands in one of two positions – one is a child of God or of the devil. In an age dominated by inclusivism and pluralism Jesus' language seems harsh and unbending.

Jesus' words, however, build on an earlier distinction made in 8:23 – Jesus and the Jews have different origins.

Jesus' reference to the devil as a murderer from the beginning is likely an allusion to the story of Cain and Abel (8:44b; cf. Gen. 4:8-16), the Bible's first murder. The Jews' desire to kill Jesus mirrors the desires of the first murderer, their father the devil. These references to the devil add a cosmic element to the conflict. The Jews that want to kill Jesus are caught up in this cosmic conflict and demonstrate their ultimate allegiance to the devil. This cosmic battle was introduced in the prologue (1:5). Unlike Jesus, who is truth (14:6), the devil has no relationship to the truth. The thought that he is 'the father of lies' is likely an allusion to Genesis 3. Jesus continues to contrast Himself and the devil (8:45-47): while the devil cannot speak the truth because of his own nature, Jesus speaks the truth; while the devil has sinned from the beginning, they cannot 'convict' Jesus of sin. The reason that they reject Jesus' teaching is because they do not belong to God. This middle section of the debate ends with Jesus' assertion that the Jews have failed the challenge of verse 31 and hence are outside its promise.

Abraham and Jesus (8:48-59)

Verses 48-59 are more heated than the earlier parts of the debate. There are six changes of speaker in this unit (vv. 48, 49, 52, 54, 57, 58) in contrast to three in verses 31-38 (vv. 31, 33, 34) and four in verses 39-47 (vv. 39a, 39b, 41b, 42).

8:48-51: The Jews now resort to name-calling (8:48).They move from a defensive posture to a more aggressive tone. Jesus said that they were children of the devil, now they accuse Him of being a 'Samaritan' and 'demon possessed'. It is unlikely that they truly believed Jesus to be a Samaritan but used the term in an attempt to insult Him. Jesus responds in verses 48-51. He does not mention the 'Samaritan' charge, but He rebuts the accusation that He has a demon by appealing to His relationship with God (8:49).[3] The Jews dishonor God because they fail to honor His chosen representative. In the ancient

---

3. It is interesting that John's Gospel is the only Gospel that does not describe Jesus casting out demons. In fact, in this Gospel the only person accused of having a demon is Jesus!

Mediterranean world, the way one treated an emissary was equal to treatment of the sender. While they dishonor God by dishonoring Jesus, He seeks God's glory (8:50; cf. 5:41, 44; 7:18). The reference to God as judge heightens the eschatological danger the Jews are in for dishonoring God and seeking their own glory. The 'truly, truly' comment of verse 51 makes the eschatological dimension even more explicit. Jesus' comment on keeping His word recalls His earlier reference back in verse 31, and suggests that truth, freedom, and eternal life ('never taste of death') belong together as Jesus' eschatological gifts.

8:52-53: 'The Jews' continue on the offense. Earlier they appealed to Abraham to defend their identity (8:33, 39), and here they appeal to him to attack Jesus' identity. Their question expects a negative answer (8:53a). Surely Jesus is not greater than Abraham and the prophets. The irony is that He is so much greater that there is no comparison! Their final question ('who do you make yourself out to be?') reveals their continued inability to grasp Jesus' true identity (8:53b). John wants those who read the Gospel to reflect back on the various statements that Jesus has made about Himself and to answer the question themselves.

8:54-57: Jesus disputes their interpretation of His words by dismissing language of self-glorification and repeating His claim of verse 50, that God is the one who glorifies Him (8:54; cf. 5:41, 44; 12:28). Strangely enough, the God they claim as their own is the God that glorifies Jesus. Their rejection of Jesus, their desire for self-glory, and their disobedience to God's word, reveal that they do not truly know God. Jesus indicts them as liars and connects them to the father of lies (8:55b; cf. 8:44). Jesus' appeal to Abraham is an important turn in the debate, because it is the first time in the debate that Jesus Himself appeals to 'father Abraham' (8:56). Prior to this verse the Jews have appealed to Abraham to prove the truth of their claims (8:33, 39, 53), but now Jesus uses Abraham as a witness against them. It is difficult to know exactly what Jesus meant when He said that 'Abraham rejoiced to see my day, and he saw it and was glad.' It could be that Jesus is referring to a specific event in Abraham's life (Gen. 12:1-3; 17:17, 20; 22:8, 13-18; cf. Rom. 4:18-21; Gal. 3:8). However, it may be that He is speaking of Abraham's life of faith as a whole.

8:58-59: Their response highlights the ridiculous nature of Jesus' comment from their perspective. The solemnity of Jesus' reply is emphasized by His use of 'truly, truly'. If there has been any uncertainty about whom Jesus believed Himself to be, He removes it (8:58). Jesus' 'I am' statement is a claim that means more than 'Before Abraham was, I *was*,' which would imply that He is more than 2,000 years old. Rather, His use of the present tense, 'I am' (*ego eimi*), is a claim to pre-existence (cf. 4:26; 6:20; 8:24, 28). Jesus' words, however, are not only a claim to being eternal, but also to being the God who appeared to Moses at the burning bush (Exod. 3:14). His opponents understood this immediately and 'picked up stones to throw at him' for His blasphemy (cf. Lev. 24:16; Deut. 13:6-11).

Reflections

The implications of Jesus' words to the Jews are stunning. The crowd considered themselves to be God's people. They claimed both Abraham and God as their father (8:39; 41). Yet, Jesus says that their true father is the devil (8:44). They give evidence that they do not truly belong to God by their words and deeds: they accuse Jesus of being a Samaritan and demon possessed (8:48; 52); Jesus' word has no place in them (8:37); they do not understand His teaching (8:43); they are seeking to kill God's Son (8:40); they dishonor Jesus (8:49); they do not know God (8:54); they are liars (8:55). The faith they are described as having (8:31) is a spurious faith evidenced by their words and deeds. This passage makes it abundantly clear that the religious leadership was unknowingly in league with the devil. As they went on rejecting the light they were pulled deeper into the darkness. Those who should have recognized God's emissary accuse Jesus of being demon possessed.

As in the previous passage (8:12-30), Jesus' relationship to the Father remains a crucial theme throughout this narrative. Jesus emphasizes the divine origin of His mission and the divine authority of His message: He speaks about the things He has seen and heard in His Father's presence (8:38, 40); He comes from and has been sent by God (8:42); He honors His Father (8:49); the Father glorifies Him (8:54); and if Jesus were to say that He did not know God, He would be a liar, like them (8:55).

Finally, John highlights the importance of Jesus' word in the narrative. Continuation in His word is a mark of discipleship (8:31) and results in the knowledge of truth (8:32). Hearing and keeping Jesus' word reveals that one is of God (8:47) and is evidence that one has eternal life (8:51). A key mark of true conversion and authentic discipleship is the abiding of Jesus' word in a believer's life.

STUDY QUESTIONS

1. In light of John's purpose (20:30-31), why do you think he included this passage?

2. What are the possible indicators of a spurious faith in this passage?

3. Why do you think that the Jews in this passage did not understand their relationship to the devil?

4. What are some marks of true conversion in this passage?

5. What does this passage teach us about the devil?

18

Jesus Heals the Blind Man
(John 9:1-41)

He had never seen his mother's face, his father's smile, the beauty of a sunrise, or any of a thousand other sights those who can see enjoy on a daily basis. He was blind from birth. He had spent every day of his life in complete darkness. His adulthood consisted of begging for alms and hoping for the pity of strangers. It is hard to believe that he would ever marry; few women would marry men with no hope of supporting them. His life was a dark and lonely existence.

As terrible and pathetic as this existence was, his state of spiritual darkness was worse. In fact, outside of Christ all people live in spiritual darkness. Blindness in the Old Testament was more than just a physical ailment. It was commonly used as a metaphor to illustrate spiritual blindness and sin.[1] This story is about how Jesus, the 'light of the world', draws people out of spiritual darkness into the light. The man in the story was physically and spiritually blind until the day he met Jesus.

John's point in the chapter is to contrast the differing effect of Jesus, 'the light of the world,' on the blind man and the Pharisees. On the one hand, the blind man receives both physical and spiritual sight from Jesus. On the other hand, the

---

1. See Isaiah 6:9-10; 29:9; 42:18-19. The Messiah was to bring light and sight (Isa. 29:18; 32:3; 35:5; 42:7).

Pharisees, who can see physically, are blind spiritually. The contrast is further illustrated in the fact that the blind man makes three confessions of ignorance (vv. 12, 25, 36), but in the end he has true vision and faith (9:34-38). The Pharisees make several confident assertions of knowledge (9:16, 24, 29), but are shown to be ignorant (9:41). The story is symbolic (although historical) of how Jesus brings spiritual light to those who are spiritually blind and at the same time passes judgment on those who see themselves as having no need.

Jesus heals a blind man (9:1-7)

An unwarranted assumption (9:1-5)

9:1-3: Jesus passes a man who has been blind from birth (9:1). It is impossible to know exactly when this event took place – it could have happened at any point during or following the Feast of Tabernacles and before the Feast of Dedication (10:22). What is clear is that John wants his readers to see the connection of this event with Jesus' declaration to be the 'light of the world' made during Tabernacles (cf. 8:12). The disciples ask Jesus if the man was born blind as the result of personal sin – either his or his parents'. In Jesus' day it was widely thought that sickness was due to personal sin (9:2). The rabbis taught that a child could suffer because of the parents' sin or that a child could sin while still in the womb.[2] Jesus' reply addresses the ultimate purpose of the affliction rather than its cause. The man's condition should not be a springboard for speculation about moral causation. It should rather be regarded in its present potential for 'displaying' (the same words is used in 1:31 and translated 'revealed') what God can do (9:3).[3]

9:4-5: Jesus tells His disciples that they must join Him in the work God sent Him to do. There is a note of urgency in His words ('we must work'). The reason for this urgency is that their time is limited. 'As long as it is day' refers to Jesus' ministry

---

2. See Exodus 20:5 and Deuteronomy 5:9 on the suffering of children due to their parents' sin and *Genesis Rabbah* 63:6 on the possibility of a child sinning in the womb.

3. We should not ignore the fact that in God's mysterious and wise providence He sometimes allows His children to go through suffering so that they can experience His mercy and grace in delivering them.

preceding His crucifixion ('night is coming'). John notes that it was 'night' when Judas left the upper room to make the final preparations for Jesus' betrayal (cf. 13:30). The disciples will be in hiding between His death and resurrection and therefore it will not be a time for work. Jesus declares to the disciples that 'While I am in the world, I am the light of the world' (cf. 8:12).

The miracle described (9:6-7)
John describes the miracle with great brevity. The question arises as to why Jesus healed him in this way (spat on the ground, made clay, applied it to the man's eyes, and had him wash in the pool). The fact is, Jesus used a variety of methods in His healings and He did something similar to this on at least two other occasions (cf. Mark 7:33; 8:23). More important here is the washing in the pool of Siloam, which was the source of water for the ceremonies at the Feast of Tabernacles. The word 'Siloam' means 'sent', which John translates for his readers. John intends the reader to see the play on words. Jesus, the sent one (cf. 4:34; 5:23, 37; 7:28; 8:26; 12:44; 14:24), sends the blind man to the pool, which means 'sent'. As Burge notes, 'the blind man is being told to go wash in the place called "sent," by the One who was sent by God.'[4] John's point is that Jesus is the source of the man's healing rather than the pool. His description of the man's healing will be repeated several times in the chapter (cf. vv. 10-11, 15, 19, 26).

The interrogations of the once blind man (9:8-34)
At this point Jesus fades into the background until verse 35. In chapters 5–8 Jesus has been on trial, but now the healed man is on trial – first questioned by his neighbors (9:8-12) and then interrogated intensely by the Pharisees (9:13-34). He proves himself to be of a higher caliber than the man healed in chapter 5. As the story unfolds we see his understanding of Jesus slowly develop.

The man and his neighbors (9:8-12)
John begins by describing the shock of the man's neighbors. It is likely that he sat at the same place begging almost every

4. Burge, *John*, 273.

day. The crowds are divided over his identity – is he or is he not the blind beggar? He puts the question to rest with the words, 'I am the one.' The reference to the man being a beggar is not unusual. In the ancient world this was all the blind could do to support themselves. The crowd asks him to tell them his story and he recounts it succinctly. His words imply that at this point he understands Jesus to be no more than a man (9:11). They want to speak to Jesus, but the man did not know where Jesus was (in fact, he had no idea what Jesus looked like!).

The man and the Pharisees: the first interrogation (9:13-17)
We don't know why the man was brought to the Pharisees. Perhaps they brought him because the healing took place on the Sabbath, although it does not seem to bother the crowd as it did the Pharisees (9:13-14). For a second time he is asked to recount the events of his healing. His response is brief – 'He applied ... I washed ... I see' (9:15).

There was a division among the Pharisees over whether Jesus was from God or not (9:16). Some deduced that He could not be from God since He did this miracle on the Sabbath, while others contended that He must be from God because of His signs.[5] The plural use of 'signs' indicates that they were aware of more miracles performed by Jesus. Those who thought Jesus came from God began with the signs, while those who thought Him a sinner began with their Sabbath traditions. They ask the 'blind man' for his opinion and he confesses Jesus to be 'a prophet' (9:17; cf. 4:19). This is an advance in his thinking having previously referred to Him as 'the man who is called Jesus' (v. 11).

The man's parents are interrogated by Pharisees (9:18-23)
Jesus' opponents are now referred to as 'the Jews' (9:18). This is certainly a reference to the religious leadership since everyone involved in the drama is a Jew. The Pharisees as such are not mentioned again until 9:40. Those who discount the miracle do not believe that the man was blind and sought

---

5. Jesus apparently broke the Sabbath in three ways: (1) by kneading the clay; (2) by placing the mud on the eyes He broke the prohibition of anointing; (3) healing was permitted only in matters of life and death (Morris, p. 480 fn.17).

to expose the miracle as a sham by calling in the man's parents (9:19). In essence, they want to know if he is their son and if he was born blind; and if so, how did he receive his sight. His parents acknowledge him as their son, that he was born blind, but they put on him the burden to explain his healing. The parents clearly lacked the temperament of their son (9:20-23). One should note their use of pronouns in distancing themselves from him. John explains that the parents feared being expelled from the synagogue.

The man interrogated by the Pharisees again (9:24-34)
The man is recalled a second time by the Pharisees in order to find evidence to condemn Jesus, even although the plain fact of the miracle now cannot be denied. The back-and-forth between the man and the religious leaders becomes very intense (note the use of the personal pronouns and the repeated use of 'know'). The more pressure the leadership puts on the man to denounce Jesus, the more the man speaks out in defense of Jesus.

9:24-27: They demand that the man 'give glory to God' for the healing, because ('we know') Jesus is a sinner who violated the Sabbath traditions (9:24). The phrase, 'give glory to God,' is a call for the man to answer honestly (cf. Josh. 7:19; 1 Sam. 6:5). The man responds that he does not know if Jesus is a sinner, but he does know one thing, 'that though I was blind, now I see' (9:25). Once again, they ask him to repeat how Jesus healed him (9:26). At this point the man's frustration causes him to become more aggressive in his responses (9:27). He asks them (sarcastically) if they want to become Jesus' disciples. The question is stated in a way that anticipates a negative answer. Maybe more importantly, he seems to be putting himself in the position of a disciple of Jesus.

9:28-34: The leadership respond by polarizing everyone's commitment into one of two camps: you are either Jesus' disciple or Moses' disciple (9:28-29). Verses 30-33 contain the man's final defense. Rather than being intimidated, he takes the initiative. His logic seems irrefutable. God does not listen to sinners (cf. Pss. 34:15; 66:18; 109:7; 145:19), but He does listen to those who fear and obey Him. No one knows of anyone who has ever been healed that was born blind. Jesus opened the blind man's eyes. Therefore, Jesus must be from God or He couldn't have healed him. The Jews' frustration reaches the boiling point, and they resort again to name-calling ('you were born in sins') and put him out of the synagogue.

Jesus, the man, and the Pharisees (9:35-41)

John is interested in the way the coming of Jesus divides people (cf. 6:60-71; 7:12-13, 30-31, 40-44; 10:19-21). We see another example of it in the conclusion of this passage: a confession of faith by the once blind man, and a statement of condemnation of the Pharisees.

9:35-38: As in the story with the lame man, Jesus finds this man (9:35a; cf. 5:14). The purpose of Jesus' signs was to elicit faith (cf. 20:30-31), so Jesus asks him, 'Do you believe in the Son of Man?' The reason Jesus refers to Himself as 'Son of Man' is likely because of the discussion of judgment that follows. The man's first use of 'lord' (*kyrios*) should be understood more as a polite form of address ('sir'). It must be remembered that he has never seen Jesus. Jesus' words to the man, that he has 'seen' Him must have been especially meaningful (9:37). The man responds, 'Lord, I believe.' John suggests that the man worshiped Jesus, indicating that he is no longer in spiritual darkness.

9:39-41: The story concludes with an ironic but somber utterance from Jesus: 'For judgment I came in the world ...' Once again, we are faced with the issue: did Jesus come to judge or not? As noted earlier, salvation is the primary intent of Jesus' incarnation, but since salvation calls for faith and subsequent obedience, rejection of the saving revelation entails God's rejection of those who reject Him. The Light of the world illuminates the darkness and the way out of it. Those who refuse to see the Light are confirmed in their darkness. Jesus' words, 'you would have no guilt,' does not mean that they would be free of a sinful nature inherited from Adam, but that they would not be guilty for transgressing the specific teachings they had received from Jesus.

Reflections

The drama of chapter 9 plays out what it means that Jesus is the 'light of the world'. The light has overpowered the darkness in both the man's physical and spiritual healing. One wonders if the progression of titles used by the once blind man is intended by John to show how a person is slowly but deliberately drawn out of the darkness and into the light as they come to 'see' more and more clearly Jesus' true identity. The progression of titles throughout the narrative reveals how the man's understanding slowly came to the 'light' – Jesus is a man (v. 11), a prophet (v. 17), one who is to be followed (v. 27), from God (v. 33), the 'Son of Man' and 'Lord' who is to be worshiped (v. 37-38). An implication of this passage seems to be that if a person will respond to the light they have been given, God will give them more light. As a person walks in the truth, their capacity for understanding truth is enlarged. For many, faith in Christ is a journey toward Him, moving to the point of personal commitment (v. 38). We should give people who are in darkness and moving toward the light time to make the journey. We should pray for them, love them, and share the gospel with them as God's Spirit works in them. This story should encourage those who have loved ones who are in spiritual darkness that God can draw them into the light of the gospel.

Finally, the light of Jesus has a twofold effect – it brings sight to the blind and a shadow of judgment to those who refuse to believe. But light is also a symbol of judgment as demonstrated in the Pharisees' rejection of it. While salvation is the primary reason for Jesus' first coming (cf. 3:17), yet since salvation calls for faith and obedience, rejection of the saving revelation entails God's rejection of the rejecter. The Light of the world illuminates the darkness, and the way out of it, but those who refuse to see the Light are confirmed in their blindness (9:40, 41).

STUDY QUESTIONS

1. Why do you think John included this story? How does it fit in with his purpose statement in 20:30-31?

2. What is the relationship between this chapter and chapter 8?

3. How does the healing of the blind man illustrate the truth that Jesus is the light of the world?

4. How does John bring out the difference between the Pharisees and the blind man?

19

Jesus is the Good Shepherd
(John 10:1-21)

This chapter is best known for its descriptions of Jesus as 'the good shepherd' (10:11, 14).[1] The imagery of Jesus as Shepherd has brought comfort and hope to God's people throughout the ages. However, in this chapter, Jesus also refers to Himself twice as 'the door' (10:7, 9). Both metaphors have to do with His role as Savior. The imagery of 'the door' presents Jesus as the only way to God, and His role as 'good shepherd' depicts His securing of salvation by the laying down of His life (10:11, 15, 17).

The shepherd imagery, as well as being very familiar to Jesus' audience, has rich Old Testament overtones. In the Old Testament God is described as the shepherd of His people (Pss. 23; 77:20; 79:13; 80:1; 95:7; 100:3; Isa. 40:10-11). The religious leaders were often chastened by God for their failure to be faithful shepherds, while in contrast the promised Messiah would shepherd faithfully God's people (Ezek. 34:1-23; Isa. 56:9-12; Jer. 23:1-4; 25:32-38; Zech. 11). Ezekiel 34 is the most important passage standing behind Jesus' words here. Just as the religious leaders in Ezekiel's day failed to care for God's people, so the religious leaders in Jesus' day failed to carry out their responsibilities for His people. This is seen most clearly in

---

1. The imagery of Jesus as shepherd can be found in the Synoptic Gospels as well. There Jesus is depicted as a shepherd that searches for lost and wandering sheep (Matt. 18:12-14; Luke 15:3-7).

the narrative of the rejection of the blind man by the religious leaders in chapter 9.

There is some debate as to whether 10:1-21 is more closely related to chapter 9 or 10:22-42. We should probably understand these verses to be more closely related to chapter 9.[2] Chapter 9 shows the religious leaders' failure to shepherd the healed blind man, describes them throwing him out of the synagogue, and concludes with Jesus affirming their blindness. The strongest piece of evidence relating the two episodes is the reference to the healing of the blind man in 10:21, pointing back to the events in chapter 9. Therefore, chapter 10 opens with Jesus contrasting His care of God's people with that of the religious leaders. While the events likely did not happen without any time between them, John saw the connection between the two events. Those who connect 10:1-21 more closely with the events in 10:22-42 and the Feast of Dedication point to 10:27 and the reference to Jesus' sheep hearing His voice and following Him. It is possible that John intends 10:1-21 to be a bridge passage connecting the events of the Feast of Tabernacles with the Feast of Dedication.

How to recognize the true shepherd from thieves and robbers (10:1-6)

The opening paragraph, be it an 'illustration' (NLT) or a 'figure of speech' (NASB; ESV), contrasts a shepherd with thieves and robbers. Clearly, Jesus is the shepherd and the thieves and robbers refer to the blind religious leaders from the previous passage.

10:1-4: The seriousness of Jesus' words is seen in His use of 'truly, truly' (cf. 1:51). He begins by contrasting a shepherd with a 'thief and robber' (10:1). What distinguishes the shepherd from the thieves and robbers is the way they enter the sheepfold. Those who wish to harm the sheep do not enter through the door, but climb over the wall. In contrast, the true shepherd enters through the door, having gained access by the gatekeeper (10:2). The gatekeeper should be understood as part of the imagery of the illustration and

---

2. Darrell L. Bock, *Jesus according to Scripture: Restoring the Portrait from the Gospels,* Grand Rapids: Baker Academic, 2002), 473, understands 10:1-21 to be a commentary on the confrontation of John 9.

not interpreted as carrying a special meaning. The shepherd is further identified by the recognition and response of the sheep to his voice (10:3-4).[3] It was common for more than one flock to be kept in an enclosure for safety and convenience. The gatekeeper would allow in a true shepherd, who would call his own sheep to follow him. It was not uncommon for shepherds of small flocks to name their sheep, identifying them by distinguishing marks. The sheep would recognize their shepherd's voice and follow him.

10:5-6: In contrast to the way sheep respond to their shepherd, they flee from a stranger because they do not recognize his voice (10:5). So, a true shepherd enters through the door and his sheep recognize his voice, while a false shepherd enters in a forbidden way, and his voice is not recognized by the sheep. John refers to Jesus' teaching as a 'figure of speech'. The term 'figure of speech' here functions somewhat like a synoptic parable, but the term 'parable' is not used in John. It is difficult to know for certain who it was that did not understand what Jesus was saying, but in light of the context it is best to understand it to refer to the crowds (cf. 8:19, 22, 27, 33, 41, 52, 57; 9:40-41).

Jesus is the Door (10:7-10)
10:7-8: In light of the imagery in the previous verses, one would assume that Jesus would expand on the contrast between true and false shepherds. However, instead He focuses on the image of the door of the sheep pen. Jesus again uses 'truly, truly' to stress the soberness of His words (10:7a). He identifies Himself as 'the door of the sheep' (10:7b). This is the third of Jesus' seven 'I am' statements. His point is that He is the exclusive way to salvation. His comment, 'all who came before me...' may refer to messianic pretenders or, more likely, to the religious leaders of His own time – note the use of the present tense, 'are thieves and robbers' (10:8).[4] They are following in the steps of those God condemned as failed leaders in the past (Ezek. 34). Jesus repeats the thought that these failed leaders are

---

3. Jesus' voice is a common theme in John (5:46-47; 8:37, 45, 47).

4. Contra Carson, *John*, 384.

'thieves and robbers' and that His sheep will not listen to them (10:8).

10:9-10: For a second time Jesus identifies Himself as 'the door' (this time without the reference 'of the sheep') and goes on to contrast Himself with 'the thief'. The definite article highlights again the exclusive nature of His claim. The imagery of a door is used in other places in the New Testament (Luke 13:24; Acts 14:27; 1 Cor. 16:9), but only here is Jesus described in this way. Jesus goes on to say that those who enter through Him 'will be saved, and will go in and out and find pasture' (10:9). The verb 'to save' is used only six times in the Gospel, but this does not mean that John is less interested in the concept of salvation than the other evangelists. As we have noted before, he prefers to speak of eternal life. The two concepts are equated in 3:16-17. One should not over-interpret the imagery of Jesus' words, 'go in and out and find pasture.' These words emphasize the freedom and provision found in salvation.

Jesus does not call His followers to a life of drudgery, but to abundance. In verse 10 He contrasts the purpose of His coming with that of Satan ('the thief'). Earlier He spoke of thieves and robbers (plural), but here He refers to 'the thief' (singular). The contrast between 'the thief' and Jesus could not be greater. The thief comes 'only to kill, steal, and destroy', but Jesus 'came that his followers might have life abundantly' (10:10). The history of the world bears this out. All one needs to do is to look around and see how the devil has brought chaos and devastation to the world. Satan is like a wolf that seeks to destroy the sheep. The imagery is not far removed from Peter's description of the devil as a 'roaring lion seeking whom he may devour' (1 Pet. 5:8). On the other hand, Jesus came to give abundant life to His followers. The life Jesus offers is full, spiritually satisfying, and free. This goes far beyond the usual thought of salvation blessings as being something in the distant future, but instead also promises a fullness of life in Jesus here and now.

Jesus is the Good Shepherd (10:11-18)

Jesus now describes Himself as 'the good shepherd' (10:11, 14). This title has meant much to believers throughout the ages. It communicates Jesus' deep love and concern for His people. It reminds us that, as our shepherd, Jesus watches over us and cares for us. The imagery of Psalm 23 fits so well with the portrait of Jesus in these verses. The fact that God refers to Himself as the shepherd of His people in the Old Testament reminds us that Jesus' language here is not the way that people normally speak about themselves (unless they are not in their right mind!); it is the language of deity. As we read this passage we should be overwhelmed with the depth of love the Savior has for His people, and the extent to which He went to save them. The doctrine of the substitutionary atonement of Christ is prominent in this passage. As it unfolds there are several references to the shepherd laying down his life 'for' the sheep.

The Good Shepherd and the hired hand (10:11-13)
'The good shepherd' demonstrates his commitment to his sheep by his willingness to lay down his life for them. While death for a Palestinian shepherd would spell disaster for the flock, the death of Jesus, 'the good shepherd,' means life for His sheep. Jesus makes repeated reference to His coming death in these verses (10:11, 15b, 17, 18). This is important for two reasons. First, it demonstrates that Jesus was aware that His mission as Savior involved His death. Second, the fact Jesus laid down His life 'for' (*huper*, 'on behalf of') His sheep teaches the doctrine of the substitutionary nature of Jesus' death. While hirelings, or hired hands, may have no malicious desires toward the sheep, in contrast to 'thieves and robbers', they also lack the love and concern of one who owns the flock (10:12-13). A hireling will not risk his life for the sheep; his main thought is on his wages.

The Good Shepherd and his flock (10:14-18)
As 'the good shepherd', Jesus knows His sheep and they know Him (cf. 10:2-4). The verb 'know' is used four times in verses 14-16 (cf. 10:2-4). The thought carries the idea of intimacy. It is not that they merely 'know about' one another, but that they *truly* know one another. The shepherd knows his sheep because he loves them. Jesus' knowledge is so intimate that

an appropriate analogy for this knowledge is His relationship to His Father (10:15).

The 'other sheep', not of this fold, point to the Gentile mission and a future community of faith where there is no distinction between Jew and Gentile. Furthermore, the use of *must* highlights the certainty of this inclusion. It is by the Son's death that this community of faith is born.

The Father loves the Son because of the Son's utter dedication to the Father's will (10:17). We have noted already the repeated references that Jesus laid down His life of His own volition (10:11,15b, 17a, 18b, 18c). He now declares that He not only has complete control of when He dies, but that He will also take up His life again (10:17b, 18d). The Son is able to take up His life again because He and the Father possess the same powers (10:28, 30).

The reaction of the Jews (10:19-21)
The response to Jesus' discourse here follows a similar pattern of rejection and acceptance (6:41, 60; 7:25, 45). There seems to be no neutral position when faced with Christ's revelation – either hostility (10:20) or openness (10:21). Some believe Him to be demon possessed (cf. 7:20; 8:48, 52). In John, demon possession is associated only with Jesus. Others in the crowd point to His words and deeds (7:30; 9:16). Yet, even then their position is not a completely positive one. They say what Jesus is not, but they make no attempt to say who He is. Jesus again eludes an attempt to arrest Him (cf. 5:18; 7:44, 45; 8:20; 8:59; 10:39; 11:53, 54).

Reflections
Christology, soteriology, and missions are all intertwined in this passage. Jesus uses the imagery of a door and shepherd to describe Himself. As the door Jesus presents Himself as the only means by which a person can be made right with God. If Jesus is the door, and we believe that He is, then all other religions are false and Christianity alone is true.

Jesus identifies Himself with God when He calls Himself the good shepherd. As mentioned earlier, God is depicted as the shepherd of His people in the Old Testament. Jesus is both Savior and Shepherd to those who believe in Him for salvation.

As Shepherd He dies for His sheep, He knows them by name, His sheep know His voice, He guides them and they follow Him.

In contrast, false shepherds care nothing about the sheep. Like the false shepherds in Ezekiel's day they care only for themselves. This is a timely word for young ministers who must decide if they will care for God's people as under-shepherds of Christ, or if they will use God's people to build a resume and a career. If Jesus willingly chose to lay down His life for the sheep one wonders how ministers can see as mere stepping stones those for whom they have been entrusted to give oversight. This passage teaches Jesus' love for the church.

Jesus makes it clear from a missiological perspective that He intends His church to be made up of all kinds of people (10:16). All of Christ's people will come to know Him in the same way; that is, they will enter through the same door. They will trust in His death for their salvation. He will be the shepherd of all His people and they will all be one flock. God's people must embrace Christ's mission of worldwide evangelization – all God's people brought into God's kingdom.

Yet, the passage ends with a Johannine reminder that Jesus divides. The accusation that Jesus is demon possessed reveals the cosmic nature of the dispute. The reference back to the blind man ties this section with the previous chapter (10:21). The light has come and men loved the darkness more than the light (cf. 3:19-21). The battle being played out on earth was a reflection of a battle being fought in the invisible world of spiritual reality.

STUDY QUESTIONS

1. How is John's purpose statement in 20:30-31 brought out in this passage?

2. Why do you think the imagery of Jesus as shepherd has meant so much to believers?

3. How does Jesus' imagery of the door/gate affect your view of other religions?

4. Why do you think Jesus' mission brought such division among the Jews?

20

The Feast of Dedication

(John 10:22-42)

This passage culminates the Festival theme that began in chapter 5: Sabbath (5), Passover (6), Tabernacles (7:1–10:21), and here the Feast of Dedication, also known as the Festival of Lights, or Hanukah. Another crucial theme in these chapters has been Jesus' identity. Who does He claim to be? In this passage Jesus identifies Himself as both the Messiah and the Son of God. The Jewish response once again is to try to stone Him for blasphemy. The conclusion to this passage, and the entire section beginning at 5:1, is Jesus' departure from Jerusalem. He will not return there until Passion Week.

It is essential to understand the background to the Feast of Dedication if one is to grasp the full import of this passage. There is no reference in the Old Testament to this Feast. Its origin is found in one of the most courageous episodes in Israel's history (see 1 Maccabees 3–4; 2 Maccabees 8:1–10:8). Antiochus Epiphanes, one of the successors to Alexander the Great, sought to unify his empire by establishing a single religion. Consequently, Judaism was outlawed, and the people were commanded to worship Zeus. The religious reformation included a pagan altar bearing the image of Zeus being placed in the Jerusalem temple. In addition, a pig was sacrificed to Zeus in the temple, as well as the outlawing of Sabbath observance, Scripture reading, and the circumcision of baby boys.

Under the leadership of Judas Maccabee ('the hammer'), the Jewish people revolted against the Syrians, fighting something akin to a guerrilla style war. Greatly outmanned, the Jewish rebels amazingly defeated the Syrians. On the 25th of Kislev 164 B.C. the desecrated temple was cleansed and sacrifices were offered in accordance to the Law. The people rapturously celebrated the rededication of the temple and its altar for eight days, and it was decreed that a similar festival should be held annually beginning on the 25th of Kislev (1 Macc. 4:56-59). The festival remains to this day as one of Judaism's most important celebrations, not least because it can be observed in people's homes. It is characterized by the use of lights. Josephus called it the Festival of Lights 'because such freedom shone upon us'. A lampstand with eight lights was used, one candle being lighted on the first day of the festival, then another each succeeding day, until all eight were lit. The word that best described the celebration was rejoicing.

John 10:22-39 takes place during this festival. As the people celebrate their deliverance from a destroyer of their religion and the rededication of their temple for true worship, Jesus declares that God has sent Him as the ultimate deliverer. His victory will usher in the inauguration of the kingdom and the worship of God under the new covenant. As the people celebrate their past deliverance from an antichrist, Jesus declares victory over a more terrible and tyrannical power, the devil. Jesus fulfills Hanukah!

The Setting: In the portico of Solomon (10:22-23)
Massive colonnades surrounded the central courtyard of the temple. Solomon's colonnade, located on the east side of the Court of the Gentiles, provided shelter from the winter weather (cf. Acts 3:11; 5:12). The reference to it being winter may be nothing more than a chronological indicator of the time of year, or it may be intended by John as a description of the coldness of the people's hearts.[1] It is impossible to know whether the crowds surrounding Jesus reflect their desire to hear Him speak or are more hostile in nature.

1. Beasley-Murray, *John*, 173.

Jesus the Messiah and Son of God (10:24-39)

Two matters dominate Jesus' teaching at the Feast of Dedication: messiahship (vv. 24-31) and sonship (vv. 32-39). The two sections unfold along parallel lines: Jesus is the Messiah/Son of God (vv. 24; 32-33); Jesus' discourse (vv. 25-29; 34-38a); Jesus' unity with the Father (v. 30; 38b); and the Jews' reaction (vv. 31; 39).

Jesus the Messiah (10:24-31)

The Jews can stand it no longer and want Jesus to tell them forthrightly if He is the Messiah (10:24). This is the crucial question of the Gospel. Up to this point in the Gospel the Samaritan woman is the only person Jesus explicitly told He was the Messiah (4:26). Jesus' response is in verses 25-29. He has answered their question already; it is likely that He does not mean that He has told them sufficiently 'plainly' (10:25). Jesus points to His signs as an indication of His identity. Their failure to believe in Him is not an intellectual issue, but is because they are not His sheep. If they were His sheep, they would recognize His voice and follow Him (10:26-27; cf. 6:35-44; 10:3-4, 8, 14-16). In contrast, His sheep are eternally secure in their relationship with Him (10:28-29). The eternal destiny of His sheep does not depend on their feeble efforts but on Christ's firm hold on them. Jesus says 'my hand' in verse 28 and the 'Father's hand' in verse 29. The believer's eternal destiny is based on this twofold grip. Eternal life is both a present reality (3:15-16, 36; 5:24; 6:40, 47, 51, 54, 58; 20:31) and a future promise to be realized (5:28-29; 14:2-3). The thought of being snatched away is a violent one. Jesus' point is that the salvation of His sheep means that they are eternally secure (cf. Rom. 8:31-39).

In verse 24 the Jews ask Jesus for a plain assertion of His messiahship; in verse 30 He gives them the answer 'plainly'. Jesus declared a functional unity between the Father and Himself in verses 28-29, but here He presents something more akin to an ontological unity. The two are one in essence and nature, but not identical persons. Jesus is affirming a deep unity that goes beyond what we can comprehend. We are created beings and we are talking about our Creator. Maybe the most we can say here is that in light of verses 28-30,

Jesus is teaching that He and the Father are two separate persons with one nature and purpose (1:1, 14; 14:9; 20:28). The important and reassuring aspect of Jesus' words is that He and the Father are one in keeping believers safe in their hands. The Jews understand Jesus to be claiming equality with God, thus explaining their attempt to stone Him (10:31; cf. 5:17-18; 8:31, 58-59).

Jesus the Son of God (10:32-39)
Jesus' courage is remarkable. He does not flinch, but instead speaks with a note of irony, asking for which miracle they are going to stone Him (10:32). They respond that it is for blasphemy (10:33). We are reminded once again of the spiritual darkness of the Jewish leadership in Jerusalem. They consider Jesus' sign-miracles irrelevant and focus directly on His claim of equality with God. Jesus' reply to the charge is to quote and interpret Psalm 82:6 (10:34-36). While the passage is difficult, the most likely interpretation is that it speaks of Israel's leaders (judges) in terms of gods. They fulfilled their God-given role by their judicial function. Jesus' argument is from the lesser to the greater. If God called Israel's leaders gods, how much more appropriate is it for the Son of God to speak of Himself in this way. Jesus concludes His words by challenging them to believe in Him in light of His works. His sign-miracles are a clear indication of His mutual indwelling with the Father (10:37-38; cf. 14:10-11; 17:21). They try to arrest Jesus but He eludes their grasp again (10:39).

Jesus departs beyond the Jordan (10:40-42)
Jesus leaves Jerusalem (late November–December) for Bethany 'beyond the Jordan'. It was there that John the Baptist once ministered (cf. 1:28). Jesus will not return to Jerusalem until the Triumphal Entry in the following spring. The reason many go to Jesus there is because of John the Baptist's earlier ministry. This is the first reference to the Baptist since 5:36. Even though he is dead, his words and influence live on. He is praised for the fact that his witness to Jesus was entirely true. While John's testimony led the people to Jesus, it was while they were 'there', with Jesus, that they came to believe. How ironic – in Jerusalem they rejected Jesus as a blasphemer

and sought to stone Him, but in the wilderness many believe in Him.

Reflections

Jesus will not address the Jewish leadership again until He stands trial before them after His arrest. Their response to Jesus highlights the darkness of the human heart. They seek to stone Him because He told them the truth about Himself. They saw His signs and heard His words, but still they refused to believe in Him. They consider their Messiah, God's Son, to be nothing more than a blasphemer deserving death. What a tragedy to have seen what they saw and to have heard the things they heard but to have been both blind and deaf.

In Jesus' final visit to Jerusalem before Passion Week, He affirms His messiahship and His sonship. Both His words and deeds show Him to be both Messiah and Son of God. Even more, He associates the Father and Himself so closely that He can say, 'I and the Father are one.' As mentioned above, the full import of this six-word sentence is beyond comprehensive explanation. John the apostle wrote so that his readers might believe that 'Jesus is the Christ, the Son of God' (20:31). As the aged apostle reflected on Jesus' ministry he longed that his readers would believe what Jesus says here about Himself. These are either the words of a man gone mad, or they are the words of the incarnate God.

Finally, in light of the setting of the Feast of Dedication, we are reminded that Jesus Christ is our great deliverer. The foe that He defeats to secure His people's salvation far surpasses the Syrian forces of Antiochus Epiphanes. Try as he may, our arch-enemy, the devil, is unable to snatch us away from God. Our salvation is eternally secure because God's people are firmly in the twofold grasp of the Father and Son.

STUDY QUESTIONS

1. What is the main point that you think John wants to make in 10:22-42?

2. How does an understanding of the Feast of Dedication help in getting a richer understanding of the passage?

3. Do you think John's reference to the 'winter' is anything more than a chronological indicator (10:22)? Why or why not?

4. How would you explain to someone what Jesus meant when He said, 'I and the Father are one'?

21

'I am the Resurrection and the Life'

(John 11:1-57)

The resurrection of Lazarus is the seventh and culminating sign in John's Gospel. This sign-miracle is unique to this Gospel.[1] Jesus, the source of life (cf. 1:4; 10:28; 11:25), gives life to a dead man.[2] Yet, even this ultimate sign is condemned, leaving Jesus a judged man worthy of death (11:53). In addition, Lazarus' resurrection foreshadows Jesus' own death and resurrection: the description of Lazarus' tomb (11:38, 44) prefigures Jesus' tomb (20:1, 7), shortly after Lazarus' resurrection Jesus is anointed for burial (12:3), and the hour of His glorification begins shortly thereafter (12:23). Most importantly, Lazarus' resurrection demonstrates what it means that Jesus is 'the resurrection and the life' (11:25). This is the fifth of Jesus' seven 'I am' statements. The statement and the sign are inextricably linked.

---

1. Resurrection stories are rare in the Bible. In the Old Testament God used Elijah (1 Kings 17:17-24) and Elisha (2 Kings 4:32-37; 13:21) in bringing people back from the dead. In the Gospels, Jesus is described as bringing Jairus' daughter (Mark 5:38-42) and the widow's son at Nain back from the dead (Luke 7:11-15). In the book of Acts, God used both Peter (9:36-42) and Paul (20:7-12) in bringing people back from death.

2. As mentioned earlier, 'life' is a distinctive theme in John's Gospel. The word occurs thirty-eight times. By comparison, it occurs in Matthew only seven times, in Mark four times, and in Luke five times. As early as 1:4 the reader is informed that 'in him was life'.

The setting (11:1-3)

The setting is the village of Bethany, two miles east of Jerusalem. Jesus' friend Lazarus (means 'God helps') is sick. Word of Lazarus' illness comes to Jesus while He is in the Jordan River valley. Lazarus is mentioned only in John's Gospel.[3] His sisters, Mary and Martha, are mentioned also in Luke 10:38-42. The profile of the two sisters in Luke (the compulsive Martha; the contemplative Mary) is paralleled in John 11 and 12. John describes Mary by an incident that he has not yet recounted (cf. 12:1-11); apparently her anointing of Jesus' feet was well known.

The death of Lazarus (11:4-16)

11:4-6: Jesus' response to Lazarus' illness is similar to His comments concerning the blind man's situation in 9:1-5. His comment that Lazarus' sickness will not end in death does not mean that he will not die, but that the ultimate outcome will be glory for the Father and the Son (11:4; cf. 7:39; 12:41; 13:31). How Jesus is glorified in this event is multifaceted: Jesus will be glorified because God the Father will be glorified in the miracle (11:40); many will come to believe in Jesus (11:45); and this event initiates actions leading to the cross (11:53). John explains that Jesus' two-day delay in leaving was not because He did not love the family but that He followed the Father's timing (11:5-6; 2:4; 7:5-9). The journey from where Jesus was staying (cf. 10:40) would have only taken one day.

11:7-10: There was a clear danger in returning to Judea (11:7-8; cf. 7:25; 8:37, 44, 59; 10:31, 39). The disciples address Jesus as 'Rabbi'. This is the last usage of the term in the Gospel. Jesus' courage to return into a dangerous setting is seen here. His comment that 'there are twelve hours in the day' refers to more than just sunlight but to the necessity of doing God's will while there is still opportunity. If one does not walk in obedience to God's will, he or she will walk in spiritual darkness and will certainly stumble and fall.

11:11-16: Jesus' victory over death is foreshadowed in His reference to the believer's death as 'sleep'. In the ancient

---

3. Lazarus was a common name in the first century. It is used in a parable in Luke 16:19-31.

world everyone feared death, but for the believer the sting of death has been removed (cf. 1 Cor. 15:55). John explains Jesus' words for his readers in verse 13. Jesus makes the situation clear that Lazarus is already dead (11:14). This is another example of Jesus' supernatural knowledge. The disciples would have been surprised with Jesus associating joy with Lazarus' death (11:15). His joy, however, is that the disciples' faith in Him will deepen as a result of the ensuing events (11:16; 11:42, 45, 48). The disciples were already 'believers', but their faith was still weak. Thomas (cf. 14:5; 20:24; 21:2), nicknamed Didymus ('twin'), demonstrates both bravery and extreme pessimism by his response ('that we may die'). Nevertheless, he was willing to choose death with Jesus rather than life without Jesus.

Jesus and Martha (11:17-27)
The story unfolds in several scenes: Jesus and Martha (11:17-27), Jesus and Mary (11:28-32), Jesus and Lazarus (11:33-44), and various reactions to the miracle (11:45-57).

11:17-19: The reference to 'four days' implies that Lazarus died shortly after the messengers departed: there was a one-day journey for the messengers to reach Jesus, a two-day wait by Jesus, and a one-day journey back to Bethany. The reference to Lazarus being dead four days suggests that decomposition had begun. This will be another one of Jesus' 'hard' miracles. The dead were buried on the day of their death. John's reference to 'Jews' here lacks its usual negative overtones. Jewish custom provided for a seven-day mourning period.

11:20-24: When Martha hears that Jesus has arrived she goes out to meet Him. Her words of regret to Jesus are repeated later by Mary (11:21, 32). Martha's words express a deep faith in Jesus ('I know that whatever you ask of God, God will give you'); however, it is doubtful she thought Jesus would raise Lazarus from death (cf. 11:24, 39). Jesus turns her thoughts toward resurrection (11:23). She understands Jesus to be speaking of the resurrection at the end of the age (11:24). This is another example of John's use of misunderstanding (2:20-21; 3:9; 4:15).

11:25-26: Jesus' statement, 'I am the resurrection and the life,' is the fifth of His 'I am' statements. Jesus' words mean more than He gives resurrection and life. Resurrection and life are so closely associated with Him that He can say, 'I am....' In verses 25b and 26 Jesus explains His comment. His point is that final death (eternal separation from God) is impossible for the believer; physical death for the believer is the gateway to eternal life. Jesus makes Himself the object of the believer's faith ('in me') in verses 25 and 26. Although Jesus' followers are still mortal, they will enjoy eternal life after death. When Jesus asks Martha if she believes, He does not mean that He can bring Lazarus back from the dead, but that life itself is linked to Him. Jesus' 'I am' statement is once again a claim to deity.

11:27: Martha's response is emphatic and reveals her faith in Jesus. Her statement ('I have believed that you are the Christ, the Son of God') corresponds to John's purpose in writing. While she agrees with Jesus' words she certainly does not understand all their implications. Her faith has content and doctrinal substance. Her declaration highlights three great truths: Jesus is the Christ; Jesus is the Son of God; and Jesus is the one who has 'come into the world'. In this moment of deep grief, Martha expresses a high view of Jesus.

Jesus and Mary (11:28-32)
John's description of Jesus' encounter with Mary is much briefer than the one with Martha and lacks the theological depth of the previous discussion. She refers to Jesus as 'teacher' and expresses the same regret as Martha concerning His failure to arrive in a timely manner.

Jesus and Lazarus (11:33-44)
11:33-38: The two references to 'weeping' denote a loud expression of grief (11:33a). One unique feature of the story is the way Jesus expresses His emotion over Lazarus' death (11:33b). He did not approach suffering dispassionately: 'a deep anger welled up within him and he was deeply troubled' (NLT). Jesus was not angry at Martha and Mary, but at the heartache that sin and death had brought into God's world.[4] John describes Jesus also as having 'wept'. The word should

---

4. The Greek term translated 'deeply moved' is used elsewhere in the New Testament in verse 38, Matthew 9:30, Mark 1:43 and Mark 14:5. It carries the thought of feeling something very strongly. The point is that Jesus' grief ('wept') was mingled with deep anger.

probably be understood as less intense than the word used in verse 33. We see Jesus' humanity expressed in His sorrow. Although He knew what was going to happen, He was moved to tears over the grief of those He loved. The crowds recognize both His love for Lazarus and the fact that if He had arrived earlier He could have healed him. They make another reference to the healing of the blind man in chapter 9.

11:39-40: Lazarus was buried in a typical first-century tomb cut from the rocky hillside. A rolling stone was placed over the entrance so it could be reopened for other burials. A central door led into the burial room where benches were carved in stone along the inner walls. Martha's response not only confirms Lazarus' death but that she was not expecting Jesus to resurrect him from the dead. Her point is that decomposition has begun. Jesus' words are a reminder that the glory of God was Jesus' unfailing aim (cf. 11:4). Much good would come of the miracle, but the most important thing to Jesus was the glory of God. While many would see the miracle, only those with faith would see the glory of God.

11:41-44: Note the repeated reference to 'believing' (11:15, 25, 26, 26, 27, 40, 42, 45). This is Jesus' purpose in His audible prayer (cf. 20:31). He adds drama to the moment by crying out in a loud voice for Lazarus to come out of the tomb. Our familiarity with the story diminishes the astonishment felt by those watching. Lazarus' body had been wrapped for burial and the linen wrappings had to be removed. Oddly, John does not describe Lazarus' reaction to being brought back to life or any discussion as to what he experienced after his death.

The reaction to the miracle (11:45-57)
11:45-46: As with so many of Jesus' signs the onlookers divide into two camps (cf. 6:66-69; 7:43; 9:16; 10:19; 11:37). Interestingly, although Martha has been in the forefront in the narrative, the Jews who believed are associated with Mary (see also verses 31 and 33). This may not be the highest level of faith, but John communicates that it is better than no faith at all. Others went to the Pharisees and reported what Jesus had done.

11:47-48: In all four Gospels the Pharisees are presented as Jesus' primary opponents throughout His public ministry.

They lacked political power, however, and it is the chief priests who will be prominent in the events leading up to His death. The Sanhedrin realized that it was futile to deny the reality of His miracles. If they didn't act soon His following would be too large for them to do anything. They feared that if Jesus gained a following and was declared to be the Messiah the Romans would take action against them.

11:49-52: Caiaphas was the high priest from A.D. 18–36 and worked closely with the Roman governor Pontius Pilate (11:49). He was the son-in-law of Annas (cf. 18:13) who had been removed as high priest by the Romans in A.D. 15. Caiaphas was interested only in political expediency, not with guilt or innocence. Ironically, the Jews went ahead with the execution of Jesus and the nation still perished (11:50). Caiaphas himself misunderstands the prophecy (11:51). John adds his own reflections on the meaning of Caiaphas' words (11:52). They were prophetic in a way he did not understand. Jesus would die not only for the Jews, but for all, including the Gentiles scattered around the world.

11:53-57: John, now finished with his comments, returns to the Sanhedrin's meeting. The determination is made that Jesus must die and they begin to plot His death. In response, Jesus makes a judicious move to withdraw from Jerusalem and go to Ephraim. Ephraim was located approximately twelve miles north of Jerusalem, far enough away to be safe from the Sanhedrin but close enough to return to Jerusalem for the Passover. His disciples stuck closely with Him during these difficult days (11:54). As the crowds begin to pour into Jerusalem to prepare for the Passover Jesus remains the center of conversation (11:55-56). The religious leaders, however, want anyone who sees Him to report it so that they can arrest Him (11:57).

Reflections

The most important point made in this chapter is that Jesus is the resurrection and the life. John stated in the prologue that in Jesus [Him] was life (1:4). Later Jesus claimed that He had life in Himself (5:26). He declared that He came so that people may have life and have it abundantly (10:10). Because Jesus is the life, and has life in Himself, He is able to give abundant life that begins now and continues into the future (cf. 3:16; 10:10). Jesus' show of power over 'the last enemy' (1 Cor. 15:26) is depicted with dramatic force as the climax of His signs. John's purpose in recording this sign-miracle was that his readers 'may believe that Jesus is the Christ ... and that believing have life in his name' (20:30-31). This sign is a powerful encouragement to trust in Jesus. If Jesus is able to give life to Lazarus' decomposing body, He can give spiritual life to the spiritually dead.

We also see how suffering comes to all people, including believers. Mary and Martha loved the Lord and they loved their brother. They watched as his life slowly slipped away. They were confident that if Jesus could arrive in time then Lazarus could be healed. They learned that when delay comes God has a better time and a better way. Jesus' plans sometimes appear strange to us. The disciples must have been stunned when Jesus decided not to go to Lazarus' aid immediately but after he died. Faith in Jesus includes trusting in His timing. Christ's plan for His people is not for their ease but to develop their faith. There is no better way for faith to mature than to have to trust in God's timing.

Finally, Caiaphas' response reminds us of the wickedness and darkness of the human heart apart from divine grace. Although he was the high priest of the Jewish people for eighteen years he chooses political expediency over faith. He refuses to believe the implications of Jesus' signs and determines that He must be killed. Caiaphas is a solemn reminder that a person can rise to the highest levels of religion and yet have a life devoid of divine grace.

Study Questions

1. Why do you think John included the story of Lazarus in his Gospel?

2. What do you think the most important point in the story is? Why do you think this?

3. Can you relate to a time in your life when you felt that God had forgotten you but you eventually saw His timing was perfect?

4. How are Jesus' humanity and deity demonstrated in this chapter? Give specific verses to support your thoughts.

22

The Anointing and Entry of the King
(John 12:1-19)

John 12 brings to a close both Jesus' public ministry and 'The Book of Signs'. The chapter can be divided into four sections: the anointing at Bethany (12:1-11); the triumphal entry (12:12-19); the request of some Greeks to see Jesus and the following conversation (12:20-37); and an explanation for the unbelief of the Jews, followed by a final passionate appeal for faith (12:38-50). In this study we will examine the first two sections and in the next the other two.

Mary anoints Jesus in Bethany (12:1-11)
In our current age of financial insecurity, Mary's act of devotion seems too extravagant and over the top to be sensible. How could anyone justify expending a vial of perfume, that was equal to a year's wage, on someone's feet, even Jesus' feet? All four Gospels have an account of a woman anointing Jesus. The most likely scenario is that John, Matthew (26:6-13), and Mark (14:3-9) describe the same scene, albeit from their own perspectives, while Luke's account is an entirely different event (Luke 7:36-50).

The setting and anointing (12:1-3)
12:1-2: John's use of 'therefore' (*oun*) ties this episode to the previous section. Despite the fact that the religious leaders

are looking for an opportunity to seize Jesus, He nevertheless openly returns to Bethany. He arrives there six days before the Passover. This is the third Passover in John's Gospel (2:13; 6:4). The reference to the Passover being six days away suggests that this event takes place on Saturday evening. This is Jesus' first visit back to Bethany since He raised Lazarus from the dead. John notes that Lazarus is present (12:1). John will refer to Lazarus again in verses 8-11. Obviously Lazarus' resurrection made quite an impact! Jesus' return to Bethany was worthy of a joyful celebration (12:2). John gives no clear indication of where the meal (*deipnon*) was held; only that Mary, Martha, and Lazarus were present. The fact that they are described as 'reclining' may indicate that it was a banquet rather than a regular meal. Martha is busy serving and Mary preparing to worship, both corresponding to the descriptions we find in Luke 10:38-42.

12:3: Mary's anointing of Jesus is one of the most moving expressions of devotion in the Gospel. John's description of the perfume (fragrant oil) as 'very costly' is somewhat of an understatement. Judas estimates the value at three hundred denarii (v. 5). A common laborer's wage was one denarius a day, making the value approximately equal to one year's salary for a laborer (cf. Mark 14: 3; Matt. 26:7). The perfume was imported from northern India, which contributed to its worth. Nard was the name of both a plant and the fragrant oil it yielded. The costliness of the perfume suggests it was a family heirloom. Mark notes that Mary poured it over Jesus' head (Mark 14:3; Matt. 26:7), while John states that she anoints His feet. The bottle was large enough for her to begin at His head and anoint His feet as well. John focuses on her anointing Jesus' feet and wiping them with her hair to highlight her humility. Jewish women did not normally let down their hair in public. The fragrant aroma from the perfume fills the home. In the next chapter Jesus performs a similar act when He washes the disciples' feet.

Judas rebukes Mary (12:4-6)
12:4-5: Mark records that several of Jesus' disciples became indignant toward Mary (Mark 14:4). John, however, puts the focus on Judas. John contrasts Judas with Mary. Their

thoughts are completely different on this occasion. On the one hand, she demonstrates that no expense is too great to express her love for Jesus. Judas, on the other hand, is concerned with the financial loss. This is only the second reference to Judas in the Gospel (cf. 6:71); however, John cannot refer to him without mention of his horrific act of betrayal. So while Mary worships, Judas scorns and seethes at the loss of potential income into the coffers. This could explain in part Jesus' warning concerning greed (Luke 12:15), and Paul's statement that 'the love of money is the root of all kinds of evil' (1 Tim. 6:10).

12:6: John indicates for the reader that Judas is not concerned about the poor but that he steals from the money box. This is the first clear hint that Judas has a serious character flaw. Scholars debate why Judas betrayed Jesus and how it was that Satan was able to possess him (John 13:27); at least part of the answer was his covetousness. Matthew indicates that Judas asked the chief priests what they would give him to betray Jesus to them (Matt. 26:14-15). John states plainly that Judas was a thief. The fact that he served as the treasurer for the group suggests he was a person of some ability. Every one of the disciples must have felt he was trustworthy. Judas' fate is a striking reminder of the danger of greed and how easily it can capture a person's soul.

Jesus defends Mary (12:7-8)
Jesus defends Mary against Judas' attack. The language here is somewhat difficult and open to various interpretations ('Let her alone, so that she may keep it for the day of my burial'). The most likely explanation is that Jesus is implying that Mary's act is more important than she knows. Her act of humble worship in anointing Jesus was symbolic of His coming burial, which was something she did not comprehend. The thought is similar to Caiaphas' prophecy concerning Jesus' death (cf. 11:49-50). The perfume had providentially been saved by her for this purpose. Normally an anointing like this was associated with festivity; however, here, Jesus' thoughts are clearly on the cross. Thus, to those who heard His comment His words must have seemed out of place. Jesus' statement about the poor certainly does not mean that He is

discouraging His followers from helping the poor.[1] Rather, He is saying that the events of these days are particularly significant, and this anointing is entirely appropriate in light of them.

The coming of the crowds (12:9-11)
It is unclear if this was a community-wide dinner or for a smaller group. Either way a large crowd begins to assemble wanting not only to see Jesus but Lazarus as well (12:9). Lazarus is becoming a celebrity in his own right and this leads the chief priests to the decision that Lazarus must also be killed. One murderous plot now becomes two as the wickedness grows (12:10). Because of Lazarus, more Jews continue to believe in Jesus (12:11). The attitude of the religious leaders once again stresses the sinfulness of the human heart. Their hatred of Jesus was so intense that they refuse to believe the undeniable miracle of Lazarus being raised from the dead.

The Triumphal Entry (12:12-19)
The next day Jesus enters Jerusalem riding on a donkey. This event is known as the Triumphal Entry and is recorded in all four Gospels (Matt. 21:1-11; Mark 11:1-10; Luke 19:28-40). Its importance is seen in the fact that not since the feeding of the five thousand has an event been found in all four Gospels. While John's account is more succinct than the Synoptic Gospels, he does add some points of his own: he alone dates the incident on the Sunday preceding Passover, the laying down of the palm branches, the reference to the raising of Lazarus (he does not want his readers to lose sight of this important sign-miracle!), the fact that the disciples do not understand the significance of these happenings until later, and the Pharisees' pessimistic words.

Jesus' entry into Jerusalem (12:12-14)
12:12-13: John indicates that the entry took place the day after the anointing in Bethany; therefore Jesus enters Jerusalem on Sunday. In the Christian celebration of Passion Week

---

1. The book of Proverbs is filled with statements encouraging assistance to the poor.

this day has become known as Palm Sunday. When word reaches the city that Jesus is arriving, a large crowd greets Him waving palm branches – a Jewish symbol of nationalism (12:13). The exuberance of the crowd is evident in their enthusiastic response as they shout out 'Hosanna' ('Save' or 'Save now'), 'Blessed is he who comes in the name of the Lord' (Ps. 118:25-26), and 'the King of Israel'. While not everyone in the crowd thought Jesus to be the Messiah, clearly many of them did.[2] The irony is that He truly is the King of Israel. Nathanael used this title for Jesus (1:49). Jesus' kingship is a motif that runs throughout the Johannine passion narrative.

12:14-15: When this event is examined in all four Gospels it becomes clear that Jesus was making a messianic statement. The Gospels indicate that Jesus intentionally sought to fulfill Zechariah 9:9 by entering the city on a donkey. Both Matthew (21:5) and John specifically quote Zechariah 9:9. Jesus' entry on a donkey rather than on a war horse suggests that He comes not as a militaristic messiah but rather as the Prince of Peace.

The response of the disciples, the crowds, and Pharisees (12:16-19)

John describes the response of various groups to Jesus' entry into the city. The disciples fail to understand the significance of the moment (12:16), the continuing witness of those present when Jesus resurrected Lazarus (12:17), the crowds who have learned of Lazarus' resurrection continue to flock to Him (12:18), and the Pharisees are utterly frustrated at Jesus' increasing popularity, 'the world has gone after him' (12:19). John illustrates this in the next verse when he describes 'some Greeks' (likely Gentile God-fearers) who want to 'see Jesus'.

It must have been an electrifying moment when the crowds burst forth and the people began waving the palm branches in the air. It is difficult to know how many people were involved in the celebration; however, John clearly wants the readers to grasp the magnitude of the event. In this most momentous of occasions, when Jesus the Messiah enters Jerusalem in direct fulfillment of Zechariah 9:9, His disciples fail to grasp the importance of the event, the crowds misunderstand what kind

---

2. Psalm 118 is one of the Hallel Psalms.

of messiah He is presenting Himself to be, and the religious establishment is furious at the commotion. The King of Israel has arrived in the Holy City and Passion Week begins!

Reflections
Both the anointing and the triumphal entry are filled with much material worthy of serious reflection. Mary's act of devotion is a helpful example of heartfelt love and worship. It is obvious that she planned this expression of love. One would not go to a dinner party with an alabaster vial of perfume unless one intended to do something with it. Apparently she thought about the act and decided beforehand that she would anoint Jesus during the evening.

It was not only a planned act of devotion but one that was quite costly. She had contemplated the cost and found Jesus worthy of the extravagant nature of her action. So often we play our finances so close to the vest that we fail to see that some expressions of worship, although costly, are worth it. Obviously, the point can be overstated, but the truth is most of Jesus' followers will never be accused of being too generous in the expenditure of their money for kingdom causes.

The contemporary church has too few people with Mary's devotion. Her love was deep, intense, and unmistakable. Her passion for Jesus moved her to fall at His feet. This kind of love is a rarity today. If the church is to recover her passion for Jesus, then we need more people who are willing to humble themselves and fall at His feet and stop criticizing those who do.

Moreover, those we think will be the most supportive of our sacrificial acts of devotion often fail to understand. Yet, even as she was being criticized by the disciples, Jesus defends her.

Mary expressed her devotion individually in Bethany; some in the crowd expressed their devotion in Jerusalem. While many saw Jesus as a prophet; others saw Him as a nuisance. Yet, there were those in the crowd that saw Him as the 'King of Israel'. While the disciples missed the significance of the moment Zechariah 9:9 was being fulfilled. If you were to take a poll on the day the likely vote would have been that Jesus was a great prophet. Opinion polls are the way that many today determine truth; not so for the followers of Jesus.

STUDY QUESTIONS

1. Why do you think John included the story of Mary's anointing of Jesus?

2. Why do you think people have such a difficult time being extravagant occasionally with their funds for kingdom causes?

3. Can you think of a time in your life when you gave sacrificially to a kingdom cause? Why did you do it?

4. Why do you think the disciples did not grasp the significance of the moment as it unfolded?

5. Do you think Jesus was making an overt messianic statement in the triumphal entry or a more subtle statement?

23

'The hour has come'
(John 12:20-50)

This incident is unique to John's Gospel. For John, the coming of the Greeks is significant. The fact that 'the world' (the Greeks) has gone after Jesus is a sign to Him that His 'hour' has arrived (12:23). The passage can be divided into two sections: the lifting up of the Son of Man and the consequences of it (12:20-36), and a final summary of Jesus' ministry (12:37-50). In the opening section we learn that the lifting up of Jesus is the means by which God draws people of every kind to Himself. And in the final section we learn why so many rejected Jesus' offer of salvation and failed to see Him as the long-awaited Messiah.

The lifting up of the Son of Man (12:20-36)

Request of Greeks to see Jesus (12:20-22)
The coming of the Greeks (i.e. Gentiles) illustrates the Pharisees' frustration that 'the whole world' (NIV) is going after Jesus. It is impossible to be certain exactly when this event took place during Passion Week. Bruce suggests it followed the cleansing of the temple (Mark 11:15-17).[1] The important point to note is where John places it, after the Pharisees' comment. The reason the Greeks approach Philip

---

1. Bruce, *Gospel & Epistles of John*, 1:263.

may be because he is from 'Bethsaida of Galilee', and his name is Greek. Interestingly enough, Philip goes to Andrew before approaching Jesus. Andrew and Philip played a prominent role as two of Jesus' earliest followers in bringing people to Him – Andrew brought his brother Peter and Philip found Nathaniel (cf. 1:35-46). The Greeks fall out of the story in verse 23.

Jesus predicts His death (12:23-26)

In response to the Greeks' request to speak to Jesus, He announces the arrival of His hour (12:23). He explains its significance in a parable (12:24), and applies it to His followers (12:25-26).

12:23-24: Jesus seemingly ignores the Greeks' request and indicates 'the hour has come for the Son of Man to be glorified' (12:23). After repeated references that His hour had not arrived (2:4; 7:6, 8, 30; 8:20), He announces that finally it has come. Jesus' crucifixion is not only the pathway to glory, but it is glory itself. He explains the significance of the hour's arrival in a parable setting forth the result of His death (12:24). He emphasizes the importance of the parable by the use of 'truly, truly.' The parable's point was easily discernible to a first-century agrarian society. The death of a single seed (Jesus) brings about much fruit (salvation of sinners). Therefore, Jesus' death will bring much glory and fruit to God.

12:25-26: Jesus next applies the implication of His death to His followers. His point is spiritual death is the pathway to spiritual life. On the one hand, those who focus their lives on the here and now ultimately lose what really matters most; on the other hand, those who love Jesus more than their own lives will have eternal life. The love-hate language is a Semitic idiom that refers to an essential preference more than to love-hate in an unqualified sense. However, this should not be understood to diminish the seriousness of the contrast. This approach to discipleship is common in Jesus' teaching (Mark 8:34; Matt. 10:39; 16:24-28). Jesus makes the choice quite clear. One may love the worldliness of this world and lose their soul, or reject the worldliness of this world for Christ's sake and enjoy the glories of heaven.

The personal pronouns in verse 26 emphasize a disciple's relationship to Jesus. The servant *must* serve and follow his Lord. In light of the previous verses, the implication is that this entails a willingness to suffer and die for Jesus. If we are to serve Christ, we must follow Him. As the old hymn goes, 'Wherever he leads I'll go!' As soldiers follow their General, servants their Master, students their Teacher, and sheep their Shepherd, so believers must follow Christ. To follow Jesus is to live life for Him as His disciple. Christian discipleship in John's Gospel is characterized by servanthood. Jesus' promise to His servant-follower is not only eternal life (as glorious as that is!) but also that 'the Father will honor him'.

Jesus' agony of soul (12:27-29)
Jesus' words ('Now my soul has become troubled') indicate His struggle over His approaching death. This agony of soul was not something that only transpired in the Garden of Gethsemane (12:27a). He knows the crucifixion is imminent and He is deeply troubled. It is not that His heart is merely disturbed, instead it is in great turmoil. This verse should not be understood to be John's version of Gethsemane; however, it depicts the same kind of anguish of soul. The agony that Jesus experienced was the result of the sinless Son of God bearing the penalty for the sins of the world. The phrase, 'Father, save me from this hour,' can be understood as a question or a prayer.[2] It seems best to understand it as part of the question. If it to be understood as a prayer, it would be similar to Jesus' prayer in the garden ('Father, take this cup from me' – Mark 14:36). Either way it demonstrates His deep anguish. Jesus' death is the purpose of His coming (12:27b). The old saying that 'Jesus was born to die' could not be stated any more clearly than here. He does not pray for deliverance but for the Father to be glorified (12:28a). This has been Jesus' driving passion (cf. 7:28; 8:16, 50). The thunder from heaven is God's response (12:28b-29). Jesus is told by the Father that He has glorified Himself in Jesus' ministry (cf. 1:14; 2:11;

---

2. Burge, *John* 344-45, and Carson, *John*, 440, understand the phrase, 'Father, save me from this hour,' to be an actual prayer, like Jesus prayed in Gethsemane. Most commentators seem to take the phrase as a part of the question (NIV, NLT, and ESV).

11:40) and will do so again. This is the only time in the Gospel that God speaks 'audibly'. God speaks audibly twice in the Synoptic Gospels, once at Jesus' baptism and again at the transfiguration. Only Jesus' understands what the Father says (12:28b). The crowd recognizes the thunder as either God or an angel answering Jesus' prayer (12:29).

Jesus addresses the crowd (12:30-36)
12:30-33: Jesus explains to the crowds that the voice of God, which they heard as thunder, was meant for them (12:30). Interestingly enough, only Jesus actually understands what God says. Yet, even though they know that the thunder was of heavenly origin, they refuse to believe in Jesus. The reason for this becomes clearer in the conclusion of the passage.

Jesus goes on to describe the effects of His death on the cross. The cross is God's judgment on the world. If one looks at the cross from a worldly perspective, it looks like the defeat of Jesus and a victory for Satan; however, it is Satan's defeat (12:31). The repetition of the word 'now' indicates the immediate and complete nature of Christ's victory. The title, 'the ruler of this world,' is used of the devil elsewhere in John 14:30 and 16:11. Strangely, John does not describe any of Jesus' exorcisms, as do the Synoptic Gospels; however, John presents the cross as the ultimate exorcism (cf. Col. 2:14-15; Heb. 2:14-15).

The cross was not only the overthrow of Satan, but the means of salvation for sinners (12:32). The 'I' is emphatic in verse 32. This is the work of Christ alone. 'Lifting up' is a reference to the crucifixion (cf. 3:14; 8:28). Jesus communicates the effect of His death, rather than the mere fact. He goes on to say that as a result of being lifted up He will draw people to Himself. The words 'all people' mean all people without regard to nationality or status. This is seen in a preliminary way with the approach of the Greeks (12:20; cf. 10:16). The cross demonstrates both Jesus' grace in His substitutionary death for sinners and His power in their salvation. John indicates for his readers that Jesus is referring to His death by crucifixion when He speaks of being 'lifted up' (12:33). The likely reason John feels it is so important to clarify what Jesus means by being 'lifted up' is that in the minds of many the thought of exaltation did not include crucifixion.

12:34-36: The crowd understands ('we' in contrast to 'you') Jesus' teaching to contradict the Scriptures concerning the Messiah.[3] They anticipate a triumphant Messiah, but Jesus speaks of death. Death at the hands of the Romans was clear proof, in their minds, that one was not the Messiah. Jesus does not answer their question directly. Rather He concludes His discussion by making an impassioned appeal for faith. The term 'light' is used five times in verses 35 and 36. They should give up their preconceived notions of messiahship and act on the revelation Jesus has given them.

Jesus refers to Himself as 'light' in terms reminiscent of 9:4-5. 'To walk in the light' is to believe in the light, and to live in a way fitting for people of the light. Time is of the essence; they must respond quickly, because the time is soon coming when the light will be taken from them (12:35a). Darkness is encroaching on them and will soon overtake them (12:35b). Those who live in spiritual darkness are like those who are physically blind; they do not know where they are going. Darkness is a vivid description of the perilous state of the unconverted. What physical blindness is to a blind person, spiritual darkness is to an unregenerate person (cf. John 9). The final verse of the section is Jesus' final dramatic call for faith. It is urgent that they believe in the light (12:36a). His self-disclosure is finished (12:36b). He now hides Himself from public view, symbolically illustrating His previous comments. He will not appear publicly again until He is arrested.

A summary of Jesus' public ministry (12:37-50)

An explanation of the Jews' rejection of Jesus' ministry (12:37-43)
John has a high view of God's sovereignty. He quotes Isaiah's words (12:37-40) to explain why so few Jews believed in Jesus despite His signs. Jesus and Paul also quote these verses (Matt. 13:14-15; Mark 4:12; Luke 8:10; Acts 28:26-27). The words 'could not believe' do not mean that they had no choice (12:39), but in response to their rejection God in turn

---

3. It is impossible to know which Scripture specifically they were referring to, but some that might have been in their minds are Psalm 89:36, Isaiah 9:7, and Daniel 7:14.

brought on them a judicial blinding and hardening of heart. They had rejected God and chosen evil because they loved the darkness (cf. 12:37).[4]

Isaiah referred to God's glory (Isa. 6:3), but John makes no distinction between the glory of God and of Jesus. Yet, there might be a reference to the fact that when Isaiah saw the rejection of Christ (Isa. 53:1) he saw the glory of Christ (12:41). Not everyone rejected Jesus' signs and John has described many that believed in Him.

A final appeal for belief (12:44-50)
Jesus' public ministry closes with a stirring call to faith. The passage reiterates much of what has been said earlier: Jesus is light; He reveals God and disperses the darkness (1:9; 8:12); He has not spoken on His own authority; He is God's agent in the world; belief in Christ is belief in God; to see Christ is to see the Father (12:44-45); Jesus' words are not His own but stem from what the Father directed (12:49-50). The book of signs is closed now. The evidence has been presented. The Sanhedrin has made its decision about Him (cf. 11:53). For John's readers, however, a decision must still be reached.

Reflections
There are two major themes that run throughout this lengthy passage: the significance of Jesus' death and people's response to Him. Jesus recognizes that the coming of the Greeks to Him is the arrival of His hour. The Son of Man is to be lifted up and the world is being drawn to Him. While Jesus is fully aware that He has come to die, at the same time the thought of it is agonizing. The sinless Son of God will bear the sins of the world on the cross. While the world sees the cross as His defeat, in reality it reveals God's glory. In addition, the cross is the means by which God draws all kinds of people to Himself, brings judgment on the world, and defeats Satan. The reference to the casting out of Satan is another example of the cosmic conflict that has been described in John's Gospel. The reader is reminded that the darkness cannot overpower

---

4. Other references to hardened hearts are Exodus 9:12, Romans 1:24-28; and 2 Thessalonians 2:8-12.

the light, especially at the cross. The cross is a picture of discipleship as well. Those who trust in Christ for salvation must be willing to take up their cross daily and follow Him.

John is very interested in showing how Jesus' coming divided people. People fall into one of two categories: either they believe in Jesus or they reject Him. John knows of no other option. But Jesus is not unconcerned about people's response to Him. He makes a passionate call for faith while there is still time. Throughout Jesus' public ministry He has demonstrated a desire to see people believe in Him. Some, like the Greeks, desire to see Him, while others, like the Pharisees, reject Him. On the one hand, it is not surprising that many rejected Him, for it was foretold in the Scriptures. Yet, as the Gospel has unfolded, many have trusted in Him.

All of this should be an incentive to make a lifelong study of the doctrine of the atonement. Christ's death is the manifestation of God's glory. Our faith in Jesus' death and resurrection is the means of our salvation. The better we understand Christ's work the more secure we will be in His salvation. In addition, Jesus' sense of urgency for the salvation of sinners should motivate us to the same sense of urgency. His impassioned call for people to believe should fuel the evangelistic fervency of the church.

STUDY QUESTIONS

1. Why do you think John included verses 20-36 in his Gospel?

2. Why did Jesus compare His death to a seed being planted in the ground (12:24)?

3. Why do you think John included 12:37-43 in the Gospel?

4. Which verses in 12:37-50 highlight human responsibility in response to the gospel and which ones highlight God's sovereignty in salvation?

24

Basin and Towel Christianity
(John 13:1-17)

The second half of John's Gospel divides into three main sections: Jesus' Farewell Discourse (13–17), Jesus' passion (18–19), and Jesus' resurrection (20–21). John devotes an unusually significant amount of space to the events in the upper room demonstrating how important those few hours were in his thinking (13:1–17:26). John devoted twelve chapters to approximately three years of ministry, but he devoted five chapters to Jesus' ministry in the upper room.

John moves from the conversation that follows the Triumphal Entry (12:20-50) immediately to the events in the upper room. John's presentation of the upper room is quite distinctive when compared with the Synoptics. The Synoptic Gospels describe the preparations made for the evening, the institution of the Lord's Supper, the prediction of Judas' betrayal and Peter's denial. While John includes the prediction of Judas' betrayal and Peter's denials, he does not make mention of the preparation for the Passover meal or of the institution of the Lord's Supper. What he does is devote significant attention to the words Jesus spoke to the disciples shortly before His arrest. This is the beauty of the fourfold Gospel witness. Without the Synoptic Gospels we would know very little about the institution of the Lord's Supper, but without John's Gospel we would know almost nothing about the extensive teaching Jesus gave the disciples before the onslaught of His passion.

John's Gospel describes some of the most dramatic encounters and moments in Jesus' life – turning the water into wine at Cana, the conversations with Nicodemus and the Samaritan woman, and the healing of the man blind from birth. Maybe the most dramatic moment, outside Jesus' death and bodily resurrection, took place in the upper room when Jesus washed His disciples' feet. One can only imagine how the twelve must have sat there in stunned silence (except for Peter's usual misstatement!) as Jesus washed their dirty feet. Jesus uses the footwashing in two ways. On the one hand, it symbolizes the spiritual cleansing that will take place through His cross-work (13:8-10); on the other, it teaches the importance of humble service (13:11-17).

Foot-washing was a common custom due to the wearing of sandals and the dry dusty roads. A good host would provide a servant to wash his guests' feet, but if none were there he would not do it. The rabbis taught that this was one task that a disciple was not to perform for his teacher.

Origin and Destiny (13:1-3)

John makes several references in these opening verses to what Jesus knew: He knew His origin and destiny – that He came from the Father and was returning back to His Father; and that the Father had 'given all things into his hands'. With that knowledge in hand, Jesus arose from the meal, donned the garb of a slave and washed His disciples' feet.

13:1: The chapter opens with a time reference. Biblical scholars are divided over the chronology of the Last Supper. John 13:1 is the first of several verses that lead some scholars to think that John wants to portray Jesus as spending His last night with His disciples *before* the Passover, with the crucifixion taking place the next day while the Passover lambs were killed. However, the most likely understanding is that John, in agreement with the Synoptics, presents the Last Supper as taking place on Thursday night and Jesus' crucifixion on Friday.[1] Jesus knew that the time was at hand for Him 'to

---

1. The discussion on the relationship of the meal and crucifixion in John and the Synoptics is voluminous. For a recent discussion of some of these issues, see Andreas J. Köstenberger, 'Was the last Supper a Passover Meal?' in *The Lord's Supper* ed. Thomas Schreiner and Matthew Crawford (Nashville, B & H Academic, 2010): 6-30.

depart out of this world to the Father' (13:3; cf. 16:28; 17:11).[2]
John does not say that Jesus is about to die, but that He is about
to return to the Father. He directs the reader's attention past
the events of the cross to Jesus' glorious return to the Father.
There is not the slightest hint at the possibility of defeat. Jesus'
love and commitment to His disciples was unquestioned. The
idea that He loved them 'to the end' (*eis telos*) has a double
meaning. Jesus loved His disciples 'to the end' – the end of
His life, and He loved them 'to the utmost' – as much as He
could possibly love them (13:1c).[3]

13:2: The events about to be described took place just after
supper had been served. Twice in this chapter we discover
that Satan is the true power behind Judas (13:2, 27). As for
the person of Judas, it may be that we should understand
the reference to his 'stealing' (12:6) to be the avenue through
which Satan entered his life. Willful sin is dangerous. The
point being made in this verse is that at this sacred gathering
a spiritual war is being waged and Satan is working behind
the scenes through Judas.

13:3: As the events of the passion are about to begin Jesus
knows that all authority has been given to Him and that He
will soon return to the Father. He could have defeated His
enemies with only a word, but John makes it clear that Jesus
was not overwhelmed by evil men or unable to defend Himself;
instead He chose to suffer and die for the salvation of sinners.
As the author of Hebrews brings out, 'for the joy set before
him [Jesus] endured the cross, despising the shame, and is
seated at the right hand of the throne of God' (Heb. 12:2b).

Humility and Salvation (13:4-11)

This section can be divided into two parts: a description of
the foot washing (13:4-5) and the theological interpretation
of it (13:6-11).

---

2. Carson, *John*, 461, notes that the term 'world' occurs forty times in John
13–17 and is intended to highlight the sharp distinction between it and His disciples.

3. C. H. Dodd, *Interpretation of the Fourth Gospel* (Cambridge: Cambridge
University Press, 1953), 398, made the interesting observation that in chapters
2–12, words for 'life' (fifty times) and 'light' (thirty-two times) dominate words for
'love' (twelve times, including both *agapao* and *phileo*). In chapters 13–17, however,
words for 'love' (thirty-seven times) dominate over 'life' (six times) and 'light' (no
uses). Jesus' love for His disciples dominates these chapters.

13:4-5: It is amazing what Jesus does in light of the knowledge that He had all authority and was to soon return to His Father – He washes the disciples' feet, including the feet of Judas! John was so stunned by what he saw happen that he described it in 'slow motion'. He carefully records each movement Jesus made. The footwashing was another demonstration of how much Jesus loved His disciples. The washing of feet was a task that was reserved for the lowest slave. Jesus breaks the mold of what is taught in contemporary models of leadership, even in the church. There is no better example than this event, except for the cross itself, that Jesus came not to be served, but to serve.

13:6-11: While the other disciples sit in stunned silence, Peter recognizes the awkwardness of the situation and objects to it (13:6). Jesus explains that this event has a much greater significance and will become clearer later (cf. 12:16). Peter tells Jesus forcefully that he will 'never' allow Jesus to wash his feet (13:8a). Jesus' response is also forceful and indicates again that there is much more to this act than meets the eye. The footwashing symbolizes the cleansing that will take place through Jesus' cross-work. When Jesus tells Peter that if he will not allow Jesus to wash his feet he will 'have no share with me', He is saying in effect that Peter will not belong to Him (13:8b). If this is the case, then Peter wants more than his feet washed (13:9). Jesus responds by changing the imagery slightly (13:10a). The point that Jesus makes next is that God cleanses/bathes us at conversion. But, as we walk through this world, we pick up its dirt. What we need then is not another bath (conversion), but a cleansing of our feet; confession of sin for a clean conscience and maintaining close fellowship with the Lord (1 John 1:9).

Jesus closes this part of the discussion by indicating that He knew that one of them was not clean (did not believe in Him) and would betray Him. Judas did not belong to Jesus because he did not believe in Jesus (13:10b-11). Jesus was fully aware of what was taking place. Judas' betrayal did not take Jesus by surprise; rather, Jesus went to the cross voluntarily, not under compulsion.

Leadership and Servanthood (13:12-17)

In our day of self-aggrandizing ministry servant-leadership is a concept that needs to be recaptured, that is Christians living in obedience to the will of God for the glory of God, even at great personal expense. Self-preservation and self-promotion cannot co-exist with a passion for God's glory in God's servants. Far too many Christian leaders are more concerned about the 'perks' of leadership than of serving God's people.

After Jesus puts back on His outer garments and returns to the table He asks His disciples if they understand what He has done for them (13:12). Before they can answer, Jesus explains a practical implication from the act. If they call Him 'Teacher and Lord' – and they did – and He washed their feet, they should wash one another's feet (13:13-14). It is interesting that they call Jesus 'Teacher and Lord', but when He refers to Himself He says 'Lord and Teacher'. It could be that His reversal of the order suggests more of what their attitude toward Him ought to be. One might have thought that Jesus would tell them that since He washed their feet, they should wash His feet, but instead He says that they ought to serve one another (13:15).

Verse 16 is one of Jesus' favorite sayings. It is found with minor variation in John 15:20, Matthew 10:24, and Luke 6:40 (cf. Luke 22:27). The words 'truly, truly' mark its solemnity. If their master served in this way, then lowly service is not beneath them (13:16).

Blessing comes from obeying Jesus' instructions on servanthood and not just learning about it (3:17). In an age filled with technological advances and the possibility of accumulating more and more knowledge, it is easy for a person to think they are what they know. While Jesus obviously does not depreciate knowledge, He does suggest that knowledge which does not lead to humble service does not bring God's blessing.

Reflections

This passage is rich in practical application. First, when we reflect on this passage and examine the glorious portrait of Jesus in it, our hearts cry out, 'Give me Jesus!' How can we not love the One who died for us so that we can be washed? It is amazing to see what Jesus 'knows' as the chapter begins. He knows that He came from the Father, that He is returning to the Father, and that all authority has been given to Him. Yet with that knowledge He wraps Himself in a towel and washes His disciples' feet. Even though He will be arrested in a few hours His attention is on His disciples.

Second, we learn that even those who appear to walk closely with Jesus may not truly know Him. Judas had spent as much time with Jesus over the previous few years as anyone had. Yet his greed gained mastery over him and he willingly betrayed Jesus for thirty pieces of silver. Judas is a reminder that we must be constantly vigilant to watch over our souls. But Judas did not act alone. Satan took advantage of Judas' sinful behavior and used him as his instrument in Jesus' betrayal.

Third, the theological significance of the foot-washing is often overlooked in favor of its practical application. This is unfortunate because the foot-washing is a window into Christ's cross-work. Our sin has caused us to be dirty and guilty before God. Yet those who receive Jesus are washed clean in the blood of the Lamb.

Fourth, as we reflect on this event, we should be overwhelmed by its theological significance and soundly rebuked by its practical implications. God's people are seldom more Christ-like than when they humbly serve one another. God is looking for basin-and-towel Christians. This model of leadership is a stern rebuke of the C.E.O. model practiced in many churches and Christian organizations. On numerous occasions Jesus taught His disciples that if one wants to be first in the kingdom he must be slave of all; that He came not to be served but to serve, that the first would be last and the last would be first. One of the great dangers of ministerial 'success' is pride. Those who serve Jesus must see themselves as His servants and demonstrate it by humble service of God's people.

STUDY QUESTIONS

1. Why do you think John included this episode in the Gospel in light of his stated purpose in John 20:30-31?

2. How would you explain in your own words the theological implications of the foot-washing?

3. Can you describe the last time someone 'washed your feet'?

4. When was the last time you performed an act of humble service in ministry to a fellow-believer? What did you do?

5. Why do you think Jesus made the specific point that you are blessed if you do these things?

25

The Betrayal of the Son of God
(John 13:18-30)

In one sense this passage depicts the tale of two men. Judas is identified as the one who will betray Jesus and Peter is identified as one who will deny Him. One leaves the upper room to carry out his diabolical plan and the other stays while insisting on his devotion to Jesus. The passage begins with Jesus identifying Judas as the traitor (13:18-20). Verses 31-38 described the moments after Judas has departed. These verses can be divided into four thoughts. First, Jesus describes the glory of the cross (13:31-32). Next, Jesus tells the disciples that they will not be able to follow where He is going (13:32). Third, Jesus gives a new commandment (13:33-35). Finally, Jesus predicts Peter's three denials (13:36-38).[1] Note how beginning in 13:36 the narrative is moved forward by questions from the disciples (13:36; 14:5, 8, 22).

The betrayal announced (13:18-20)
It is difficult to know if one should place verses 18-20 with verses 1-17 or verses 21-30.[2] Grammatically they are tied

---

1. Some, like Grant Osborne, *The Gospel of* John, Cornerstone Biblical Commentary (Carol Stream, IL: Tyndale House Publishers, 2007), 208 and Carson, *John*, 476 understand the Farewell Discourse to begin here since Judas has left the upper room. Others (Blomberg, *Jesus and the Gospels*, 388) think it begins at 14:1.

2. The NIV, NASB, Carson *John*, 470, and Köstenberger, *John*, 410-18, place verses 18-20 with verses 21-30; however, the ESV, NASB, and Morris, *John*, 550-54, place them with verses 1-17.

more closely to verses 12-17 but conceptually they are with verses 21-30. It is best to understand these verses as serving a transitional function moving from the foot-washing to the prediction of Judas' betrayal. They will be examined with verses 21-30 since Judas' betrayal is mentioned again there. The main thoughts in these verses are: Judas' betrayal fulfills the Scriptures (v. 18), Jesus tells the disciples about what is going to transpire in order to strengthen their faith (v. 19), and how people respond to their mission is how they respond to Him (v. 21).

13:18: Judas is brought once again to the forefront (cf. 13:10-11). His betrayal must have made a huge impression on John, for he refers to it so often (6:70; 12:4; 13:10b, 11b). Immediately after describing Jesus' humility in the washing of the disciples' feet, John describes Judas putting the plan of betrayal into action. Jesus makes it clear that He is not speaking of all the disciples in what He has just said. Although He had chosen them one of them would betray Him. Jesus' purpose in the choosing of Judas can be seen in the fact that his betrayal fulfilled the Scripture. Judas' actions will typologically fulfill Psalm 41:9.[3] Just as David was opposed by an unnamed enemy, so David's Son will be betrayed. The fact that Judas' betrayal was prophesied in the Old Testament is affirmed by a number of New Testament texts (Acts 1:16ff; Matt. 26:15; 27:3-10). The eating of bread with someone communicated friendship. The lifting of the heel speaks of the treacherous nature of Judas' act.

13:19: Jesus explains that the reason He is telling them this is so that 'when this takes place you may believe that I am he'. This is one of several references to Jesus' foreknowledge in the upper room (cf. 14:29; 16:1, 4, 32, 33). Jesus wants to strengthen the faith of the disciples during these events. Specifically He wants them to believe that 'I am he'. This statement should be understood to have overtones of deity (cf. 8:24, 28, 58; 18:5, 6, 8; cf. Exod. 3:14; Isa. 41:4; 43:10). When they look back on these events (especially after the giving of the Spirit at Pentecost) it would confirm to them that Jesus was in control of these events as they unfolded.

---

3. See the discussion in Carson, *John*, 470, on the typology of the scene.

13:20: Jesus concludes this section with a heightened sense of seriousness by His use of 'truly, truly.' He ties His mission to the mission of His followers. Jesus' disciples (and indeed all of His followers) are a people on mission (cf. 13:14, 16). The close relationship between Jesus and His followers is a picture of the even closer relationship between Jesus and the Father (cf. 5:19ff). To receive Jesus' messengers is to receive their message, to receive their message is to receive Jesus, and to receive Jesus is to receive the Father.

The traitor identified (13:21-30)
This passage can be understood to fall into two main thoughts. The first is the conversation between Jesus and the beloved disciple as to the identity of the traitor (13:21-26); in the second, Jesus identifies Judas as the traitor (13:27-30).

Jesus and the Beloved Disciple (13:21-26)
13:21-22: Once again Jesus is described as being 'troubled in spirit' (cf. 11:33; 12:27). John indicates that Jesus did not go through life emotionless. Although He believed and trusted in His Father's sovereign plan He was still deeply grieved by the betrayal of a friend. Jesus has hinted at the fact of betrayal a number of times, but He now declares it unambiguously: 'Truly, truly, I say to you, one of you will betray me.' The disciples are stunned and look at one another wondering which of them it may be. An interesting point is that they do not assume He was speaking of Judas.

13:23-26: Verse 23 introduces the first of the five 'Beloved Disciple' passages (19:26-27, 34-35 [at the crucifixion]; 20:2-5, 8 [at the empty tomb]; 21:7, 20 [fishing in Galilee]). The beloved disciple must have been on Jesus' right and able to lean back on His chest (13:23). Peter could not have been sitting next to the Beloved Disciple because Peter 'motioned to him' to ask Jesus of whom He was speaking (13:24). The Beloved Disciple leans back and confidentially inquires as to the traitor's identity (13:25). It may be that Judas was reclining just to the left of Jesus, which was considered by many to be a place of honor.[4]

---

4. Carson, *John*, 474.

Jesus responds to the question of the traitor's identity by an action. It is likely that no one heard what Jesus said to John. One wonders why John did nothing after Jesus identified Judas as the traitor. Jesus' words and actions may not have added up in John's mind. First, Judas' placement to the left of Jesus meant he sat in a distinguished position. He may have been placed there because he was the treasurer of the group. Second, Jesus' giving of the morsel (vv. 26, 27, 29) was thought to be an act of honor. Carson understands the giving of the morsel to be a 'final gesture of supreme love'.[5] Third, Jesus' instructions to Judas may have made John think that the betrayal was not imminent. Finally, there is no indication that Judas' betrayal would involve Jesus' arrest and culminate in His execution. John's use of Judas' full name brings a certain sobriety to the moment.

The plot is put into motion (13:27-30)
13:27-29: After Judas takes the morsel Satan enters into him (13:27). Judas is possessed by Satan. This is the first use of the name Satan in the Gospel. Satan will leave nothing to chance at this point. However, Jesus, in control of the situation, tells Judas to act immediately. These are Jesus' final words to Judas in this Gospel. In a very short time both Jesus the Savior and Judas the traitor will be dead. No one is suspicious when Judas leaves – again possibly indicating that no one heard what Jesus said to John (13:28). John explains what was going through the disciples' minds as Judas left (13:29).

13:30: John mentions again that Judas took the morsel in order to emphasize the significance of the act. The reference to Judas departing into the night is true chronologically, but is intended also to make a powerful theological statement. In a very real sense this was the darkest night in the history of mankind. On this night the Son of God will be handed over to His enemies. One is reminded of the battle between light and darkness (1:5). Darkness has captured Judas because he has rejected the light. The hour is soon approaching when the Light of the world will be extinguished for a season (9:4; 12:34-36). When Jesus is arrested in Gethsemane, Luke

---

5. Ibid.

records Jesus saying to those who arrested Him, 'this is your hour, and the power of darkness' (Luke 22:53).

The glory of the cross, a new commandment, and the denial of a friend (13:31-38)
Now that Judas has departed, Jesus begins to prepare the disciples for what is ahead of them. This is where the Farewell Discourse officially begins. In this opening section Jesus speaks about the glory of the cross (13:31-33), the new commandment that they are to love one another (13:34-35), and He predicts Peter's denials (13:36-38).

The glory of the cross and the reality of separation (13:31-33)
The departure of Judas means that the act of betrayal is underway. The word 'now' indicates that the events culminating in Jesus' death and resurrection have begun. Because Christ's death is a part of God's plan and nothing can stop it from taking place, Jesus speaks as if it has already occurred ('Now is the Son of Man glorified'). The glorification of the Son and Father are intricately connected together in the cross of Christ (13:31-32).

Jesus' tender love for His followers is expressed in His reference to them as 'little children' (13:33). He expresses to them that very soon He will be separated from them during the time between His death and resurrection. The thought of separation will be a constant theme throughout the discourse. Earlier Jesus had made similar statements to the Jews: 'You will seek me, and will not find me; and where I am, you cannot come' (7:34); 'I go away, and you will seek me, and will die in your sin; where I am going, you cannot come' (8:21). A striking difference now is that Jesus does not tell His disciples that they will die in their sins. Furthermore, in a few moments He will tell them that He is going to prepare a place for them and that He will come again for them (14:1-3). The pain of separation for them would have been slightly mitigated by these promises.

A new commandment (13:34-35)
The new command to 'love one another' was in one sense an old one (Lev. 19.18), but for His disciples it was new in

the standard Jesus has set ('as I have loved you'). He is not asking them to do anything He has not already done. While Jesus' entire ministry to them has been saturated in love, the greatest expression of His love for them will be on the cross (13:33). Love will be the distinguishing mark of Christ's followers (13:34; cf. 1John. 3:23; 4:7ff).[6] The love that Jesus calls His followers to express is not controlled by emotions but is rather one of action. Christian love is characterized by sacrifice (13:4ff) and obedience to Jesus (14:15). Genuine discipleship exemplified by sacrifice and obedience is at the heart of evangelism.

The denial of a friend (13:36-38)
Peter ignores the words about love and reverts to the matter of Jesus' departure (13:36). Apparently Peter knows that danger must be involved. His words ('I will lay down my life for you') are similar to those used of the Good Shepherd (13:37; cf. 10:11). The irony of the situation is that the opposite is true. Jesus is about to lay His life down for Peter. The impact of Peter's denial is seen in the fact that it is recorded in all four Gospels (Matt. 26:33-35; Mark 14:29-31; Luke 22:31-34). The solemnity of the prediction is seen by the use of 'truly, truly.' The prediction must have shocked Peter. He became quite subdued, for he remains unusually silent throughout the rest of the time in the upper room. We do not hear of him again until 18:10.

Reflections
John 13:18-30 reveals the cosmic drama going on behind the scenes in the upper room. The cosmic drama begins early in the chapter with the reference that Satan put into the heart of Judas to betray Jesus. Then later in the evening, Satan enters into Judas while he was sitting at the table next to Jesus. Satan did not intend to leave anything to chance. He could not afford to allow Jesus to slip away as He had so many times when the Jews wanted to stone Him. Then when Judas leaves the upper room John declares, 'and it was night.' As

---

6. The Latin for 'new commandment' (*mandatum novum*) led to this day being called Maundy Thursday in the Christian calendar.

mentioned earlier, this is clearly more than a chronological indicator, but refers to the power of darkness' great attempt to overpower the light. Yet, even as Satan's diabolical plot to betray the Son of God is undertaken, God remains in control. Jesus is fully aware of what is transpiring and even initiates the process ('What you do, do quickly'). Let us never forget that God often uses Satan as His errand boy. God is never caught off guard.

How are Peter's and Judas' acts different? Judas betrayed Jesus and Peter denied Jesus in His hour of need. Peter betrayed Jesus by the taking of an oath and the calling down of curses upon himself in his insistence that he did not know Jesus. Yet, Judas' name, on the other hand, has become synonymous with being a traitor. What is the difference between Peter and Judas? The difference is that Judas' act was carried out in cold blood. It was the result of careful thought and planning and in the end he deliberately and callously refused the outreach of Jesus' hand. But Peter's actions were anything but cold and calculating. His actions were the result of fear and cowardice. He was overwhelmed in a moment of weakness, paralyzed by the horror of being discovered to be Jesus' disciple. Peter's grief led to tears of repentance, while Judas' actions led to remorse and regret, but not to true repentance.

Finally, the thought that Christ and God are glorified in the act of crucifixion goes against the way people normally think of glory, even in the church. Glory in the contemporary church is exemplified by big budgets, large crowds, famous preachers and the like. God's greatest glory shone out from the cross on a hill called Golgotha. His triumph of redemption is achieved through betrayal, denial, crucifixion, and death. We are not comfortable with that kind of glory. So the church turns from the gospel message to gimmicks and games. Yet God is not glorified by gimmicks and games but by the proclamation of the cross – 'to Jews a stumbling block and to Gentiles foolishness' (1 Cor. 1:23).

Study Questions

1. What is the main point John wants to communicate in this passage?

2. What verses in this passage indicate that Jesus was not caught off guard by the events that were about to transpire?

3. Why is it hard for the church to understand the thought that God was greatly glorified in the cross? How is this counterintuitive to the world's thinking?

4. Why is love such a powerful means of evangelism?

5. How can the church better demonstrate Christ's love to one another and be a better witness to the world?

26

A Cure for Troubled Hearts
(John 14:1-14)

Life is filled with many low points – the heartbreak of losing a loved one, the shattering of a dream, or the disappointment of a broken relationship. These low points seem to come at the worst of times and often they come like unceasing waves of the sea. We sometimes think things could not get any worse, and then they do! The disciples must have felt like that in the upper room.

Chapter 14 opens with Jesus' words, 'Do not let your hearts be troubled' (14:1). Near the conclusion of the chapter He repeats the same advice: 'Do not let your hearts be troubled and do not be afraid' (14:27). The disciples must have felt that their world was crumbling around them. Jesus has informed them of Judas' betrayal, Peter's denial, and His own departure. They had left virtually everything in order to follow Him and now it appears that He is abandoning them. How is it possible for them not to drown in a sea of hopelessness? The answer must have sounded shocking to them – it is better for Jesus to go than for Him to stay. How could it possibly be better for Him to depart than to remain with them?

In this passage Jesus answers the question, 'Why would it be better for the disciples when He went away than it would be for Him to remain with them?' He sets forth five reasons why His departure will be for their advantage: first, to prepare a better place for them (14:1-4); second, to show them the way to the Father (14:5-7); third, to provide greater intimacy of relationship (14:8-11); fourth, to enable them to do greater works (14:12-14); and, fifth, to send another divine Helper (14:15-31). In this study we will examine the first four reasons and in the next study the fifth one.

This portion of the Upper Room discourse unfolds through a series of questions that began with Peter's question in 13:36 (cf. 14:5, 8, 22). We need to catch something of the atmosphere. The air is tense. The disciples feel as if Jesus' mission is unraveling right before their eyes. Nevertheless, even though Jesus Himself is facing His greatest crisis, His concern is for His disciples.

Jesus must depart so He can prepare a place for them (14:1-4)

14:1: Jesus continues to answer Peter's question from the previous chapter ('Where are you going?'). His response is that He is returning to the Father in order to prepare a place for them. He exhorts them not to allow their hearts to be overwhelmed by sorrow (cf. 11:33; 12:27; 13:21) and gives four arguments why this should be the case.

First, they can trust in Jesus even as they trust in the Father.[1] Jesus' words would have sounded shocking to the disciples. Everything about the circumstances – betrayal, denial, arrest, and crucifixion – argued against their trusting in Him. In time, they would see more clearly that Jesus deserved their absolute faith. His advice to the disciples in the midst of their turmoil and fear is still good advice for us today. The antidote to anxiety and hopelessness is faith in God and in Jesus.

14:2: The second argument as to why they should take heart is because Jesus is going away in order to prepare a place for them. The place to which Jesus is going is heaven, which He describes as 'my Father's house'.[2] The imagery is

---

1. The two verbs can be understood in three different ways. One is to understand the verb 'to believe' as an imperative in both instances ('believe in God, believe also in me'). The context seems to favor this understanding. However, it is possible to take both as indicatives ('You are trusting in God and trusting also in me'). A third possibility is to translate the first verb as an indicative and the second as an imperative ('You are trusting in God, now trust in me').

2. The older English translation 'mansions' is incorrect. The term simply refers to 'dwelling places'.

of a spacious home with room for all of God's children. What a beautiful picture of heaven! Jesus will prepare a place for them through the cross and resurrection (14:2b).

14:3: The third argument Jesus mentions as to why they should not be troubled is because He will come back for them. In what senses will He come to them and take them to be with Him (14:3a)? Some understand this to be a reference to His post-resurrection coming to them. Others understand Him as referring to the coming of the Spirit mentioned in 14:15-29. However, it is more probable, in light of His comments in verse 2, that Jesus is referring to his Second Coming. This promise that He will take His followers to be with Him satisfies the deepest longings of each believer's heart (14:3b).

John, in the Revelation, boldly declares: 'And I heard a loud voice from the throne saying, "Behold, the dwelling place of God is with man. He will dwell with them, and they will be his people, and God himself will be with them as their God"' (Rev. 21:3). One glory of the new covenant is that God's presence is a present reality. The manifest presence of God in the life of a believer now satisfies the deepest longing of the heart. Nevertheless, what believers experience now is merely a foretaste of the greater manifestation of God's presence with His people throughout eternity.

14:4: The fourth argument mentioned by Jesus as to why they should not be overwhelmed by sorrow is because they at least had an inkling of the place to where He was going. While they might not grasp fully His teaching at that moment, the Spirit would eventually make it perfectly clear to them. Because of these four reasons, Jesus' disciples can trust in Him.

Jesus must depart so He can show them the way to the Father (14:5-7)

Thomas is befuddled as to how they could possibly know the way (14:5). His simple question led to one of the greatest statements Jesus ever made concerning Himself ('I am the way, and the truth, and the life'). This is Jesus' sixth 'I am' statement. 'I am the way' sounds a note of exclusivity (14:6). The point is that Jesus is the only way to the Father and no one can know God except through Him. The early church was known as 'the Way' (Acts 9:2; 19:9, 23) and they boldly proclaimed that there was 'no other name given among men whereby they must be saved' (Acts 4:12). In a pluralistic first-century world Christianity declared that the way of salvation was through Christ alone. What was true in the first century is equally true in the twenty-first century.

Jesus is also the only way to God because He is 'the truth'. Each of the three nouns (way, truth, life) is preceded by the definite article. 'Truth' and 'life' should not be thought merely as modifying 'the way'. He is the only way to God because ultimate truth resides in Him. Jesus not only taught the truth and lived the truth, but He perfectly revealed the true God.

Furthermore, Jesus is 'the life' (cf. 1:4). To know Jesus is to know eternal life (17:3). Apart from Him one is spiritually dead. Jesus understood that the disciples did not fully grasp His identity. If they had really understood who He was they would have known the Father, for He came to reveal the Father (14:7a). In anticipation of the resurrection Jesus could say, 'From now on you do know him and have seen him' (14:7b). [3]

Jesus must depart so that they may experience a greater intimacy of relationship (14:8-11)

Philip then requests that Jesus would show the Father to them (14:8). If they could only see the Father it would be enough. Philip likely desires a theophany as experienced by Abraham (Gen. 18:1), Moses (Exod. 3), Elijah (1 Kings 19:9-14), and Isaiah (Isa. 6:1-3). Jesus' response reveals some frustration and disappointment in them – 'you' is plural (14:9a). What Philip and the other disciples had failed to understand was that when they looked at the face of Jesus they saw God's glory (14:9b). Jesus' claim is incredible in its implications. One must either dismiss his claim as the ramblings of a lunatic or one must embrace it as truth. Jesus' point is that He came to reveal God's nature and character.

---

3. Carson, *John*, 493, and Köstenberger, *John*, 430, understand the 'if' clause as a first class condition. The idea is 'if you had known me, and you do.' The NLT, NASB, NIV, Brown, *John*, 2:621, and Morris, *John*, 570, understand it to be a second class condition, contrary to fact, 'if you had known me, but you do not.' A rebuke seems less likely at this point in the narrative than words of reassurance.

Philip's lack of perception reveals a lack of faith. The word 'believe' is used three times in verses 10 and 11.The unity of the Father and the Son is one of John's central themes (14:9b-11). This crucial issue was a source of conflict between Jesus and the Jewish leadership (cf. 5:18; 10:30). Four times, in very brief order, Jesus reveals how close and mysterious His relationship to the Father is: 'He who has seen me has seen the Father' (14:9b); 'Do you not believe that I am in the Father, and the Father is in me?' (14:10a); 'but the Father abiding in me does his works. Believe me that I am in the Father and the Father is in me' (14:10b-11). Although there is a mutual indwelling between the Father and the Son, the Father and the Son remain distinct persons within the Trinity. This is equally true of the Holy Spirit.

If Philip finds Jesus' words too difficult to believe, then he should believe Jesus' works. The Father has done those miracles through Jesus (14:11). While faith based on miracles is not the greatest kind of faith, it is better than no faith at all (cf. 20:29; Matt. 11:2-5). Although miracles were never intended to coerce belief they did provide support for faith.[4] Jesus' miracles are 'non-verbal Christological signposts' that reveal His true identity.[5] His words concerning the mutual indwelling of the Father and Son clearly suggest an ontological unity (unity of being) between the Father and the Son, but the emphasis here lies in their functional unity, that is, the way in which God is revealed in Jesus' words and works (cf. 10:38).

Jesus must depart so that they can perform greater works (14:12-14)

14:12: Jesus here gives the fourth reason as to why it is better for Him to leave than to remain. His use of 'truly, truly' heightens the significance of His comments. His point is that His departure to the Father will enable the disciples not only to perform the works He did, but to perform even 'greater works' (14:12a); these 'greater works' are seen in the narrative of Acts. While there are numerous miracles recorded

---

4. Robert H. Mounce, *John, The Expositors Bible Commentary*, rev. ed. (Grand Rapids: Zondervan, 2007), 562.

5. Carson, John, 495.

in Acts, they seldom rise to the level of the miracles Jesus performed. It is best therefore to understand 'greater works' as demonstrated in the geographical spread of the gospel and in the large number of converts to Christ. Jesus ministered in one place at a time, and to a limited number of people; His disciples would take the gospel to the ends of the earth and see significant numbers converted to Christ. These 'greater works' will occur because Jesus will go to the Father (14:12b).

14:13-14: Jesus speaks next of prayer. The 'greater works' will be performed through answered prayers. Jesus makes several promises in the upper room concerning prayer (14:13, 14; 15:16; 16:23, 24, 26). For Jesus to tell them to pray 'in my name' must have sounded crazy to the disciples. The ultimate reason that Jesus will answer prayers in His name is because the Father is glorified by answered prayer. Jesus' greatest passion is the glorification of the Father (cf. 5:41; 7:18; 8:50; 12:28; 17:4).

What does it mean to pray 'in Jesus' name' (14:14)? It is certainly not a magical formula that one mindlessly repeats at the end of a self-serving prayer. Four characteristics of a prayer offered in Jesus' name are: (1) God's glory is the prayer's goal (14:13); (2) Christ's person and work are its basis; (3) being filled with God's Word and living in obedience are the prerequisite to it (cf. 15:7); (4) the request is in accordance with Jesus' character and will. Twice Jesus promises He will answer their prayers (14:13a, 14b). The openness of what can be requested is staggering and is limited only by the request corresponding to Jesus' person ('name'). Although the 'health-wealth' gospel has distorted Jesus' words, nevertheless we should not back down from the possibilities that are open to us in prayer. When God's people are filled with God's Spirit and Word they will pray 'big prayers' to their listening Father. Jesus is not stingy toward His people. He desires to answer prayer so that the Father may be glorified.

Reflections

Jesus' disciples were on the verge of entering that interim period of darkness between His death and resurrection. He did not want them to be hopeless but instead to understand that this separation between the cross and resurrection, as well as the time between His first and second comings, was for their benefit.

This passage is rich in teaching on soteriology, Christology, and discipleship. From a soteriological perspective we learn that Jesus is the only way to God. The way of salvation is a narrow way that leads through the cross of Christ. From a Christological perspective John highlights again the fact that God's glory is seen most clearly in the person of His Son. John has maintained this perspective from his prologue onwards. As for discipleship this passage emphasizes the close relationship between prayer and ministry ('greater works'). It is stunning that Jesus' followers do not spend more time praying in light of the magnificent promises He made in the upper room concerning prayer. Jesus' promises should embolden us to pray 'big prayers' in His name.

Finally, what Jesus says about heaven is profound in its implications. His words probably did not make a great impact on the disciples at the time, but later on they became precious to the disciples and to all of God's people. Jesus promised that He would go to heaven in order to prepare a place for all his followers. Heaven is like a home and God has prepared for each of them a room there. The fact that heaven is compared to a home reminds us that believers are a part of God's family and that heaven will be lived in God's presence surrounded by brothers and sisters.

STUDY QUESTIONS

1. Why do you think Jesus described heaven as a home? What images does that bring to your mind?

2. Why do you think the exclusive claim made by Jesus here ('I am the way ...') was so controversial in the first century and continues to be so in the twenty-first century?

3. Why do you think so many Christians pray so little when Jesus has made such stunning promises about answering prayer?

4. What are examples of 'greater works' in our day?

27

The Promise of the Spirit

(John 14:15-31)

Jesus continues to help the disciples understand why it is better for Him to leave than to stay. Here John introduces the first two of five 'Paraclete' passages in the Farewell Discourse. The Greek word *parakletos* can mean comforter, counselor, advocate, strengthener, or exhorter. In these passages we see the Holy Spirit introduced as such a person, a replacement for Jesus who functions as a helper (14:16), an interpreter (14:26), a witness (15:26), a prosecutor (16:7), and a revealer (16:13).[1] Only if Jesus goes can He send the Spirit. The Paraclete's coming ensures that the disciples will not be left as orphans when Jesus departs.

The Spirit as Helper (14:15-21)
14:15-17: This is the first of several instances in the discourse where Jesus links love and obedience (14:15; cf. 14:21, 23; 15:14). It is a contradiction for someone to say that they love Jesus but yet live a lifestyle characterized by disobedience.

Jesus will ask the Father to give the disciples 'another Helper' who will never leave them (14:16). Once given to believers, the Spirit will never be taken away. Jesus refers to the Spirit as the 'Spirit of truth' in that He conveys truth (14:17; cf. 15:26; 16:13). Moments earlier Jesus had declared

---

1. Bruce, *Gospel and Epistles of John*, 1:302.

Himself to be 'the truth' (cf. 14:6), and previously He had associated truth with the Father (cf. 4:23-24). The 'world', which stands in opposition to Jesus, cannot receive the Spirit. In contrast, the Spirit is with the disciples and after Pentecost He will be in them.

14:18-21: The disciples must have felt abandoned with Jesus' talk of leaving. How comforting it must have been to them for Jesus to promise that He will not leave them as orphans but will come to them (14:18-19). Is Jesus referring to His resurrection, or to the coming of the Spirit, or to His Second Coming? The most straightforward understanding is His resurrection ('on that day'), with the possible implication of the coming of the Spirit on the day of Pentecost in light of the immediate context. Verse 19 supports this understanding. Jesus will not appear again to 'the world' after His death but He will appear to His disciples after the resurrection. His victory over death will result in eternal life for His followers. In verses 20 and 21 Jesus connects loving obedience with enjoying the experiential knowledge of God's presence. In verse 15, love is the motivation to obey; in verse 21, obedience is the test of true love. Jesus' teachings were not given to make us only more knowledgeable scholars but also more godly disciples (14:21a).

Jesus promises a special reward to a person whose life is characterized by loving obedience (14:21b). That person will not only be loved by the Father and the Son, but Jesus will reveal Himself to him or her as well. Jesus' point is that He will make Himself known in a special way through the ministry of the Spirit. This is an immeasurably gracious incentive to walk in loving obedience to the Savior. Apathy and disobedience keep many believers from ever knowing the blessedness of the manifest presence of God in their lives.

Love and Obedience (14:22-24)

Jesus is interrupted again by one of His disciples. This final question comes from Judas, 'not Iscariot' (14:22; cf. Luke 6:16; Acts 1:13). Each interruption provides Jesus with an opportunity to address a significant spiritual truth. Judas wonders why Jesus will show Himself to the disciples but not to the world. Why such exclusivity? Jesus does not directly

answer Judas' question, but He encourages him to understand
the promise along the lines of the abiding presence of the
Father and Son. Jesus again links love and obedience (vv. 15,
21). Those whose love is genuine and demonstrated by
obedience experience the reality of God's presence in their
lives. In many ways this is what separates one believer from
another. Every believer is indwelt by God's Spirit, but not
every believer is filled with the Spirit and knows the blessing
of God's manifest presence in his or her life (cf. Eph. 5:18-21).

In contrast to the disciples, those who do not obey Jesus'
words do not obey God's; for Jesus' words are God's words
(14:24). The world, unlike Jesus' followers, does not obey Him
because it does not love Him.

While Jesus is preparing a future home in heaven for
His disciples, the Father and Son make a present home (the
same word used in verse 2) in the believer's life through the
indwelling Holy Spirit (14:23). In the Old Testament God dwelt
among His people first in the Tabernacle (Exod. 25:8) and later
in the temple (1 Kings 8:10-11), but God's presence will now
abide in His people.

The Spirit as Interpreter (14:25-31)
14:25-28: Jesus' final words in the chapter are not an answer to
a specific question but function as a summary of what He has
taught, with an emphasis on the idea of assurance. The clause
'these things I have spoken to you' refer to this discourse. This
expression is found seven times in the Farewell Discourse
and nowhere else in the Gospel (14:25; 15:11; 16:1, 4, 6, 25, 33).

Jesus' departure remains in the forefront of the discussion
(14:25). When the Spirit comes He will remind and interpret
Jesus' words and ministry to the disciples (14:26). This is a
reminder that the disciples often did not grasp the full import
of Jesus' teaching until after the coming of the Spirit (cf. 2:22;
12:16). The disciples would be reminded of what Jesus taught
them and they then would understand His intended meaning.

Jesus returns to the topic of peace (Hebrew, shalom) with
which the chapter begins (14:27). In Hebrew thought 'peace'
was more than the absence of strife but referred also to the
thought of well-being and blessing. Jesus blesses them with
His ('my') peace, the well-being that is the result of being in a

right relationship with God. Paul teaches that Jesus is peace, that He proclaimed peace, and that He gives peace through His death on the cross (Eph. 2:14-17). Isaiah predicted that the Messiah would be the 'Prince of Peace' (Isa. 9:6). It is His peace because He will purchase it with His own blood.

The peace the world gives is tied to circumstances. When life gets hard the world's peace quickly disappears. Since Jesus has blessed the disciples with His peace they need not be afraid of talk concerning His departure. He understands that they do not grasp fully what He means about His going away and coming again. If they did they would have rejoiced. It is not likely that Jesus thinks they have no love for Him ('*if* you loved me'), but if they loved Him more they would be more concerned about what is best for Him than what is best for themselves (14:28a).

Jesus' teaching concerning His subordination to the Father ('the Father is greater than I') has been noted several times in the Gospel (14:28b; cf. 5:19-30; 8:29; 12:49-50). Verse 28 was seized on in the fourth century by the heretic Arius and is followed by modern-day Arians such as Jehovah's Witnesses who believe that the statement teaches that Jesus is not divine. Yet John's teaching on the oneness between the Father and the Son is the strongest in the New Testament (1:1, 18; 8:58; 10:30; 20:28). At the same time Jesus referred numerous times to being sent on a mission by His Father (3:17; 4:34; 5:19, 30, 36; 6:38; 7:16, 33; 8:29; 12:48-49). John's Gospel teaches an ontological equality and a functional subordination.

14:29-31: All that Jesus has told the disciples has been to strengthen their faith in the midst of coming trials. Satan ('the ruler of the world') has assembled his forces and is preparing to arrest Jesus. He has no legal claim on Jesus because He has never sinned. Even as Jesus told His disciples that they will demonstrate their love by obedience, so too He has demonstrated His love for the Father by obedience. It is possible that the remainder of the discourse took place on the way to Gethsemane.[2]

---

2. Some scholars understand the transition between 14:31 and 15:1 to be evidence of a literary seam indicating that John's Gospel was pieced together from different sources. It is more likely that John is just recording Jesus' transition from the upper room to Gethsemane.

Reflections

Two thoughts, among many that stand out in this passage, are love demonstrated by obedience and the ministry of the Spirit. Jesus makes it perfectly clear that heartfelt love cannot be separated from obedience. The one who obeys out of heartfelt love for Jesus will experience more deeply the love of God and the presence of Christ. The obedient believer sees God at work in ways that others do not. In addition, obedient disciples will experience the great privilege of Christ's presence in their lives. It is a wonder that many believers are willing to give up life's greatest blessings for lesser things.

A second important theme in the passage is the ministry of the Holy Spirit. The Spirit will enable Jesus' followers to live for Him and carry out His mission to the world. Five aspects of the Spirit's ministry to Jesus' followers are set forth in this passage: (1) the Holy Spirit will unite disciples to Jesus in a new intimacy of communion (vv. 17-21); (2) the Holy Spirit will unite disciples to the Father in a deeper way (v. 23); (3) the Holy Spirit will support them in their loving obedience to the teaching of Jesus (vv. 21-24); (4) the Holy Spirit will teach them (v. 26); and (5) the Spirit will impart the gift of Jesus' own peace (v. 27).

STUDY QUESTIONS

1. Why do you think love for Jesus and obedience to Jesus are so closely linked?

2. Can you think of a time in your life when you had an unusual sense of God's presence?

3. Why do you think many evangelical Christians seem to minimize the significance of the Holy Spirit in a believer's life?

4. Which aspect of the Spirit's ministry to believers do you find most meaningful and why?

28

Abide in Me

(John 15:1-17)

The allegory of the vine teaches the importance of fruitfulness in a believer's life.[1] However, this fruitfulness is not the result of a believer's self-effort but by his or her abiding in Christ. The concept of abiding in Christ is in some ways the Johannine counterpart to the Pauline doctrine of 'in Christ'. Both authors seek to bring out the vital relationship that exists between Christ and the believer.

The expression 'to abide in' appears ten times in 15:4-10. Another important term in this passage is 'fruit'. It is used eight times in 15:1-16, but only twice in the rest of the Gospel (4:36; 12:24). This passage can be divided into two main sections (15:1-11 and 15:12-17). The two sections are not unrelated as the terms 'abide,' 'fruit,' and 'love' appear in both. In the opening section Jesus establishes the close personal relationship that exists between Himself and each believer (15:1-11). There is a mutual indwelling – Christ is in the believer and the believer is in Christ – that is expressed in the imagery of a vine and its branches. The second section focuses on the theme of love (15:12-17). Those who abide in Christ demonstrate their

---

1. In light of Jesus' words in 14:31b, 'let us go from here,' scholars debate the setting for this passage. The debate centers around whether Jesus left the upper room or not. At the end of the day it is impossible to know if Jesus spoke these words in the upper room or on the way to Gethsemane. Either way it does not affect the interpretation.

abiding by being people of love – love for God and Christ, as well as love for one another (15:11, 17).

Abide In Christ (15:1-11)

This section can be divided into two parts: Jesus establishes the principle of abiding (15:1-6) and then He describes the practice of abiding (15:7-11).

'I am the true vine' – The principle of abiding (15:1-6)
15:1-3: Jesus refers to Himself as the true vine (15:1). This is the seventh of Jesus' 'I am' statements in the Gospel (see 6:35; 8:12; 10:7, 11; 11:25; 14:6). Vine imagery is frequently used in the Old Testament as a symbol for Israel (Ps. 80:8-18; Isa. 5:1-7; 27:2; Jer. 2:21; 5:10; Ezek. 15; 17:1-6); however, Israel's failure to produce good fruit resulted in divine judgment. Jesus is the fulfillment of God's true intentions for Israel. The Father, as the caretaker of the vineyard, 'takes away' dead fruitless branches and 'prunes' the fruitful ones so that they 'may bear more fruit' (15:1b-2).

Scholars debate what the imagery of being 'taken away' means (15:2a). Some understand it to be a reference to believers who lose future rewards. The difficulty with this interpretation is that in verse 6 the branches themselves are judged because they do not abide in Christ. The intensity of the language in verse 6 strongly implies eternal judgment.

A second interpretation is that the imagery in verse 2 suggests that a believer can lose their salvation. Support for this interpretation is found in the phrase 'every branch in me'. If the branch is 'in Jesus', then the imagery must reflect that of a believer who fails to bear fruit and does not continue to abide in Christ, thus forfeiting salvation. Yet the interpretation of this passage must be examined in light of the entire Gospel. It has been argued earlier that John's Gospel teaches the eternal security of every true believer (cf. 10:27-29). Interpreters must be careful not to press an analogy beyond the author's intentions. The reference to 'every branch in me' is a part of the viticulture imagery and thus is necessary to complete the analogy. The imagery does not refer to believers who lose their salvation, but to those who appear to believe but who in reality do not (i.e.

Judas).[2] The point is that those who experience mutual indwelling bear fruit demonstrating their salvation.

God prunes the branches so that they are as fruitful as possible (15:2b). The image of fruit should be interpreted in rather broad terms and not only as the fruit of the Spirit. Jesus has in mind all of the fruits of a Christian life lived in intimacy with Him. Their acceptance to God, that is, their cleanliness, is a work God has already accomplished (15:3; cf. 13:10-11).

15:4: The mutual indwelling of Christ and the believer is an objective truth. There is no Christian of whom this is not a reality. However, there does appear to be degrees of abiding in Christ as seen in the present imperative. Paul communicates a similar thought in Ephesians 3:17 when he prays 'that Christ may dwell in your hearts through faith'. Christ already dwelt in the Ephesians through the Holy Spirit, but Paul still wants them to be filled with the Spirit (Eph. 5:18). To abide in Christ means to live in a close relationship to Him. The means by which this intimate relationship is maintained is through trust, prayer, the Word, and obedience. The results indicated in this passage are fruitfulness characterized by Christlikeness, answered prayer, and joy. Jesus states as a principle that fruitfulness is not possible apart from the believer's union and fellowship with Him. He then makes direct application to His disciples, 'neither can you unless you abide in me' (15:4b).

15:5-6: Jesus states again that He is the vine (this time without the adjective 'true') and the disciples are the branches (15:5a). A living intimacy with Christ is absolutely essential if one's life is to bear fruit. Mutual indwelling is the key to fruitfulness (15:5b). Apart from this mutual indwelling the believer can do nothing of eternal significance (15:5c). Those who do not abide in Christ (do not have saving faith) will be judged like the fruitless branches (15:6; cf. Ezek. 15:1-8; Heb. 6:7-8). Fire is a common symbol for divine judgment. Some understand the fire to refer to the loss of rewards for believers, but this fails to take into account that it is the

---

2. Other passages that seem to indicate that a person can appear to be a Christian for a period of time but in the end demonstrate that they were never truly converted are: Matthew 13:18-23; 24:12; John 8:31ff; Hebrews 3:14-19; 1 John 2:19; 2 John 9.

branches that are burned up. This is another warning against the sin of presumption (cf. 15:2; 2:23-25).

The principle of abiding illustrated (15:7-11)
In the verses that follow we see both the results and means of abiding intermingled. The passage carefully balances our mutual participation with God. We do have a part to play; yet we must keep in mind 'that apart from him we can do nothing' (v. 5b).

15:7: An alteration to the immanence formula occurs in this verse. No distinction should be made between the indwelling of Christ and His words. Thus, Christ's words play a crucial role in abiding. To abide in the word is a mark of real discipleship (cf. John 8.31-32). To abide in the word 'signifies a settled determination to live in the Word of Christ and by it, and so entails a perpetual listening to it, reflection on it, holding fast to it, and carrying out its bidding' (15:7a).[3] As believers hide God's Word in their hearts and meditate on it they are in communion with Christ.

One of the most magnificent promises related to abiding is answered prayer. This is especially true since Christ's words are active in the disciple's life guiding their prayers. Three things can be said about the relationship between abiding and prayer: first, prayer is one means of maintaining a close abiding relationship with Jesus; second, answered prayer is a form of fruit-bearing and this brings glory to the Father; and third, by bearing 'much fruit' individuals prove that they are Jesus' disciples (15:8). It is amazing that God is glorified both in the work of the Son (cf. 13:31-32) and in the fruit-bearing of the disciples. While this point can be pushed too far, we should not minimize how much it means to the Father to see people redeemed by the blood of His Son bearing fruit to God's glory.

15:9-11: Jesus confesses that He loves His followers with the same love that the Father has for Him (15:9; cf. 3:35; 5:20; 10:17; 17:24, 26). The cross proves the veracity of Jesus' claim. In light of this, He commands the disciples to abide in His love. Brown suggests that to abide in Jesus' love means 'to live rejoicing in its reality, depending upon its support, doing nothing to grieve

---

3. Beasley-Murray, *John*, 133.

it, but on the contrary engaging in what delights the love.'[4] A means of abiding in Jesus' love is to obey His commands even as He obeyed the Father's commands and abided in the Father's love (cf. 4:34; 5:19ff; 6:38; 8:29, 55; 10:17-18; 12:27-28; 14:31).

The importance of obedience is repeated often in this discourse (15:10; cf. 14:15, 21, 23). Jesus wants His followers to understand that on the one hand love is more than mere sentimentality but on the other hand it is not robotic obedience. Love and obedience are so intertwined that a believer's obedience to Christ arises out of a heart filled with the deepest affection for Jesus.

The Savior has a twofold purpose in telling the disciples these things (15:11). First, He told them these things so that '[his] joy may be in them'. Joy has been mentioned earlier only in 3:29, but it is found several times in the farewell discourse (15:11; cf. 16:20-22, 24; 17:13). As believers abide in Christ they will exhibit the joy of Jesus in the midst of life's daily grind. The obedience of Christians to Jesus is not a joyless journey, for they have the Savior's joy ('my joy'). Earlier Jesus made reference to 'my peace' (14:27) and 'my love' (15:10), and now He offers His joy; truly the way of Jesus is a life filled with His peace, love and joy!

Jesus' second purpose is that '[their] joy may be full'. A causative relationship exists between the two parts of this verse. Fullness of joy is only possible in the lives of believers because they have Jesus' joy in them. Our joy is Jesus' joy in us! Our joy is not the result of an easy life but of a life wholly devoted to Christ.

Love one another (15:12-17)
These verses are bracketed by commands for the disciples to 'love one another' (vv. 12, 17). As mentioned above, these verses are not completely disconnected from the preceding as evidenced by references to 'love,' 'fruit,' and 'abide' (translated as 'remain' in verse 16).

15:12-15: The believer's standard of love is Christ's love (15:12; cf. 14:31). Christ's love is demonstrated in His sacrificial death (15:13). Christ's love for each believer further expresses

---

4. Brown, *John*, 2:273.

the intimacy of friendship and confidentiality (15:14a, 15). A believer, however, must never forget that Jesus is Lord and that His followers are to live in obedience to Him (15:14b).

15:16-17: Jesus makes it plain that He initiates His relationship with His followers (15:16). He chooses them and appoints them to be His emissaries. As they go on mission for Him they are to bear lasting fruit (15:17). The thought of fruit-bearing is related closely to evangelism and answered prayer. He encourages His followers to hold nothing back when they pray ('whatsoever'). Here the Father is the One who answers the prayer, earlier it was Jesus Himself (cf. 14:14). The section closes as it began, with an admonition that the disciples are to 'love one another' (15:17).

Reflections
The relationship between Jesus and His followers is one of mutual indwelling – Christ in the believer and the believer in Christ. This relationship is true of every believer without exception. Abiding in Christ is one of the most important concepts in Johannine theology. It is at the heart of Christian living in John's thought. Jesus sets forth the means by which believers can deepen the degree of their abiding in Him. The 'how' of abiding involves: reading, studying, meditating on, and obeying the Word; having a regular prayer life; and loving fellow believers. Obviously, this means more than robotically carrying out a list of spiritual disciplines. It entails a heartfelt love for Jesus that reads the Bible with an open heart and an intention to obey it, regularly pouring one's heart out to the Savior in prayer, and loving people with the sacrificial love that has been poured out upon us by Jesus.

The results of abiding are delineated in the passage as well: prayer with confidence (15:16; cf. 14:12-14);[5] an assurance of Christ's love and a deep experience of it (15:10; cf. 17:26); a joy that runs deeper than pain or pleasure (15:11), a new depth

---

5. The number of promises related to answered prayer in the upper room discourse indicates the great importance Jesus wanted prayer to hold in the life of the church. Significant kingdom advancement will not take place apart from prayer. Given the extent of apathy regarding prayer, one wonders how much more Jesus would have to say in order to show to His people the potential power of answered prayer.

of fellowship with fellow-believers that transcends the casual way the term is often used in churches today (15:12, 17), an evangelistic zeal expressed in sharing the gospel with the lost (15:16), and a depth of relationship with Jesus as friend (15:15).

STUDY QUESTIONS

1. Why do you think that Israel as God's vineyard failed to produce the kind of fruit God desired from them?

2. Why do you think Jesus included in His teaching such a stern warning about the danger of not bearing fruit?

3. How can you deepen your level of abiding in Christ in light of the teaching of this passage?

4. Is your life characterized by joy? Why or why not?

29

The World Hates You!

(John 15:18–16:4)

Jesus explains in this passage why it is so important for his disciples to love one another. The reason is because the world will hate them, persecute them, put them out of their synagogues, and try and kill them. They must love one another because the world will not love them. Jesus had stated elsewhere that His followers will be persecuted (Matt. 10:17-25; 24:9-14; Mark 13:9-13). In this passage, Jesus sets forth the reason for the world's hatred and God's provision of the Spirit to aid them in the face of persecution. The term 'world' dominates this passage. It is used in a number of different ways in the Gospel, but in this passage it characterizes a system and people of rebellion, hatred, and persecution. The passage can be divided into four sections. First, Jesus begins by not only stating the fact of the world's hatred but the reason for it (15:18-20). Second, the world's guilt is seen in their rejection of God evidenced by their rejection of Jesus (15:21-25). Third, Jesus encourages His followers that they will receive the Spirit's help to bear witness to Him in their suffering (15:26-27). Finally, Jesus sets forth some specific ways that the world will persecute His followers (16:1-4).

The world hates them because it hates Jesus (15:18-20)
The term 'world' is used seven times in verses 18-25 (five times in verse 19). The conditional phrase should be understood

as corresponding to reality – 'If the world hates you' – and it does (15:18a). The world's feelings toward Jesus and His followers are stated in the strongest possible term, 'hate.' The word is used six times in verses 18-25. Revelation 12 takes us behind the scenes into the origin of the world's hatred of the church.[1] Persecution of God's people is satanic in origin. Jesus' disciples should not be surprised at the world's hatred, for it had hated Christ. Jesus tells them to 'know' that it hated Him first (15:18b). While it might not make their suffering easier it will be comforting to them to know that they are being treated in the same way that their Savior was treated.

Jesus' followers can know they are not 'of the world' because the world loves its own. Jesus chose them out of the world, so they are not 'of the world', and as a result the world hates them (15:19). Jesus never seems to tire of reminding His disciples that He took the initiative in saving them; they were in the world and of the world, but He chose them out of the world. To be 'of the world' is to be characterized by the desires and attributes of worldliness. The world hates the countercultural nature of Christianity. Jesus reminds them that a slave is not greater than his master (15:20; cf. 13:16). In the previous context the point was that the disciples were to serve one another as their master served them. Here the thought is that since the world persecuted Jesus and rejected His message it will persecute His followers and reject their message (15:20).[2]

The guilt of the world (15:21-25)

The world's root problem is its rejection of God (15:21). Verses 22-25 divide into two parallel thoughts: (1) Jesus came speaking the words of God (15:22a) and performing the works of God (15:24a), and (2) the Jewish people rejected both (15:22b, 24b). Jesus equates 'the world' here with the Jewish persecution of

---

1. Morris, *John*, 678, writes, 'It is significant that the disciples are to be known by their love (cf. 13:34-35), the world by its hatred.'

2. Carson, *John*, 526, interprets the latter part of the verse positively. This understanding suggests that there are two sides to ministry; the negative (persecution) and the positive (some will listen to me and some will listen to you). The context seems to favor a negative interpretation – 'if they had listened to me' (which they have not); 'they would listen to you' (which they will not). The negative interpretation is favored by Burge, *John*, 420-21.

His people. The world's guilt is based on its accountability to divine revelation (15:22b, 24b). The specific sin that they are guilty of is rejection of the ministry of God's incarnate Son. This demonstrates the darkness of the human heart. Jesus' contemporaries heard Him speak and saw Him perform miraculous deeds (however, the use of 'works' suggests more than Jesus' miracles), but they rejected Him nonetheless. Their hatred toward Jesus is also hatred toward the Father because they are one (15:23). The Jewish hatred of Jesus was foretold in their own scriptures (15:25). The expression 'They hated me without cause' is a reference to Psalm 69:4 (cf. Pss. 35:19; 109:3). This Davidic Psalm depicts a righteous sufferer who is passionate for God but is persecuted by God's enemies for no acceptable reason. This reminds John's readers that the same will be true for them. The world's hatred toward God is so intense that they will persecute His people even though they have no reason to do so. In addition, the Old Testament quotation reminds John's readers that God was in control and His plan was being fulfilled even when it looked like the darkness was overcoming the light.

The Spirit as witness (15:26-27)

The believers will not be alone in these conflicts. Jesus refers again to 'the Helper' (Paraclete) He will send to them (15:26a; cf. 14:16, 26). The Helper is referred to as 'the Spirit of truth' (15:26b; cf. 14:17; 16:13). The Spirit's witness and the disciples' witness are placed side by side in verses 26 and 27. When the Spirit comes (Acts 2) to the disciples He will be a witness to Jesus (v. 26) through the disciples (v. 27). It is hard to overemphasize the importance of 'witness' in this Gospel. While the latter part of verse 27 points to the disciples, the implication is that all of Jesus' followers are to testify to Him (Matt. 28:16-20). They will be able to do this because Jesus sends the Spirit who is 'from the Father' and 'proceeds from the Father'.[3] The main point here is that the Spirit is sent by the Father.

---

3. The phrase 'proceeds from the Father' was understood by the Eastern Church to teach the eternal procession of the Spirit from the Father alone. The Western Church, following the Nicean Council (A.D. 325), added to the Nicean Creed what is known as the *filioque* clause ('and from the Son') to safeguard the truth that the Son is consubstantial with the Father.

Final thoughts on the world's persecution (16:1-4)

There is an unfortunate chapter break at this point since the discussion continues concerning the world's persecution of Jesus' followers. As the disciples take the gospel to the world (15:26-27) they will experience persecution. At this point Jesus becomes more specific about the persecution that awaits them. It would not be very long until faithfulness to Jesus would cost some of His followers their lives. The reason Jesus is telling them these things is so they will not fall away (16:1).[4] The way ahead has many difficulties and He does not want them taken by surprise or to go astray. Jesus delineates for them some of the ways they will soon be persecuted.

First, 'they will be put out of the synagogues' (16:2a). It is hard for us to understand how profoundly troubling it would be for a first-century Jewish Christian to be excommunicated. Earlier, John noted that many of the religious leaders who heard Jesus speak 'believed in him', but 'because of the Pharisees they would not confess their faith for fear that they would be put out of the synagogue' (12:42; cf. 9:22). If they were put out of the synagogue it meant being cut off from family and friends; a reminder that devotion to Jesus must surpass every other human relationship.

Second, some in the world will believe that they are carrying out the will of God in their persecution of believers (16:2b). The apostle Paul was an example of this mentality and Stephen is an example of one killed for his commitment to the Lordship of Christ (Acts 7:57-60). The reason for the persecution of Christians is because the persecutors do not know either the Father or Jesus (16:3; cf. 15:21). It is stunning to contemplate the fact that those who carried out the persecution were people that knew the Scriptures and obeyed outwardly the requirements of the Law, but they did not know God.

We are reminded that man's greatest need remains the miracle of grace. Orthodoxy without a heart transformed by God's grace can result in a mean and cruel disposition. Jesus tells them these things so that when persecution comes

---

4. The phrase 'I have said all these things to you...' is used seven times in the discourse. The use of the perfect tense verb gives a certain permanence and solemnity to Jesus' words here.

they will not be caught off guard (16:3). Jesus refers to the time of persecution as 'their hour'. Even as Jesus' hour refers to His passion, so His people have an hour when they will experience suffering for their faith. They can gain comfort in the fact that they are following in their Master's footsteps. The reason He is giving them these details now is that He will soon be leaving them (16:4).

Reflections

Nobody likes to be disliked or hated, especially when they've done nothing to deserve it. But the darkness hates the light and the sons of the light. Jesus made it perfectly clear in this passage that believers should not be surprised by the world's hatred (cf. Matt. 5:10-12; 10:16-23). Paul stated the matter plainly as well: 'All who desire to live godly in Christ Jesus will be persecuted' (2 Tim. 3:12). What was true in the first century is equally true in the twenty-first century. Believers around the world are paying the ultimate price for their commitment to Jesus. Jesus' comments remind us that persecution does not surprise Him, nor should they surprise His people. Ultimately enemies of the gospel respond as they do, not because they hate them, but because they hate Him.

How should we respond to these attacks? Jesus teaches us that we should love our enemies and pray for them (Luke 6:27). Never underestimate the power of prayer. We should state our positions clearly and present our arguments persuasively. We should remember that we battle not against flesh and blood, but against spiritual forces of wickedness. Furthermore, we should intercede and speak out for brothers and sisters around the world who are suffering for their faith.

Study Questions

1. Why do you think John included this section in his Gospel?

2. What does Jesus say about why the world will perse-cute His followers (15:21-25)? Does anything stand out about the kind of language Jesus uses to describe the relationship between the world and His followers?

3. What is the Holy Spirit called by Jesus (15:26-27)? Why do you think Jesus gives Him that title? What does it say His role will be as it relates to the mission of the disciples?

4. What does Jesus say is the reason He has shared all these things with them? What stands out to you about this section (16:1-4)?

30

'When the Helper Comes'
(John 16:5-33)

Jesus has finished describing to the disciples the world's hatred of them and returns to the theme of His departure. They must have felt He was adding insult to injury. But He encourages them that despite His return to the Father (16:5, 17, 28) He will send the Spirit to them (16:5-15), turn their grief into joy (16:16-24), and ensure their ultimate victory despite tribulation (16:25-33).

The Spirit as Prosecutor: Ministry to the World (16:5-11)
Jesus focuses again on the Spirit's coming: 'for if I do not go away, the Helper will not come to you' (v.7a) ... 'I will send him to you' (v. 7b) ... 'And when he comes' (v. 8) ... 'When the Spirit of truth comes' (v.13). Jesus wants there to be no doubt in the disciples' minds that He will send 'another Helper' to them. The two ministries of the Spirit mentioned here are His convicting of the world (16:5-11) and His revelatory ministry to the apostles (16:12-15).

16:5-7: After Jesus states that He will soon return to the Father, He chastens the disciples for not asking where He is going (16:5). Peter, however, did ask this question earlier (cf. 13:36; 14:5). Yet, Peter seemed less interested in where Jesus was going and more interested in why he couldn't accompany Him. Perhaps Jesus' point here is that this is a more appropriate time to ask Him. Jesus knows that as a result of His words their hearts are filled with sorrow (16:6). Therefore He solemnly affirms that it is better for them that He leaves than stays. In those moments, that assessment would have been difficult for them to believe (16:7a). The reason it is better is that if He leaves He will send the Helper (16:7b; cf. 7:39; 14:16-17; 15:26).

16:8-11: Jesus explains that part of the Helper's ministry will be to 'convict the world concerning sin and righteousness and judgment' (16:8). The parallelism in verse 8 is unpacked in verses 9-11. This is the only explicit passage in the Gospel that describes the Spirit's ministry to the world. However, in John 3, it is implied that to be 'born from above' is a work of the Spirit in the life of one who is of the world. When the Helper comes 'he will convict the world' (16:8a). The imagery is a courtroom where the world is proven guilty. The Paraclete is depicted as a prosecuting attorney.[1] Carson notes that the Paraclete is not arguing His case before God the judge, but rather 'shaming the world and convincing it of its own guilt, thus calling it to repentance'.[2] If this is the correct understanding, then many who are in the world will not be held captive forever but will be convicted of their sins, repent and trust in Christ.

There are three areas in which the Spirit's convicting powers are at work (16:9-11). First, the Paraclete convicts the world concerning sin because it does not believe in Jesus (16:9). The world refuses to believe in Christ and apart from the Spirit's work people will never see themselves as sinners.

Second, the world is convicted of 'righteousness' (16:10). Scholars debate whether to understand this to be a reference to the 'shame righteousness' of the world[3] or to Christ's righteousness demonstrated in His resurrection and exaltation.[4] The former seems to be slightly favored by its placement between sin and judgment. If this is the case the Spirit convicts the world that its good deeds, apart from commitment to Christ,

---

1. Köstenberger, *John*, 471.

2. Carson, *John*, 537.

3. Craig L. Blomberg, *The Historical Reliability of John's Gospel: Issues and Commentary*, (Downers Grove, IL: InterVarsity Press, 2001), 214; Carson, *John*, 537-38.

4. Köstenberger, *John*, 472; Keener, *John*, 2:1034.

cannot merit salvation and are as 'filthy rags' (Isa. 64:6). The reference to Jesus going to the Father is the reason that the Spirit is carrying out this ministry rather than Jesus.

Third, the world is convicted 'concerning judgment, because the ruler of this world is judged' (16:11). At the cross Jesus defeated Satan and his demons. Just as the people of God benefited from Christ's victory on the cross, the followers of 'the prince of this world' were judged and defeated with him at the cross. While Satan is still a foe with considerable power, his ultimate defeat was accomplished at the cross.

The Spirit as Revealer: Ministry to the Church (16:12-15)
The main thrust here is that the Spirit will guide the disciples into the truth. Jesus says it in a number of different ways and the repetition of the thought is impressive. 'When the Spirit comes' – 'he will guide you (16:13) ... he will not speak on his own authority (16:13) ... whatever he hears he will speak, and he will declare (16:13) ... and declare it to you (16:14) ... and declare it to you' (16:15).

It makes perfect sense that the disciples cannot handle much more instruction now (16:12). Soon the 'Spirit of truth' (cf. 14:16-17) will be their guide 'into all the truth' (16:13a). The latter part of the verse indicates that the Spirit will continue the revelatory work of Jesus (16:13b). This promise is directed most specifically to Jesus' disciples, and finds its particular fulfillment in their subsequent work of the writing of the New Testament (cf. 14:26). Just as Jesus spoke what He heard from the Father, so the 'Spirit of truth' will speak what He hears and not act independently (16:13c; cf. 8:26-28; 12:49; 14:10). The Spirit draws no attention to Himself but focuses on Jesus (16:14). The Spirit will glorify Jesus by drawing out the implications of Christ's teaching and revealing Christ's glory to His followers – 'he will take what is mine and declare it you' (16:15).

Jesus comforts the disciples to offset the pain of separation (16:16-33)
This final section of the discourse can be divided into two parts. First, Jesus explains that His separation is temporary ('a little while') and a new relationship will exist between Jesus'

followers and the Father in prayer (16:16-24). Second, Jesus concludes with a final prediction and words of encouragement (16:25-33).

Sorrow turns into joy (16:16-24)

Jesus makes two main points in these verses. First, now is a time of intense sorrow for the disciples, but their sorrow will soon become joy (vv. 15-23a). The word 'sorrow' (vv. 20, 20, 21, 22), and related ideas such as 'weep and lament' (v. 20) and 'anguish' (v. 21), highlight the intense pain that the disciples will experience with Jesus' death. The thoughts of 'joy' and 'rejoice' are equally pervasive in this paragraph (vv. 20, 21, 22, 24) and emphasize the dramatic transformation that the resurrection will bring. Second, the new age inaugurated by the resurrection results in a greater intimacy with God (vv. 23b-24).

16:16-18: Jesus' words, 'A little while, and you will see me no longer; and again a little while, and you will see me,' confuse the disciples (cf. 7:33; 12:35; 13:33; 14:19). The first part of the statement refers to Jesus' death and burial, while the second part refers to the disciples seeing Him again after His resurrection.[5]

16:19-24: Jesus explains that the world will rejoice at His death but although the disciples will grieve, their sorrow will turn into joy (16:19-20). The very thing that caused them sorrow will be the same thing that brings them joy. The cross that caused them to weep and lament will be the source of their rejoicing. Jesus illustrates His point by comparing the agony of childbirth to a mother's joy at holding her newborn baby in her arms after delivery (16:21; cf. Isa. 26:17-21; 66:7-14). While they already are experiencing sorrow ('so also you have sorrow now') they will soon know a joy that will never be taken away (16:22). One should not think that believers will never again experience heartache or disappointment; rather, they will know a joy in their hearts that the world cannot take from them. It is interesting that Jesus changes 'You will see me' (cf. 16:16b; 17b; 19b) to 'I will see you' (16:22).

---

5. Some commentators understand the phrase to be a reference to Jesus' ascension and His second coming; while others understand it to be a reference to Jesus' ascension and the coming of the Holy Spirit.

It is difficult to know if 16:23a goes with the proceeding discussion or the following one on prayer.[6] It seems more likely that 'in that day' refers to the resurrection and that the disciples will not have to ask Jesus the kinds of questions they have been asking.[7] He explains another implication of His resurrection as it relates to prayer (16:23b-24). The importance of the statement is underscored by the use of 'truly, truly' (cf. 16:20). This is Jesus' fourth promise concerning prayer in the upper room (cf. 14:13-14; 15:7, 16). As a result of the dawning of the new age Jesus promises a new intimacy in prayer between the Father and His followers. The disciples had not previously prayed to the Father 'in Jesus' name', but that is about to change. These two verses are a marvelous encouragement for believers to pray. Jesus says that whatever the disciples ask of the Father in His [Jesus] name 'he [the Father] will give it'. Jesus promises them that if they ask they will receive, with the result being that they will be bursting with joy! One wonders why the people of God pray so little when they have promises like this.

Tribulation but Victory (16:25-33)
Jesus has been speaking enigmatically using 'figures of speech' (16.25a). Three of the four New Testament uses of this word are in John (10:6; 16:25, 29; 2 Peter 2:22). It refers to hidden, obscure speech that needs to be interpreted.[8] A time is coming when Jesus will speak to them more plainly. Jesus' teaching at that time will continue to focus on revealing the Father to them (16:25).

Following the resurrection the disciples will pray to the Father in Jesus' name, but they must not think that this means that Jesus must persuade the Father to answer their prayers. His point is that they will have a more intimate relationship with the Father as a result of Jesus' death and resurrection (cf. Heb. 10:19-20). The Father loves (*phileo*) them, in part

6. Blomberg, *Jesus and the Gospels*, 337, and Carson, *John*, 545, understand it as connected to Jesus' statement on prayer.

7. Köstenberger, *John*, 477, and Morris, *John*, 627.

8. Gerhard Kittel and Gerhard Fredrich, *Theological Dictionary of the New Testament* (Grand Rapids: William B. Eerdmans Publishing Company, 1974), 5:856.

because of their love and belief in Jesus (16:26-27).[9] One should not pass over too quickly the thought concerning God's love. What an amazing truth – God loves His people! To love and to be loved are two of the deepest longings of every heart. People go to great lengths to get love and sometimes they go to even greater lengths to demonstrate it. God's people should never doubt the depth of God's love for them.

Verse 28 summarizes Johannine theology in two sets of balanced clauses. The first half of the verse refers to Jesus' mission from the Father (cf. 3:16-17) and incarnation into the world (cf. 1:10-11). The latter half of the verse teaches that now that the mission is complete He will leave the world (cf. 14:19) and return to the Father (13:33, 36; 14:2, 19, 20, 28; 16:5, 16, 17, 19). The disciples respond enthusiastically that now Jesus is speaking 'plainly'. They are confident that they 'now' comprehend His supernatural insight – 'we know that you know all things' – and divine origin – 'came from God' (16:30).

Jesus' response can be taken as either a declaration (NIV) or a question (NASB; ESV). Either way there is a note of irony in His words (16:31). The truth is that they will soon abandon Him, but the Father will not abandon Him (16:32). Jesus concludes by reminding them that He has told them 'these things' so that in Him they 'may have peace' – *shalom* (16:33a). The biblical concept of peace is much more than the absence of conflict, but includes the rich blessings that come to one in a right relationship with God (cf. Num. 6:24-26; Hag. 2:9; Rom. 5:1). Jesus' followers will experience 'tribulation in the world', but (a strong adversative) they are to 'take heart' because He has 'overcome the world'. The world will do its worst to Him but He will be victorious over it. This is the only use of the word 'overcome' in John's Gospel. The perfect tense of the verb stresses the abiding nature of the victory. The cross was Satan's and the world's greatest attempt to 'overcome the light' but they were soundly and eternally defeated there. This thought brings great comfort to believers

---

9. The use of the perfect tense verbs translated 'have loved' and 'have believed' emphasize these as continuing characteristics of Christian living.

as they experience the world's hatred in their mission of taking the gospel to the nations.

Reflections

I want us to consider three thoughts from this passage: First, Jesus gives His final instruction in the upper room on the ministry of the Paraclete. He does not want them to think for a moment that He is abandoning them. He will send the Spirit to them (16:7, 8, 13). Jesus' followers are never alone. No matter how alone we may feel, the Bible teaches us that we are not alone if we know Christ. The Spirit is the presence of Jesus with His people. We may never feel more alone than when we suffer for the gospel, but as Morris states, 'The work of the Spirit in the church is done in the context of persecution... He comes to assist men caught up in the thick of battle, and tried beyond their strength.'[10]

Second, Jesus continues to make tremendous promises concerning prayer (16:23-24; cf. 14:13-14; 15:7-8, 16). Here are a few things to keep in mind when praying. Pray specific prayers – the more specific the prayer the more specific the answer! Don't be afraid to pray big prayers in Jesus' name. Big prayers in Jesus' name humble us by reminding us we can't do life on our own. Big prayers in Jesus' name drive us to the Bible to see if our requests are biblical. Big prayers in Jesus' name increase our faith when Jesus answers them. Finally, big prayers in Jesus' name involve us in kingdom pursuits. We can intercede on behalf of brothers and sisters that serve on the other side of the world.

Third, John says a lot about joy in the Farewell Discourse. Earlier we learned from John the Baptist about the joy of discovering one's role in God's plan and faithfully fulfilling that role (3:30). In 15:9-11, Jesus taught that when we abide in Him by obeying His Word we experience fullness of joy. In 16:22-24, Jesus teaches that answered prayer brings such joy. In John 17:13, we will see that trusting in Jesus' words results in His fullness of joy being real in us.

---

10. Leon Morris, *Expository Reflections on the Gospel of John* (Grand Rapids: Baker Publishing Group, 1990), 692.

STUDY QUESTIONS

1. Why do you think that John included this section in the Gospel?

2. Jesus said it was for their good that He was going away. In what ways was it better for the disciples to have the Holy Spirit than to have Jesus in the flesh?

3. What is the Holy Spirit to the world (15:8-11)? What does the Holy Spirit do in the believer (15:12 -15)?

4. What do you learn about prayer from Jesus' teaching in the Farewell Discourse?

5. What does Jesus' teaching on joy in the passage contribute to what He has said earlier in the upper room about joy?

6. How do Jesus' words, 'I have overcome the world,' give you peace?

31

Jesus' Intercessory Prayer
(John 17:1-26)

You can learn a lot about a person by how, what, and when they pray. Jesus was unmistakably a man of prayer. Even now at the Father's right hand He intercedes for His people (Heb. 7:25). Jesus' prayer in John 17 is important for several reasons. First, Jesus prays immediately after He tells His disciples that in this world they will have tribulation (16:33). Shortly, He and His disciples will experience intense tribulation in the Garden of Gethsemane (cf. 18:1). In preparation for that suffering Jesus prays. Second, this is the longest recorded prayer of Jesus in the Bible. We learn a lot about Jesus' heart from this prayer. Third, the fact that the prayer is offered in the shadow of the cross makes it significant. In chapter 18 Jesus stands strong in a moment when most people would collapse in fear. His time in prayer fortifies His soul for that encounter.

The prayer can be divided into three sections: Jesus prays for Himself (17:1-5); for His disciples, which is the longest section of the prayer (17:6-19); and finally, for future believers (17:20-26).

Jesus prays for Himself (17:1-5)
John 16 closes with Jesus' promise of peace. John now describes Jesus launching into prayer. Obviously there is a

close connection between peace and prayer. Three thoughts stand out in these verses: Jesus' confidence in the Father's plan (17:1a); His passion for the Father's glory (17:1b, 4-5); and His gift of eternal life to those given Him by the Father (17:2-3).

17:1: Jesus lifts His gaze to heaven as He begins to pray (cf. Ps. 123:1; John 11:41; Mark 7:34). He addresses God as Father, as He had taught the disciples to do (Matt. 6:9; Luke 11:2). Jesus announces again the arrival of His 'hour,' that is, the culmination of His mission (17:1a; 2:4; 7:30; 8:20; 12:23; 13:31-32). The fact that Jesus does not ask the Father to save Him from the hour indicates His complete confidence in God's plan (cf. 12:27). Instead, He prays that God would glorify Him, so that He in turn may glorify God (17:1b). The word appears as a verb or noun five times in these verses (17:1, 4, 5). To mankind the cross appeared as an instrument of shame; for Christ it was not merely the means to glory, but it was glory. Jesus' consuming passion was to glorify His Father.

Jesus' request implies His divinity since God will not share His glory with another (Isa. 42:8; 48:11). Interestingly, Jesus confidence in God's sovereignty did not stop Him from praying. We often take the attitude that God will do whatever He will do, so why pray? The answer is that God commands us to pray and has given us many promises to encourage us to pray.

17:2-3: The basis of Jesus' glory is the authority God has given to Him in order to give eternal life to those given to Him by the Father (17:2). The verb 'to give' (*didomi*) is used three times in this verse and seventeen times in the prayer (17:4, 6, 7, 8, 9, 11, 12, 14, 22, 24).[1] Believers are God's gift to His Son.

Verse 3 provides a definition of eternal life (17:3).[2] Eternal life is defined relationally as knowing God and Jesus Christ. Knowing means more than intellectual apprehension and carries the thought of intimate knowledge. It is more than

---

1. Of the seventeen uses in this chapter, in thirteen the Father is the subject of the verb, and for each one of these the gift is made to the Son. The other four usages refer to the Son giving to the disciples.

2. Some consider verse 3 to be an explanatory comment by the evangelist, otherwise Jesus would be referring to Himself as 'Jesus Christ' (17:3).

knowing *about* God and Jesus, for it is *truly* knowing them in a personal way through faith in Christ. God is 'the only true God' in contrast with all other supposed gods.

17:4-5: Jesus glorified the Father by completing the work the Father gave Him, especially the cross-work – the noun is singular (17:4). Jesus speaks as if it is finished, for there is no doubt that it will be. Among His final words from the cross are 'It is finished' (19:30). In verse 1 Jesus prayed, 'Glorify your Son,' and He concludes this opening section by asking His Father to glorify Him with His pre-incarnate glory (17:5; cf. 1:1, 14; 3:13; 6:62; 8:58; 16:28; 17:24).

Jesus' passion for the Father's glory is both refreshing and challenging. In a world where ministers easily fall into the entitlement mindset, Jesus' passion is for the Father's glory. Even on the brink of the crucifixion His mindset is on accomplishing the task for which the Father sent Him. The crucifixion appears to be the humiliation and defeat of God's Son, but in reality it will be the glorification of the Son and the Father. It is encouraging also to know that Jesus' belief in God's sovereignty did not squelch His prayer life but instead was an incentive to pray.

Jesus prays for the disciples (17:6-19)
This central portion of the prayer is the longest and focuses on Jesus' intercession for His disciples. This section can be divided into three thoughts: Jesus gives a progress report on His disciples (vv. 6-8); He prays for their spiritual protection (vv. 9-16); and He prays that they would be set apart for world missions (vv. 17-19).

Jesus' followers are characterized by faith, knowledge, and obedience (17:6-8)
These verses are something of a progress report of His ministry and at the same time a description of His followers. Jesus manifested God's name to His disciples, that is, He revealed God's essential nature to them (17:6; cf. vv. 11, 12, 26). This revelation was not made indiscriminately, but to those God gave to Him 'out of the world'. The fact that they belonged to God before He gave them to Jesus suggests divine election is meant. The evidence that they belong to God is seen in the

fact that they obeyed God's word (cf. 14:15, 21, 23), even as
Jesus did (cf. 8:55; 14:31; 15:10).

Now that Jesus has revealed to the disciples what God
is like, they are able to understand that He is the source
of everything that has been given to the Son (17:7). Jesus'
teaching is an example of this (17:8a). The disciples 'received'
Jesus' teaching and as a result they believe that He came from
God (17:8b). Jesus never forgot that He was sent on a mission
from God (cf. 17:3, 18, 21, 23, 25).

*Jesus prays for their spiritual protection from Satan and the
world (17:9-16)*
17:9-12: Jesus now prays for His disciples. He is not praying
for the world, but those God has given Him 'out of the world'
(17:9a). Even though those for whom Christ prays are a gift
from God to Him, they still belong to God – 'for they are
yours' (17:9b-10). This dual 'ownership' is another indication
of the intimacy between the Father and Son.

The fact that Jesus does not pray for the world here should
not be understood to mean that He has no concern for the
world; for He desires that the world know that the Father
sent Him (cf. 17:23). The time for Jesus' departure from the
'world' is near and He is concerned about His disciples who
remain 'in the world' (17:11a). Both references are more than
a mere geographical notation. While in the world, Jesus lived
in a spiritually hostile environment. He knows He will be
leaving His followers behind in this hostile setting. In light of
His departure He implores the Father 'to keep them in your
name', that is, that He will protect them spiritually.

Jesus addresses God as 'Holy Father' (17:11b). This is the
only time in the New Testament God is referred to by this
title. The name suggests both the separateness ('holy') and
nearness ('Father') of God.

Jesus desires that His followers will not only be protected
but that they also will remain united (17:12a). Evil powers will
attempt to destroy their unity and nothing less than God's
manifest presence and power can preserve it. The importance
of unity in the prayer is seen in the fact that it is repeated
again in 17:21-23. If Jesus thought it was necessary to pray in
this way for His followers, how much more necessary is it for

us (cf. Ps. 133)! While Jesus was with them He protected them and He did not lose a single one the Father gave Him, with the exception of 'the son of perdition'. Judas' betrayal fulfilled the Scriptures. Yet the fact that his betrayal was foretold in the Scriptures did not alleviate his guilt.

17:13-16: Jesus prays for the disciples concerning the conflicts that they will face (17:14, 16). However, before He does, He prays that they would have His joy 'made full' in them (17:13). Even though this world is a spiritual battleground, His followers can know fullness of joy. Joy is an underdeveloped quality in most believers. As Jesus moves ever closer to the cross, joy becomes a more common theme in His teaching. Before the Upper Room Discourse the word 'joy' is found only in 3:29. However, it appears seven times in the Farewell Discourse (15:11; 16:20, 21, 22, 24; 17:13). The thought is that the Christian life is not a drab, barren existence. Jesus wants His followers to experience fullness of joy despite living in a fallen world.

Jesus turns from joy to conflict (7:14-16). He prays for their protection from the evil one. Note the repetition of the word 'world' in these verses. The disciples are not to try to escape from the world because of persecution. Instead, Jesus prays that they be kept from the evil one (Matt 6:13).

Jesus prays for His followers to be set apart for a worldwide mission (17:17-19)
In a very real sense these verses are a continuation of the previous thought as seen by the repetition of the terms 'world' and 'word'. As the Father sent the Son into a hostile world, so Jesus sends His followers into it. The words 'I have sent them' are proleptic. Just as Jesus consecrated Himself, so He prays that the Father would sanctify them in the truth. Truth is important because Satan is the 'father of lies'. To be sanctified is to be set apart for God and His purposes. Jesus prays that God will set apart His disciples for His own purposes. The means of this sanctification is the truth, God's Word.

It is hard to see how there could be genuine consecration apart from God's Word. As believers absorb increasing quantities of God's Word, cherishing it because it is true, they become increasingly holy and ever more useful for God's purposes. A perpetual thinking on God's Word is used by the Spirit to mold us into Christlikeness. This is not only Jesus' desire for these disciples but also for all of His followers. The primary purpose here, that His followers are to be set apart, is for their mission into the world. Their sanctification has as its goal their witness to the world. Thus, Jesus sets apart Himself to perform His redemptive work on the cross in order that the beneficiaries of the work might set apart themselves to do the work of missions.

Jesus prays for future believers (17:20-26)
The final words of Jesus' prayer are for future believers. In a very real sense this was the night on which Jesus prayed for you, if you are a Christian!

Jesus prays our unity (17:20-23)
Jesus wants future believers to experience the unity of love that exists between the Father and the Son. The reason for this is that the world may be convinced by the church's witness to the divine revelation in Christ (17:20). The church's unity is not an option but a divine mandate (17:21-23). This unity among believers is to replicate, to a lesser degree, the unity of the Godhead. Several times in this prayer Jesus prays 'that they may be one' (17:11, 21, 22). His prayer for church unity is evangelistically motivated. He wants a unified church in order that it may be a witness to the lost world (17:21b; 23b).

Jesus has given His people His glory so that they may be one. Glory in John's Gospel is different from worldly conceptions of glory. Glory in this Gospel is demonstrated in humble service, a service culminating in the cross. When someone leaves a position of power and prestige to perform lowly service (from the world's perspective), as Jesus did, we see God's glory. Service is not a means to glory, service itself is glory. Jesus' words, 'I have given,' communicate the permanent aspect of the glory. The glory from the world comes and goes, but the glory God gives to His people remains.

Jesus adds the request that His followers would 'know that you love them as you have loved me' (17:23). What an unbelievable thought! God loves believers in a way comparable to the love He has for Jesus. Paul prays that the believers in Ephesus would be able to comprehend God's love (Eph. 3:18-19) – the staggering nature of this claim is truly incomprehensible. The greatness of God's love for His people can only be apprehended by divine revelation.

Jesus' prayer for unity is not a unity at any cost. The church cannot compromise on the truth of God's Word. The unity for which Jesus prays is a supernatural unity that exists because the church is the temple of God and indwelt by the Holy Spirit.

Jesus prays for our future destiny (17:24-26)
The desires of Jesus for His followers do not end in this life because He asks that they be with Him throughout eternity. For believers, to be in the presence of the Savior and to see His glory will cause all of their suffering and sacrifice in this life to fade into the background. To be with Jesus will be their greatest blessing – after all of the sacrifice and service of this life they will find that blessing to be more than compensating (17:24).

Jesus concludes His prayer by referring to God as 'righteous Father', the only time in the New Testament that God is spoken of in this way. While the world does not know God, Jesus knows Him and has made Him known to His followers.

The final words in the prayer are a request that His followers will be indwelt with God's love, which is the same love that the Father has for Him, and that He will indwell them as well. Only by the work of the Holy Spirit can a believer truly grasp the significance of Jesus' request. The Father's love and the Son's indwelling are virtually incomprehensible. While the words are quite easy to read, the truth of them is almost unfathomable. Only as believers pray and meditate on these things does the Holy Spirit make it a reality in their lives.

Reflections
What a privilege to listen to the Lord's heart as He prays on the precipice of His death. His prayer reveals what is uppermost on His mind: the Father's glory (17:1-5), His disciples' consecration, spiritual protection and mission (17:6-19), and the unity, mission, and destiny of future believers (17:20-26).

I want us to consider several thoughts about this prayer: First, the timing of the prayer is astonishing in that it is not a gloomy prayer of hopelessness but instead is a prayer of triumphant faith.

Second, Jesus' prayer reminds us that we live in a spiritual war zone. We must be on the alert for satanic attacks and the subtle pull of worldliness. This world is a dangerous place and the pressure of self-glorification and the avoidance of suffering for the gospel is a constant temptation. Since we live in this war zone we must follow Jesus' example and pray for one another. We must never forget that prayer is war (Eph. 6:18-20).

Third, if you isolate yourself from the body, or have a divisive disposition, you will experience spiritual defeat and divine discipline. Jesus' prayer is a community prayer and Jesus sees this community as the people of God.

Fourth, we must saturate ourselves with God's Word to prepare ourselves for God's mission to the world. We are to take the gospel into enemy territory, as Jesus did, because people's eternities are at stake. In His final prayer before His arrest Jesus still has the world on His mind.

STUDY QUESTIONS

1. How is Jesus' prayer for Himself similar to (17:1-5) and different from what He prays for His disciples (17:6-19)?

2. In what ways is the Father glorified according to Jesus' prayer?

3. Why do you think Jesus does not pray for the world here?

4. How does Jesus' concern for the world come through in the prayer?

5. Why is the unity of the church such an important part of Jesus' prayer?

32

A Study in Contrasts
(John 18:1-27)

This passage is a study in contrasts: a traitorous friend, a corrupt priest, a fallen disciple, and a courageous Savior. This is a continuing story about collusion, secret agreements concerning betrayal, conniving and conspiring. It is a story about the abandonment of leadership; about how Israel's religious leaders gave up all pretense of devotion to God, and instead decided to conspire with the Roman military. The events described take place during the Thursday night of the closing week of Christ's life. John's theological message is that despite the darkness of the hour, it is in fact the hour of glory.

This is the first of four major scenes in John's Passion story: The story begins in a garden across the Kidron Valley where Jesus is arrested (18:1-11); the scene then shifts to an interrogation before Annas, the father-in-law of the high priest (18:12-27). While Jesus is interrogated, Peter is in the process of denying his relationship to Jesus. The third scene is the most extensive of the Passion and is Jesus' trial before Pilate (18:28–19:16). John presents the action of this section with great literary skill, alternating the reader's focus from private conversations between Jesus and Pilate inside the praetorium to confrontations with Jewish leaders and the crowd outside of it. The final episode takes place on Golgotha; the events at the cross and then the burial of Jesus' body are described (19:17-42).

Return to the Garden: Jesus and Judas (18:1-11)

Jesus goes to the Garden of Gethsemane to begin to reverse what happened in the Garden of Eden. While the Synoptic Gospels describe Jesus' agonizing prayer there, John's account plunges immediately from Jesus' prayer in John 17 to His violent arrest. The verses can be divided into three sections: the dramatic confrontation between Jesus and His enemies (18:1-7), Jesus as the Good Shepherd protecting His sheep (18:8-9), and Peter's foolhardy attempt to protect Jesus (18:10-11).

The dramatic confrontation: Jesus and His enemies (18:1-7)

John begins by setting the scene (18:1-3). 'When Jesus had spoken these words' is probably a reference to all of chapters 14–17.[1] Jesus then led the disciples east across the Kidron Valley to the western slopes of the Mount of Olives (18:1).[2] The Kidron Valley is a riverbed (wadi) lying between the Mount of Olives and Jerusalem, which is dry except for the rainy winter season. Matthew and Mark refer to the site as Gethsemane ('oil press'); John simply calls the location a garden.

John escalates the drama of the arrest by his description of the forces arrayed against Jesus: a fallen disciple, the violent power of Rome, and the hatred of the religious authorities. At the head of the list is Judas (18:2); from his first appearance in the Gospel (cf. 6:71) he is identified as the betrayer (12:5-6; 13:2, 18, 19, 21, 26, 27). He knew Jesus' location because He had taken His disciples there often. Judas reminds us of the danger of failing to take advantage of one's spiritual privileges. From the highest degree of privilege to the lowest depth of sin, there is but a succession of steps. Judas had been under the teaching of the Lord Jesus, yet he did not take what he was taught to heart.

Only John mentions the presence of Roman soldiers (18:3a).[3] Jesus is confronted by the whole array of His enemies,

---

1. Carson, *John*, 576.

2. Brown, *John*, 2:806, notes that Jesus' exit from Jerusalem parallels David's flight from Absalom across the Kidron (2 Sam. 15:23) after his betrayal by Ahithophel, who later hanged himself (2 Sam. 17:23).

3. The term 'cohort' in theory was a thousand soldiers. The term could also refer to a 'maniple' of two hundred soldiers. While this seems to be a large number for

Gentile and Jewish. The Jewish authorities are described as 'officers from the chief priests and the Pharisees' (18:3b). The combination of 'chief priests and Pharisees' is characteristic of John's Gospel. Each time they are mentioned together it is at a moment when the religious authorities decide to take action against Jesus (cf. 7:31-32; 7:45-52; 11:47-53). This will be the last reference to the Pharisees in the Gospel. The probable reason for this is that they lacked the political influence of the chief priests who will take Jesus to Pilate. The 'lanterns and torches' were necessary even with the full moon of Passover in case Jesus and His followers sought to escape into the darkness. Jesus, fully cognizant of what was taking place, steps forward, and questions them as to whom they are seeking (18:4).[4] Jesus asks the question again in verse 7.

At the very moment when one might expect an unarmed victim to flee, John portrays Jesus in complete control. His enemies fall to the ground as He identifies Himself as the divine 'I am' (18:6).[5] The historicity of the event is challenged by many scholars because of its apparent supernatural nature. It is difficult to know what happened exactly, but it seems unlikely that they were merely startled and one tumbled over another in a domino effect. John, however, makes it clear that they 'drew back and fell to the ground' in response to Jesus' 'I am' (*ego eimi*) statement.[6] Something dramatic and dynamic happened when Jesus spoke those words. One thing that is clear is that the forces of darkness were impotent against Jesus (cf. 13:19). In all the commotion that was taking place Jesus asks again, 'Whom do you seek?' (18:7).

---

such a task it must be remembered that the Romans were determined to prevent an uprising during the Passover. It should be noted that 470 soldiers guarded Paul on his journey from Jerusalem to Caesarea (Acts 23:23).

4. The contrast with the Synoptic Gospels is obvious. In their accounts, Judas steps forward to kiss Jesus in order to identify Him. John does not mention the kiss but describes Jesus stepping forward and taking the initiative. John leaves no doubt that Jesus was in control of the situation and not taken by surprise. The accounts are not contradictory but complementary and when taken together they give a fuller picture of what transpired.

5. Jesus' comment here is not unlike the absolute 'I am' statements found elsewhere in the Gospel (6:20; 8:24, 28, 58).

6. Falling to the ground in God's presence is a common reaction in the Bible (Ezek. 1:28; 44:4; Dan. 2:46; 8:18; 10:9; Acts 9:4; 22:7; Rev. 1:17; 19:10; 22:8).

The Good Shepherd protects His sheep (19:8-9)

Jesus identifies Himself again to His enemies and demands that His disciples be permitted to leave (18:8). John, in contrast to the Synoptics, does not describe the disciples fleeing into the darkness. Instead, John focuses on Jesus offering Himself in their place. We should never underestimate the tender concern Jesus has for His followers. As the Good Shepherd, He stands between them and their enemies by offering Himself in their place (10:15, 17, 18, 28). Jesus' actions fulfill His earlier promise (18:9; cf. 6:39; 10:28; 17:12). If ever there was a moment when Jesus could be excused for acting selfishly this would have been it, but He thinks only of His disciples. The passage reminds us of the voluntary nature of Jesus' suffering. It becomes clear that if in this vulnerable moment His enemies are overwhelmed by His presence there can be no doubt that He willingly submitted Himself to be taken captive by them and to suffer crucifixion at their hands.

Simon's wayward act (18:10-11)

Peter's foolish act is described in all four Gospels, but only John gives the names of 'Simon Peter' and 'Malchus' (18:10). Peter's weapon was a small dagger or long knife. In all of the confusion Peter drew his sword but only managed to cut off the ear of Malchus, the high priest's slave. Luke mentions that Jesus healed the servant's right ear. Jesus rebukes Peter by telling him to put his weapon away; Jesus was to drink the cup given to Him by the Father. His response reveals that even in these moments His focus is on accomplishing the salvation the Father sent Him to secure. The drinking of the cup symbolizes Jesus bearing God's wrath for the world's sin (18:11; cf. Mark 14:36; Isa. 51:17-22; Jer. 25:15-17, 28-29). Jesus will drink it down to the dregs until the moment comes when He says, 'It is finished!' We should be astounded at the willingness of Jesus to drink the cup of God's wrath on our behalf.

A Corrupt Priest, a Cowardly Disciple, and a Courageous Savior (18:12-27)

On a literary level John alternates between the events inside Annas' home and outside in the courtyard. The alternating of focus from Annas and Jesus to Peter and his interrogators highlights the differences between Jesus and Peter.

Inside the house: Jesus and Annas (18:12-14)
Jesus is arrested, bound, and taken to Annas (18:12-13). Annas was the father-in-law of Caiaphas the high priest. It is likely that Annas still had considerable power, even though he was not the official high priest. By taking Jesus first to Annas, Caiaphas had time to assemble the Sanhedrin for a clandestine meeting. John reminds the reader of Caiaphas' earlier comment (18:14; cf.11:50).

Outside in the courtyard: Peter interrogated by a slave girl (18:15-18)
John switches from Jesus to Peter. Peter's three denials must have made a deep impression on Jesus' earliest followers because they are described in all four Gospels. This alteration of focus extenuates both Jesus' bravery and Peter's cowardice. While Jesus boldly proclaims His identity and mission before Annas, Peter crumbles in fear and denies his identity to a slave girl. John adds a new insight not found in the Synoptic Gospels, which is that another disciple accompanied Peter into the courtyard. The other disciple is probably John, though we cannot be certain. The slave girl's question to Peter is stated in a way that expects a negative response. Peter's answer is ironic considering Jesus' response in verse 5. Peter says, 'I am not,' while Jesus said, 'I am *he.*' At this point John changes back to the scene of Jesus and Annas.

Inside the house: Annas and Jesus (18:19-24)
Annas is again referred to as high priest, much like how previous presidents are still referred to by the title of their former office. Earlier in the Gospel the issue had been the identity of Jesus; now the issue is His teaching (18:19). Jesus takes the focus off the disciples and comments that His teaching was done in the open (18:20-21). The blow by one of the attendants is another evidence of their failure to recognize the truth (18:22). Jesus demands that proper judicial practice should be followed, such as the calling of witnesses (18:23-24; cf. 7:23-24). The scene concludes with Annas sending Jesus

to Caiaphas, but John does not describe the actual encounter (18:28).

Outside in the courtyard: Peter's second and third denials (18:25-27)

The earlier question about Peter's identity is repeated (18:25; cf. v. 17). John narrates Peter's denials on both sides of the interrogation of Jesus. Jesus speaks openly and not in secret (18:20), but fear drives Peter to conceal his true identity (18:25). The third confrontation escalates the drama (18:26-27). The wording of the accusation suggests that Peter is identified now positively. For a third and final time Peter denies his Lord. The sound of the cock reminds the reader of the prophecy of Jesus spoken earlier in the evening (13:38). Although Peter obviously loved Jesus he was not prepared for the intensity of this spiritual battle. There is no resolution of Peter's fate at this point, and his lack of faith will be evident again at the empty tomb.

Reflections

This scene serves well John's Christological teaching. It appears that Jesus has walked right into a trap, yet the triumphant Christ who strode victoriously through the Gospel remains victorious even now. Although bound as a prisoner and about to be condemned to death, He continues to speak boldly and shine forth brightly on the darkest of nights. Peter, however, is a different story. Under the threat of exposure and possible death, he succumbs to fear and falls into the darkness. Yet Jesus has called Peter into the light and that call will not be thwarted. Peter's longing to follow Jesus to death (6:68; 13:37) will ultimately come to pass (21:18, 19). Judas and Annas, on the other hand, demonstrate the danger of a religion that fails to transform one's heart. Judas teaches us that privileges misused will paralyze the conscience. We may bask in the full sunshine of spiritual privileges, listen to the best of Christian teaching, and yet bear no fruit to God's glory. Judas' story should be a lesson and warning to us all that truth heard should be truth obeyed. Annas, on the other hand, compromises religious conviction for political expediency.

Finally, where is God as these events unfold? He seems to be absent during this episode. This is similar to what we sometimes think when we assume that God has abandoned us in our time of need. We feel as though our prayers are not answered, our dreams are shattered, or the tragedies that have befallen us are undeserved. Yet in the midst of this apparent darkness God is not absent. We learn that even when God appears absent He is there. God's presence is subtly indicated in the reference to Caiaphas' earlier statement (cf. 11:50). These events were all a part of God's redemptive plan. As the Psalmist wrote, 'If I say, "Surely the darkness will overwhelm me, and the light around me will be night," even the darkness is not dark to you, and the night is as bright as the day. Darkness and light are alike to you' (Ps. 139:11-12).

STUDY QUESTIONS

1. What do you think is the most important lesson John wants to communicate to his readers in this passage?

2. Why do you think John did not describe Jesus' agonizing prayer in the garden as do the Synoptic Gospels, but instead focused on Jesus' protection of the disciples?

3. Do you think the actions of Jesus have any implications for those who serve in positions of spiritual authority? If so, what are those implications?

4. What principles did you discover for your own life from the various personalities in the passage: Annas, Judas, and Peter?

33

The Son of God is Convicted of Treason
(John 18:28–19:16)

The trial of Jesus before Pilate is the longest and most intricately crafted scene of John's passion narrative. He paints a masterful portrait of Jesus in apparent abject weakness – He is a prisoner, renounced by the religious leaders, abandoned by His disciples, and standing before the summit of secular power. Yet, Jesus is transparently powerful. He speaks the truth openly and boldly.

John uses a split screen to achieve his dramatic effect. The trial takes place in the praetorium (18:28), the temporary residence of the Roman Prefect while in Jerusalem. The setting shifts back and forth, from inside the praetorium, where Pilate and Jesus are sequestered, to the violent crowds who remain outside. The end result is seven brief episodes: outside the Jewish leaders hand Jesus over (18:28-32), inside Pilate questions Jesus about His kingship (18:33- 38a), outside Pilate declares Jesus innocent (18:38b-40), inside the Roman soldiers scourge and mock Jesus (19:1-3), outside Pilate declares Jesus not guilty a second time (19:4-8), inside Pilate questions Jesus about His origin (19:9-12), and outside Pilate delivers Jesus to crucifixion (19:13-16).

The reader moves with Pilate from one location to the other, hearing the revealing words of Jesus in the privacy of the praetorium counterpointed by the fury of the crowd whenever the action steps outside. But notice how the 'outside' words of the crowd seem to break 'inside' and turn the tide (19:12, 13). The major theological theme is Jesus' kingship (18:33, 36, 37, 39; 19:2-3 12, 14-15, 19-22).

Outside: The Jewish leaders hand Jesus over to Pilate (18:28-32)

John, like the Synoptic evangelists, is selective in what he reports. In 18:24 John notes that Jesus was sent to Caiaphas, but there is no report on what happened there. Pilate is brought into the drama without introduction (18:29). John presumes his reader's knowledge concerning him. The irony between the Jews' words and their actions is clear. They don't want to enter the praetorium and be defiled, but they have no qualms about handing over an innocent man to be crucified. The Jewish leaders seem intentionally evasive and provocative in their response to Pilate concerning Jesus' crime. Pilate in turn responds caustically.

Inside: Pilate questions Jesus about His kingship (18:33-38a)

After hearing the leaders' demands, Pilate goes back inside the praetorium for his first conversation with Jesus. Here the theme of Jesus' kingship is introduced (18:33). Jesus, however, turns the table on Pilate and interrogates the interrogator (18:34). Pilate's question, 'What have you done?', affords the reader an opportunity to reflect on Jesus' signs, statements, and sermons in the Gospel account. Jesus' reply moves the conversation along (18:36). His use of 'world' is full of theological meaning. The kingdoms of this world are ruled by darkness and untruth and hate the light – His kingdom is of a different kind. Pilate's response is a restatement of his earlier question (18:37a). The reply of Jesus is the most powerful statement of His royal mission in the Gospel (18:37b). The scene closes with Pilate's famous question, 'What is truth?' These words can be interpreted as an expression of cool and worldly cynicism or as agnostic futility in the search for truth.

Outside: Pilate declares Jesus innocent (18:38b-40)

Pilate declares Jesus' innocence for the first time, thus Rome pronounces Him not guilty (18:38b). In Mark (15:8) and Luke (23:18), the crowd take the initiative in reminding Pilate of the custom of releasing a prisoner at Passover, but in John's Gospel Pilate initiates the issue (18:39). The leaders choose a bandit (18:40). Earlier Jesus referred to the Jewish leaders as 'thieves and robbers' (10:18) and now they choose to set a revolutionary free and put Jesus to death. At the Last Supper, Jesus warned the disciples that the world would love its own (cf. 15:19).

Inside: The Roman soldiers scourge and mock Jesus (19:1-3)
The Romans normally used scourging as a prelude to crucifixion, but here it is another attempt by Pilate to satisfy the Jewish leadership's thirst for blood without having to crucify Jesus. The crown of thorns, the purple robe, and the taunting are all symbols of royal power and intended to humiliate Jesus. Isaiah prophesied of this brutal moment: 'I gave my back to those who strike me, and my cheeks to those who pluck out the beard; I did not cover my face from humiliation and spitting' (Isa. 50:6).

Outside: Pilate declares Jesus' innocence a second time (19:4-8)
Pilate declares Jesus innocent again (19:4). The words, 'Behold, the Man,' have taken on a life of their own in Christian art and imagination (19:5). What Pilate meant by the words and what John intended the reader to understand have been debated. Did John want to evoke 'Son of Man' imagery, or is he alluding to such passages as Zechariah 6:11, 12 or Isaiah 52:13-15? There is no way to be absolutely certain what John intended. There can be no debate, however, that Pilate presents Jesus to the world in His most humiliated and abject state – battered, abandoned, and completely vulnerable to His enemy.

The leaders respond with cries of 'crucify' (19:6). This is the first time in the Gospel that the word is used. Pilate's exchange with the leaders at this point is reminiscent of 18:30-31. The religious leaders introduce another designation for Jesus – 'Son of God' (19:7). At least three times in John's Gospel the Jews attempted to kill Jesus for this very reason (5:18; 8:59; 10:31-39). Jesus was guilty of blasphemy in their eyes and according to Scripture He had to die: 'Moreover, the one who blasphemes the name of the Lord shall surely be put to death; all the congregation shall certainly stone him. The alien, as well as the native, when he blasphemes the Name, shall be put to death' (Lev. 24:16). This designation increased Pilate's fear and anxiety (19:8).

Inside: Pilate questions Jesus about His origin (19:9-12)

Pilate and Jesus move back inside the praetorium at this point. The parallel between this episode and the second segment are striking. In 18:33-38 Pilate questioned Jesus about His kingship; here He questions Jesus about His origin and authority (19:9; cf. 7:28-29; 8:14; 9:29). Pilate, the representative of secular authority, brings up the crucial issues of authority and crucifixion (19:10). Jesus bravely replies that no human ruler has authority over His life (19:11; cf. 10:17-18). Whatever role Pilate plays in the drama is given from above. God the Father directs Jesus' destiny.

Jesus' bold statement shakes Pilate and causes him to resolve to set Jesus free (19:12). The Jews respond by threatening Pilate. The term, 'friend of Caesar,' may have originally been a title of privilege for a person favored in the imperial court. Shockingly, it is the Jewish leadership, not the Romans, which introduce the issue of loyalty to Caesar.

Outside: Pilate delivers Jesus to crucifixion (19:13-16)

Pilate capitulates to their demands when he hears the Jews' words in verse 12 (19:13). More significant is John's theological perspective by reference to the precise time when Pilate takes his seat at the sixth hour – twelve noon (19:14). The four Gospels agree that Jesus was crucified on the eve of the Sabbath, but Mark records the time as 9:00 in the morning – 'the third hour' (Mark 15:25). Matthew and Luke do not give a time but they do agree with Mark that the darkness fell at noon (the sixth hour).

The best way to resolve the apparent conflict is to remember that time designations in that day lacked the precision of today. Such designations as 10:35 a.m. were impossible. In general, one referred to the third, sixth, and ninth hours (9:00 a.m., noon, 3:00 p.m.). Almost all of the specific references to time in the New Testament use these time designations (exceptions are Matthew 20:9 and John 1:39; 4:52). A person could be more precise, but generally people spoke in broad terms concerning time. It should be noticed that John says 'about' noon.

John refers to the day of Jesus' crucifixion as the day of preparation for the Passover. The Synoptic Gospels indicate that Jesus was crucified on a Friday, the day before the Sabbath (Mark 15:42) and the day after the Passover meal was celebrated (cf. John 13:1; 18:28; 19:14, 31). So, was Passover from Thursday night to Friday night (following the Jewish custom of counting a day from sundown to sundown) or from Friday night to Saturday night? John and the Synoptic Gospels actually agree that Jesus ate the Passover meal on Thursday night and was crucified on Friday. While John 13:1-2 does not refer specifically to the Passover meal it does seem to imply it. John 18:28 can refer to the *chagigah*, a lunchtime meal on the day after the initial sacrifice of the lambs; and 19:14, 31 probably refer to the day of preparation for the Sabbath during Passover week (cf. Mark 15:42).[1] The drama ends just as Jesus had predicted it would (19:16).

Reflections
The Jewish leaders rejected the kingship of Jesus and claimed Caesar as their king. They acknowledged a human power that they thought could help them maintain their own status. Instead, Roman power ultimately destroyed Jerusalem and the temple and decimated the Jewish people. The next generation paid dearly for the sins of their fathers. Today, people refuse to allow Jesus to be their king for much the same reason; they desire to maintain the status quo in their lives. They make choices based upon short-term goals and personal comfort and, like the religious leaders,

---

1. Other suggested solutions to the issue are: (1) Jesus followed an Essene or Galilean calendar that differed from others. This explanation is unlikely because of the confusion that would have been caused in Jerusalem by different groups celebrating on different days. (2) Jesus and the disciples celebrated a day early since Jesus knew He was to die. While this is possible, there is no corroborating evidence and it contradicts Mark 14:12. (3) The Synoptic Gospels are right and John has made an unhistorical modification in order to bring out the theological significance of Jesus as the Passover Lamb, but elsewhere John brings out the theological significance of Jesus at various feasts without the falsification of the data. (4) John is historically accurate and the Synoptic Gospels are chronologically wrong. While this fits John's concern for chronology, there seems to be no motivation for the change by the Synoptic evangelists.

claim another king instead of Jesus. Let us mark, with great fear and trembling, the terrible danger one falls into when one continues to reject the light. There is such a thing as judicial blindness. The words of Solomon seem especially appropriate to such a people: 'Because I called and you refused, I stretched out my hand and no one paid attention; and you neglected all my counsel, and did not want my reproof; I will also laugh at your calamity; I will mock when your dread comes' (Prov. 1:24-26).

Pilate lets this unbelievable opportunity slip through his fingers. Three times he pronounced Jesus 'not guilty' (18:38; 19:4, 6). He even tried to set Jesus free (19:12). But Pilate would not stand for truth or justice in the face of fierce opposition; instead he did everything he could to preserve his position at the expense of doing what was right. Under pressure we too may feel our security threatened. But unlike Pilate, we must stand for what is right even if the consequences mean personal loss. If we don't, we will lose something even more valuable – our integrity. When we know what is right and do not do it we sin (James 4:17).

The most important truth in this passage is Christological. Jesus is accused of being the 'Son of God' (3:16-17; 3:35-36; 6:40; 8:35-36; 14:13; 17:1; 20:30-31). We see here the Savior of the world scourged, crowned with thorns, mocked, beaten, rejected by His own people, unjustly condemned by a judge who did not believe that He had done anything wrong, and finally delivered up to one of the most painful forms of execution the world has ever known. Yet, this was the eternal Son of God, whom myriads of angels worshiped and served. This was He who came into the world to save sinners, and after living a sinless life, He spent the final three years of that life going about doing good, teaching the crowds, feeding the hungry, giving sight to the blind, and setting free the captives. Let us all stand in amazement at the wondrous love of Jesus. Let us never forget as we consider this story of suffering that Jesus suffered for our sins, He was bruised for our iniquities, the just for the unjust, the chastisement of our peace was upon Him. When He was reviled He did not revile in return … .

STUDY QUESTIONS

1. What do you think is the major point John wants to make in this passage?

2. How do you think Pilate's question, 'What is truth?' should be understood?

3. What do you think John wanted his readers to understand by Pilate's phrase, 'Behold the man'?

4. Can you think of a possible modern day parallel to the choice of 'Caesar' over God?

34

The Death of God's Son
(John 19:17-42)

There may be no greater pain than watching a loved one die. This is especially true if you understand that person's death to be the end of your hopes and dreams. This was never truer than when Jesus died. The disciples left virtually everything to follow Him. They believed Him to be the long-awaited Messiah. They saw Him do things that no other person had ever done – turn water into wine, heal the sick, feed the multitudes, walk on water, and resuscitate the dead. His teaching was like no teaching they had ever heard. They were confident that He was going to set up an earthly kingdom. But now He hung on a cross, His life slipping away and all their dreams and aspirations were destroyed.

The 'hour' of Jesus has arrived and the Son of Man is 'lifted up'. John communicates at least three thoughts to his readers from this scene. First, by recounting Jesus' words from the cross he wants us to understand that Jesus remained in control of His destiny (19:26, 28, 30). Second, by the references to the fulfillment of Scripture he wants to communicate how God's purposes were being meticulously fulfilled in those events (19:24, 28, 36). Third, as Jesus dies, He dies as the victorious Passover Lamb.

Much of what John describes in this passage is distinctive to his Gospel. In fact, this is true of all the Gospel writers in their description of Jesus' crucifixion and death. Each evangelist focused on those aspects of Jesus' crucifixion that suited the theological points each wanted to make.[1] John's unique contributions are the exchange between Pilate and the religious leaders over the wording on the inscription (19:19-22), Jesus' seamless garment (19:23-25a), Jesus entrusting Mary into the Beloved Disciple's care (19:25b-27), Jesus' cry of thirst (19:28-29), Jesus' final words (19:30), the events immediately following His death (19:31-37), and Nicodemus' role in the burial of Jesus (19:38-42).

The journey to Golgotha (19:17-18)

Jesus begins the journey to Golgotha carrying His own crossbeam. The vertical beam remained at the crucifixion site. At some point along the way Jesus collapses and Simon of Cyrene is forced to carry the crossbeam for the remainder of the way (cf. Mark 15:21). John does not mention this but instead keeps the focus on Jesus' command of His destiny.[2]

John refers to the location by both its Greek ('Place of a Skull') and Aramaic ('Golgotha') names. 'Calvary' comes from Latin. John notes that they went outside the city. We don't know why the site was called the 'Place of the Skull'. Some suggest that the name of the site was the result of a rock formation (Gordon's Calvary). Others propose that the name derived from the terrible activity that took place there. The traditional site of Jesus' crucifixion and burial is now beneath the Church of the Holy Sepulchre.

John describes the event itself very briefly: 'There they crucified him.' The brevity of the description, which is true of each Gospel, may be due to the fact that the brutality of crucifixion was well known. In addition, John mentions two criminals were crucified alongside Jesus. The presence of the

---

1. There are several features found in the Synoptic Gospels that are not found in John's account: Simon carrying the cross-beam, the presence of the thieves, the mockery of the bystanders, the tearing of the temple veil, Jesus' cry of abandonment, and the acclamation of the centurion. There are a number of places where the Synoptics and John overlap: the journey from the praetorium to Golgotha, Jesus being crucified with others, the casting of lots for His garments, the placing of the placard over the cross, the offer of wine to drink, and the presence of women at the site.

2. Some suggest that John evokes memories of Isaac carrying the wood for his own sacrifice, but John does not refer to it.

criminals is reminiscent of Isaiah's words: 'He was numbered with transgressors' (Isa. 53:12; cf. Luke 22:37).

Pilate and the religious leaders argue over the placard (19:19-22)

It was customary to hang a sign on the cross over the victim's head indicating his name and crime. The wording Pilate chooses infuriates the religious leaders ('Jesus the Nazarene, the king of the Jews'). It is another insult to the Jewish leadership. It is written in three languages – Aramaic, Latin, and Greek, which helps explain the variation in wording between the Gospels. Aramaic was the language of the Jewish people; Latin the language of the Roman government; and Greek the language spoken by people throughout the empire. The irony is that what Pilate means as a taunt to the Jews is in reality a true statement. Even in this dark moment, Jesus is declared king to the world (cf. 12:31, 32).

The fulfillment of Scripture (19:23-37)

John states three times in this section that particular events took place to fulfill Scripture (19:24, 28, 36).

The soldiers cast lots for Jesus' seamless garment (19:23-24).
The soldiers responsible for policing the crucifixion site kept the few possessions that crucified persons brought with them to the cross. Here the soldiers divide up Jesus' outer garments but cast lots for His more expensive seamless inner garment. Only John describes this latter detail.[3] The soldiers' actions unwittingly fulfill Psalm 22:18, a fact that reinforces the reality of God's control over the events, down to the seemingly most insignificant details.

---

3. What John intended to communicate by recounting this event has been debated. Some think John may be recalling the vestments of the High Priest (Exod. 28; 39:27-31; Lev.16:4). Yet, there is no mention in the Old Testament of them being seamless (however, this detail is referred to by Josephus in his *Antiquities* 3.7.16). In addition, while John clearly exploits Passover symbolism, he does not interpret Jesus' death or ministry against a priestly background. C. K. Barrett, *The Gospel According to St. John: An Introduction with Commentary and Notes on the Greek Text*, 2nd ed. (Philadelphia: Westminster Press, 1978, 550), understands the reference to be symbolic of the unity Jesus creates through His mission to the world (since Roman soldiers do not tear the garment). However, while John stresses unity in chapter 17, one wonders if his readers would easily recognize that symbolism here.

It is striking that as the soldiers gamble for the meager possessions of a dying man, Jesus demonstrates selfless concern for His mother. There can be no starker contrast in attitude between the world's kingdom and Christ's kingdom.

The mother of Jesus and the Beloved Disciple (19:25-27)
Jesus turns His attention to His mother as death quickly approaches. One wonders why John includes this emotional exchange. It is likely another example of Jesus' selflessness. Mary would have been in a very vulnerable situation. The presence of Jesus' enemies and the Roman soldiers created a volatile situation. Jesus, it seems, wants to make sure that His mother is not caught in the middle of a potentially violent scenario. Jesus' brothers at this point did not believe in Him.[4]

The death of Jesus (19:28-30)
Jesus dies with the same deliberation and calm that has characterized His entire Passion in John's Gospel. John's description is distinctive in comparison to the Synoptics. In the Synoptics there is the intense mocking and the cry of abandonment. In John, Jesus remains in control of events. Jesus' cry, 'I thirst,' is a unique Johannine touch. In Mark and Matthew, Jesus is offered a sponge filled with vinegar. In Luke, the offer is clearly designated as an act of mockery (Luke 23:36-37). Jesus is aware that death is near. His mouth is dry and He likely was having a difficult time communicating. Thus, He asks for a drink in order to moisten His mouth and to be strengthened for a final declaration. At the same time, even this request fulfills Scripture. The Scripture is likely Psalm 69:21, or possibly Psalm 22:15. John's mention of the hyssop reminds the reader of the Passover (Exod. 12:22, 23; cf. Heb. 9:18-20). In Egypt the Jews used hyssop to brush the lamb's blood on the doorposts during the first Passover. Jesus is God's Passover Lamb (1:29, 36), and His blood likewise saves.

---

4. This is the only reference to the sister of Jesus' mother in the New Testament. She may have been the wife of Zebedee (Salome), the mother of James and John. This would have made Jesus and John cousins. Mary the wife of Clopas is mentioned directly only here in the New Testament. Mary Magdalene is present both at the cross and the empty tomb (20:1ff).

After taking a drink, Jesus cries out in victory and exhaustion, 'It is finished' (19:30). His work of salvation is complete. He has fulfilled His mission of redemption and completed the work the Father sent Him to do. Peter put it this way: 'He himself bore our sins in his body on the cross, so that we might die to sin and live to righteousness; for by his wounds you were healed' (1 Pet. 2:24; cf. Isa. 53:4).

Each evangelist crafts the final moments of Jesus' life in a manner consistent with each Gospel's overall portrayal. In John, Jesus bows His head and gives up His spirit. The wording emphasizes the voluntary nature of His death. The reference to the giving up of His spirit refers not to the Holy Spirit, but to His human spirit, which He voluntarily releases to return to His Father's presence until His bodily resurrection. The word translated 'gave up' is the same word that has been used to describe Jesus being handed over to His enemies (John 18:2, 5, 30, 35, 36; 19:11, 16).

The events immediately following Jesus' death
(19:31-37)
Once again this scene is unique to John. The Jews do not want the bodies languishing on the cross on a Sabbath during Passover. It is determined that their legs should be broken, so hastening death by asphyxiation. The legs of those on either side of Jesus are broken first. When it is discovered that Jesus is already dead, the soldiers do not break His legs, but as either a final act of brutality or in order to confirm his death, one pierces His side with a sword and out flows 'blood and water'. It is not immediately obvious what John intended by the reference to the blood and water. The spear likely pierced the pericardial sac around the heart of Jesus. The blood and water confirm both the reality of His death and His true humanity. John must have felt the incident to be very important and comments that it was well attested (19:35).

These two events are said to fulfill Scripture. The fact that the soldiers do not break Jesus' legs highlights further Passover imagery (19:36; cf. Exod. 12:46). The reference to the piercing of His side is a fulfillment of Zechariah 12:10.

The burial by Joseph and Nicodemus (19:38-42)

Joseph of Arimathea had not publicly identified with Jesus before requesting permission to bury His body (19:38). This request would put his reputation at risk. He will bury Jesus in his own tomb (cf. Matt. 27:60). Surprisingly, he is joined by Nicodemus (19:39), like Joseph a member of the Jewish Sanhedrin, which voted to seek Jesus' crucifixion. It does not appear that either of them favored the decision. This is clearly true of Joseph (cf. Luke 23:50-51).

Nicodemus provides an enormous amount of aromatic spices to be used inside the linen grave clothes in which Jesus was to be buried (19:40). The Jews did not embalm as the Egyptians, but the aromatic spices lessened the smell of decomposition and showed honor to the deceased. The significant amount was enough for a regal burial (2 Chron. 16:14).

The story of a once promising life appears over. His resting place in Joseph's tomb is not far from the site of crucifixion (19:41-42). This allowed the body to be buried before sundown.[5] Jesus' vision of the inauguration of a new kingdom is buried with Him, or so it appeared. The messianic hope of Abraham's seed is crushed once again. As the sun begins to set, His followers hide in dejection, despair, and despondency. The shattered dreams of a new day fade as the sun sets over the holy city. But, as is often the case when God is at work, human expectations and perceptions are not to be trusted. While Jesus' burial seems like the end of the story, in reality it is just the beginning!

Reflections

God's mercy was disguised on the hill called 'the place of a skull'. When Jesus said, 'It is finished,' He brought to fulfillment all that the sacrificial system required – a once-for-all sacrifice for sin that needed never to be repeated. Jesus fulfilled what the sacrificial system had pointed to from its inception.

Jesus' throne was disguised as a cross on Golgotha. John makes it clear that the crucified one was truly a king. Even before His birth the angel Gabriel told Mary that the Lord

---

5. Jewish custom recognized sunset as the beginning of a new day.

God would give to Him the throne of His father David (Luke 1:32, 33). Shortly after His birth the Magi came from the east to worship the newborn 'king of the Jews' (Matt. 2:2). Less than a week before His crucifixion, as He entered Jerusalem, the crowds cried out, 'King of Israel' (cf. 12:13). He confirmed to Pilate that He was a king, but His kingdom was not of this world (19:36. 37). As He hung on the cross His kingship was proclaimed in Aramaic, Latin, and Greek. He was born a king, lived as a king (though veiled to human eyes), was lifted up and crucified for being a king, and ultimately was buried like a king. We should take care that we know Jesus as king and His reign is established in our hearts.

Finally, this passage demonstrates the horrific nature of sin. If God allowed His Son to be tortuously treated and crucified for the salvation of sinners, sin must be more terrible than we could ever have imagined. Furthermore, people can never know the depth of God's love for them until they see it through the cross. Even then God's love is so great that it is not fully comprehensible to the human mind (Eph. 3:17-19). Whenever we feel abandoned by God, go back to Christ's cross and catch a fresh glimpse of God's boundless love for sinners. God loves you (John 3:16)!

Study Questions

1. What aspects of Johannine irony do you find in this passage?

2. What do you think Jesus meant when He said, 'It is finished'?

3. What do you think John wanted us to think about Nicodemus in light of this passage?

4. What elements in this passage contribute to the thought that Jesus is our Passover Lamb?

35

The Bodily Resurrection of Jesus Christ
(John 20:1-31)

Jesus' bodily resurrection from the dead is the cornerstone of the Christian faith. It is an essential element in the gospel message (1 Cor. 15:1-8). His resurrection is ground zero for debates over the truthfulness of orthodox Christianity. One prominent scholar has suggested that the body was thrown into a shallow grave and eaten by wild dogs.[1] Others suggest that His post-resurrection appearances to His followers were hallucinations. Yet the historicity of His resurrection has been ably defended and stands at the heart of the Christian hope. All four Gospels come to their climax in the resurrection narratives, but each does so in its own way. John's account is unique throughout. However, all four Gospels agree on the fact of the empty tomb and the bodily resurrection of Jesus from the dead.

Four major events take place in this chapter: Mary Magdalene's discovery of the empty tomb and the examination by Peter and by John, the beloved disciple (20:1-10); Mary's dramatic encounter with the risen Jesus (20:11-18); the appearance of Jesus to the disciples when Thomas is absent (20:19-23); and the appearance of Jesus a week later to the disciples with Thomas present (20:24-31).

---

1. John Dominic Crossan, *Who Killed Jesus?* (San Francisco: Harper, 1996), 187-88.

The hopelessness of an empty crypt (20:1-10)

It is hard to imagine the sense of hopelessness and despair that Mary must have felt as she made her way to the tomb that Sunday morning. Just months before no one could have dreamed that things would have turned out like they did. Little did Mary know that her despair was about to turn into inexpressible joy!

Mary Magdalene's discovery (20:1-2)
Early Sunday morning Mary Magdalene makes her way to the tomb, only to discover the stone rolled away from the entrance (20:1). The fact that she comes to the tomb 'while it was still dark' is likely a chronological reference, as well as symbolizing her lack of understanding (cf. 3:2).[2] The Synoptic Gospels mention the presence of several women, but John's focus is on Mary. The plural 'we' in verse 2 suggests Mary is not alone. While John does not report Mary looking into the tomb, it is clear from verse 2 that she does. Luke describes her as a woman once tormented by demonic possession, but who was set free by Jesus (Luke 8:2-3). Mary immediately reports her discovery of the empty tomb to Simon Peter and John, 'the disciple whom Jesus loved' (20:2-4).

Peter and John examine the empty tomb (20:3-10)
Peter and John race to the tomb in response to Mary's report. John arrives first but does not enter (20:3-4). John stresses the fact that the linen strips and the burial cloth were not in disarray (20:5-7). His emphasis suggests that the tomb was not ransacked by grave robbers. Peter, unlike John, doesn't hesitate to go right in. John then enters the tomb and the text says simply, 'he saw and believed' (20:8). It seems most likely that John believes Jesus to be alive, but he does not yet understand that Jesus' resurrection was foretold in the Scriptures. The text does not report if he said anything to anyone. The narrative concludes with the two disciples leaving, but Mary remains behind (20:10).

---

2. Brown, *John*, 2:980-81.

Jesus appears to Mary Magdalene (20:11-18)

20:11-15: The appearance to Mary is especially wonderful, for she was 'no one special'. In contrast to the two disciples, Mary refuses to leave until she finds out what has happened to the body (20:11). She is heartbroken; twice John mentions her weeping (20:11, 15). This is what Jesus prophesied in the upper room (cf. 16:20).

The presence of angels at the tomb is mentioned in all four Gospels (Matt. 28:2; Mark 16:5; Luke 24:4); however, the angels do not play a major role in John's account. Their primary function is to question Mary concerning her tears. The question may be understood as a subtle rebuke ('Why are you crying?'). She is deeply concerned that the body of Jesus should be given an honorable burial (20:12, 13). When Jesus appears He asks her essentially the same question as the angels and her reply is much the same (20:14, 15). As to why she did not recognize Him, it is difficult to say. It could be that her tears blurred her vision. Yet, several times after His resurrection those who knew Him fail to recognize Him immediately (cf. John 21:4; Matt. 28:17; Luke 24:16, 37). Apparently, there was something different about the risen Jesus so that He was not immediately recognizable.

20:16-18: Jesus calls her by name and instantly she recognizes His voice (20:16). When the Good Shepherd speaks, His sheep know His voice (cf. 10:3). Mary calls Jesus, *Rabboni,* (cf. Mark 10:51); John translates the Aramaic term for his Greek readers. It is not easy to understand what happens next. It appears Mary falls on her knees and wraps her arms around Jesus so that He cannot get away from her again (20:17). His command ('Stop clinging to me') has been interpreted in various ways. Two thoughts may be in play here. First, He has not yet made His final ascension, so she will have opportunities to see Him again ('for I have not yet ascended to the Father').[3] Second, He may be teaching her that His relationship with her is now different.[4] His words, 'my Father, your Father; my God, your God,' emphasize that

---

3. Beasley-Murray, John, 377; Carson, *John*, 644.

4. Grant Osborne, *The Resurrection Narratives: A Redactional Study* (Grand Rapids: Baker, 1984), 162; Burge, *John*, 556-57.

Jesus' relationship with God is on a different level from hers. Words cannot express the depth of feeling Mary must have communicated when she reported, 'I have seen the Lord' (20:18).

Jesus appears to the disciples, but Thomas is not there (20:19-23)

For several hours the disciples have to take Mary at her word regarding her encounter with Jesus. Later in the day, Jesus appears miraculously in the room with the disciples. John includes the fact that the doors are shut and that they are hiding out of fear of the Jews. The risen Jesus is not limited by closed doors (20:19)! They must have expected a stern rebuke, but Jesus greets them with the normal Hebrew greeting 'peace' – *shalom* (cf. 14:27; 16:33). Surely He means by it more than a simple greeting, for He says it twice (20:19, 21). He identifies Himself by His scars from the crucifixion. Luke indicates that they thought He was a spirit (Luke 24:37). Their joy is a fulfillment of Jesus' earlier prophecy (20:20; cf. 16:20-22). Jesus repeats His greeting a second time to calm their hearts after showing them the scars from His crucifixion.

He then commissions His disciples. As the Father sent Him, He now sends them (20:21). They will be a people on mission (20:21b; cf. 17:18). Jesus does not leave them on their own in the accomplishment of this mission but He equips them for it: 'He breathed on them and said to them, "Receive the Holy Spirit"' (20:22). The word translated 'breathed' is the same word used in the Greek Old Testament in Genesis 2:7 when God breathed life into Adam. It is also used in Ezekiel 37:9 when dry bones are infused with divine life. Scholars are divided on how this event is to be understood and how it relates to the Day of Pentecost in Acts 2.

It is highly unlikely that John has taken the Pentecost event and transposed it back into his narrative.[5] Some understand the relationship between Pentecost and John 20:22 to be the first of a two-stage process, with this being 'empowerment for ministry'

---

5. This seems to be Beasley-Murray's position (Beasley-Murray, *John*, 382). He understands John's narrative as a theological adaption of the historical event in Acts 2.

and Acts 2 to be the indwelling of the Spirit.[6] I think it more likely that we are to understand Jesus' actions along the lines of an enacted parable that foreshadows the coming of the Spirit on the Day of Pentecost.[7] On the basis of the gift of the Spirit, the Spirit-filled church will pronounce through the gospel the forgiveness or retaining of sins based upon a person's response to the gospel (20:23). The words literally read, 'Those whose sins you forgive have already been forgiven; those whose sins you do not forgive have not been forgiven.'[8]

Jesus appears to Thomas (20:24-29)

Jesus' encounter with Thomas is unique to this Gospel. It occurs on the Sunday following the resurrection (20:26). Thomas' fellow-disciples had reported to him the Lord's gracious appearance to them, but he steadfastly refused to believe ('I will not believe') unless he sees physical proof (20:24, 25). The group is gathered together and Jesus suddenly appears in their midst. He greets them for the third time with the word 'peace.' Then He confronts Thomas' doubts. He offers to allow Thomas to touch His scars and challenges him to stop disbelieving and to begin to believe. Thomas not only believes Jesus is alive, but brings out its implication with the words, 'My Lord and my God' (20:28). There is no higher Christological confession in John's Gospel. Thomas goes from doubt of Jesus' resurrection to confession of His deity. Not everyone will have the same opportunity as Thomas did, so those who believe without the opportunity of seeing the resurrected Jesus will be especially blessed (20:29).

John's purpose in writing (20:30-31)

John concludes this chapter by stating his purpose in writing. He indicates the selective nature of what he has written

---

6. Bruce, *Gospel & Epistles of John*, 1:392; 392; Blomberg, *Historical Reliability*, 267, Osborne, *Resurrection Narratives*, 169, understand it to be somewhat analogous to the reception of the Spirit followed by the filling of the Spirit. This approach sees this scene as the fulfillment of the Paraclete promises in the upper room discourse.

7. Carson, John, 655; Köstenberger, John, 574; Ben Witherington, *John's Wisdom: A Commentary on the Fourth Gospel* (Louisville: Westminster John Knox Press, 1995), 342-46.

8. The verbs 'forgiven' and 'retained' are in the perfect tense, emphasizing the present or ongoing result of a completed action.

(20:30). Out of all the miracles that Jesus performed John chose seven, calling them signs. His purpose was that his readers 'may believe that Jesus is the Christ, the Son of God; and that believing you may have life in his name.'

There is a text-critical question as to whether the verb 'believe' is a present or aorist subjunctive. The manuscript evidence is rather evenly divided. The former suggests the Gospel was written to strengthen the faith of believers and points to a Christian audience;[9] the latter leaves the door open to an evangelistic purpose.[10] As mentioned in the introduction, I think it is possible that John wrote with both thoughts in mind.[11] I will repeat what I wrote in the introduction: the Gospel would have likely been read in Christian churches in Asia Minor. As the book was read, believers' faith in Christ would be greatly strengthened and their love for Him would grow deeper. They would also be better equipped to share their faith by using the stories of Jesus they heard read from the Gospel. They would learn how Jesus dealt with different kinds of people, helping them as they evangelized family and friends. Furthermore, it is not unlikely that there would be seekers that would gather with family and friends to learn more about Jesus. As the Gospel was read and taught, undoubtedly many would come to saving faith. Many evangelistic Bible studies begin with the Gospel of John and many seekers begin their search for Jesus there as well.

Reflections
Several thoughts can be highlighted from this chapter. First, Mary's encounter with Jesus is quite instructive. Here is a woman who knew what it was like to be trapped in sin and possessed by demons. She experienced the freedom that comes when Jesus sets a person free. Her love for Jesus was not superficial. While His disciples left the empty tomb behind, she refused to leave. She had no insight that Jesus was alive, but she desired that His body should be given an honorable burial. Casual Christianity knows little of this kind

---

9. Beasley-Murray John, 387-88; Keener, John, 2:1215-16.

10. Carson, John, 662-63.

11. Blomberg, Jesus and the Gospels, 196, 417; Witherington, John's Wisdom, 346.

of devotion because it thinks little of its sin. The more aware we are of our sinfulness and the greater the understanding we have of God's forgiveness the more it will be demonstrated in commitment to Jesus.

Second, Jesus greets the disciples three times with 'Peace be with you' (20:19, 21, 26). Surely He intended it to be more than a mere word of greeting. They will experience peace of conscience through His death and peace of mind through His resurrection.

Third, we see evidence that supports the historicity of Jesus' resurrection. First, none of His followers anticipated His resurrection. They seem completely unprepared for it. They are described as being in hiding. Even after He appears to a number of His followers, Thomas refuses to believe. It seems unlikely that if the disciples were making up the story of the resurrection they would highlight their complete lack of understanding that it was going to happen.

Second, the first witness of the resurrection is a woman. This is not the kind of event first-century Jews would make up if they were fabricating Jesus' resurrection. Women were not considered reliable witnesses. More likely, they would have recounted an initial appearance to one of the twelve.

Third, the disciples are described as hiding in fear from the Jews. One wonders why they would describe themselves in this way if they were making up the resurrection story. One would expect that they would have described themselves as anticipating the resurrection.

Fourth, the discovery of the empty tomb and the appearance of the angels are described succinctly and without great elaboration, very unlike the apocryphal accounts of Jesus' resurrection. John's Gospel presents a historically reliable account of His resurrection.

STUDY QUESTIONS

1. Why do you think Jesus' first appearance was to Mary Magdalene?

2. Why do you think Thomas found it so hard to believe his fellow-disciples?

3. Compare Jesus' commission to the disciples in 20:19-23 with Matthew 28:16-20 and Luke 24:44-49. How are they similar? What is unique about each one?

4. What do you think is the strongest piece of evidence for Jesus' bodily resurrection?

36

'Let's Go Fishing!'
(John 21:1-23)

We can all rejoice in the fact that the God of the Bible is the God of second chances (and third and fourth and fifth…!). Chapter 21 helps us understand how Peter, after he denied Jesus three times, became a leader of the early church.

There are two main opinions concerning John 21. Some consider it to be an addendum to an already completed work. The principal reason it is thought to be supplemental is that John 20:30-31 looks like a fitting conclusion to the Gospel. It seems better, however, to understand chapter 21 as an integral part of the Gospel. As to the fact that John 20:30-31 appears to be a fitting conclusion to us, we should not impose our standards of consistency on the author. The importance of Peter's reinstatement makes it unnecessary to see this chapter as being written by a later redactor. There is really no overwhelming reason not to see it as having been written by John at the same time as the rest of the Gospel.

The most important consideration is why John included it. His primary point in the chapter is to recount Peter's restoration. Several aspects of the chapter point in that direction. First, the miraculous catch of fish harkens back to Peter's initial call in Luke 5:1-11. While the event is not described in John's Gospel, it is likely that the readers would have known of it. John was present at both events (cf. Luke 5:10). Jesus called Peter and the other disciples there to be 'fishers of men'. Thus, Jesus sets the stage to remind them of His call to fish for men.

Second, the reference to the charcoal fire and the thrice repeated question, 'Do you love me?' reminds Peter of his threefold denial by the fire in the high priest's courtyard (18:15-18; 25-27).

Finally, Jesus predicts Peter's death (21:19). In the upper room Peter boldly declared that he would die for Jesus. Eventually he will die for Jesus.

If the primary purpose of the chapter is the reinstatement of Peter, a secondary thought is the missionary outreach of the church.[1] This is not unlikely if there is a connection between Peter's initial call in Luke 5:1-11 and the miraculous catch here. A third purpose in the chapter is to affirm the truthfulness of the Gospel's witness (21:24-25).

Jesus' third appearance (21:1-14)

This is the only resurrection appearance in John's Gospel that takes place in Galilee. This opening section falls into three parts: an amazing catch after a night of futility, John's recognition of Jesus, and a divinely prepared breakfast.

An amazing catch (21:1-6)

21:1-3: The opening verse introduces the chapter. The term 'afterward' is indefinite and makes it impossible to identify with precision when this event took place except that it occurred after the events of chapter 20. John refers again to the Sea of Tiberias instead of Galilee (cf. 6:1). The phrase, 'He manifested *himself* in this way,' suggests John is stressing the revelatory nature of the event and not only its historical factuality. John lists a total of seven disciples (21:2). John himself is one of the seven, being one of Zebedee's two sons.

We should not understand Peter's decision to go fishing in a negative light. Some suggest he is returning to his old profession, but it is more probable that he was finding a way to spend the evening while waiting for another appearance from Jesus (21:3). Several of the disciples join him. The result of the expedition is the same as when they are described as

---

1. Bock, *Jesus According to Scripture*, 550.

fishing all night in Luke's Gospel (Luke 5:4). Night was a good time for fishing because the evening enabled them to escape the heat of the day and they could take their catch to the market in the morning.

21:4-6: As dawn breaks, a stranger on the shore highlights the fact that they have caught nothing. The disciples fail to recognize Jesus (21:4-5). Their failure may have to do with the fact that they are tired, combined with the early morning mist. It should be remembered that Mary, waiting at the tomb, had also failed to recognize Him initially in the garden. It must have stung a bit for the stranger to utter the words, 'Children, you do not have any fish, do you?' John is pointing to Jesus' supernatural insight. How else would he have known that after an entire night of fishing they had not caught anything? Jesus' instruction concerning where to fish is similar to what He said to them a few years before and the result is much the same (21:6; cf. Luke 5:6-7).

An unexpected appearance (21:7-9)
John ('that disciple whom Jesus loved') recognizes that it is Jesus. Peter's reaction is to put on his outer garments, jump into the water, and swim to shore. The other disciples row to shore dragging the enormous catch of fish. The reference to the distance from shore is a subtle indicator of historicity ('about one hundred yards').

A delicious breakfast (21:10-14)
When they arrive on the shore they discover Jesus preparing breakfast for them. He asks them to contribute part of their catch to the feast. While the command is addressed to the group ('Bring some of the fish which you have now caught'), it is Peter who responds.[2] The number of fish caught was 153. The number should be understood as literal rather than symbolic.[3] Like most good fishermen, when they catch a great number of fish, they count every one! As Jesus serves them none of them

---

2. Bruce, *Gospel & Epistles of John*, 1:401, suggests that Peter must have been a man of considerable size and strength to perform this task.

3. Many have tried to find a symbolic reference in the number but the failure of interpreters to agree on what it symbolizes argues against it. For a discussion on various interpretations, see Brown, *John*, 2:1074-76.

ask Him who He is – they knew it was *Him*. They have seen Him serve bread and fish before (cf. 6:11). This is the third time Jesus appeared to the disciples (20:19-23; 20:24-29), not counting His appearance to Mary (20:14).

Jesus' restoration of Peter (21:15-23)

This passage must be taken in conjunction with Peter's threefold denial. Just as Peter denied Jesus three times in the presence of their enemy, now he must affirm his love for Jesus three times in the presence of their friends.

Jesus calls Peter to love and service (21:15-17)
The dialogue between Jesus and Peter is one of the most famous exchanges in the Bible. The seriousness of Jesus' words to Peter can be seen in Jesus using Peter's full name ('Simon, son of John'). It demonstrates His desire to restore the fallen disciple to a position of service. Before this can take place Peter must admit his sin to Jesus and before the other disciples.

The dialogue is filled with numerous synonyms in the Greek text. There are two different words used for love, tending the flock, and for sheep. The only pair that gets much attention is the two words used for love (*agapao* and *phileo*). Jesus uses *agapao* the first two times he asks Peter if he loves Him. Peter responds three times using *phileo*. The third time Jesus asks Peter He uses *phileo*. The question is what should be made of this variation, if anything? In light of the fact that there seems to be no distinction in the other pairs of synonyms used, a distinction should not be made in the two words for love either. It seems most likely that John is using them for stylistic variation.[4]

The important point is that in so serious a matter as the reinstatement of Peter, the great question was whether Peter loved Jesus. Three times Jesus' response to Peter is that Peter is to care for Christ's sheep. When Jesus asks him the third time, 'Simon, son of John, do you love me?', Peter is grieved. He

---

4. D. A. Carson, *Exegetical Fallacies* (Grand Rapids: Baker, rev, 1996), 31-32, 51-55. In addition, both words are used of the Father's love for the Son (3:35; 5:20). John has a habit of introducing slight variations without any real distinction in meaning (cf. 3:5). Furthermore, their conversation would have been in Aramaic and not Greek. The word choice in Greek would be John's. Finally, it is hard to understand why Jesus would lower His standard to Peter's level in the final exchange.

certainly recognized this as an intentional reminder of his threefold denial. Peter appeals to Christ's knowledge of him to answer the question.

In the light of the bonfire, Jesus asks Peter if he loves Him more than 'these' (21:15). Jesus has masterfully recreated the scene when Peter denied Him as he warmed himself by a campfire not too long ago. The word 'these' has no clear antecedent in the sentence. Some believe Jesus was referring to the 'fishing gear'. The thought would then be, 'Do you love me more than you love your old profession?' If this is the point, then Jesus is challenging Peter not to return to his former occupation.

Another possibility is that Jesus is referring to the other disciples. 'Do you love me more than you love these men?' This seems less likely than the previous suggestion because it seems obvious that Peter loved Jesus more than them. He was willing to leave everything to follow Him.

The most likely interpretation is, 'Do you love me more than these men love me?' How could Peter know the depth of their love for Jesus? He could not. Yet, earlier he had asserted confidently, 'Whatever the others might do, I will lay down my life for you' (John 13:37).

Jesus calls Peter to suffering and death (21:18-19)
Peter's commission is followed by a prophecy. The seriousness of the moment is reflected in Jesus' use of 'truly, truly.' The early church understood this to be a reference to Peter's death by crucifixion. Just as Christ's death brought glory to God, so would Peter's. By the time the Gospel was written Peter had glorified Christ in martyrdom. Peter's words, 'I will lay down my life for you,' were ultimately fulfilled (13:37).

Peter's response (21:20-23)
Again Peter is too concerned about what would happen to the beloved disciple. The beloved disciple is doing what Peter was told to do ('the disciple whom Jesus loved following them'). Jesus makes it clear that what He does with the beloved disciple is none of Peter's business. Peter is to concentrate on following Jesus.

In verse 23 John deals with an error that had arisen. The adversative 'but' used here is very strong. It appears that some thought that Jesus suggested that John would not die before the Second Coming. John clarifies Jesus' point for the reader. This verse seems to argue against the fact that John was dead when this Gospel was written. Otherwise, how could anyone say he would not die?

A concluding note of authentication (21:24-25)

It is difficult to know if these final words are John's disciples authenticating the veracity of the Gospel and the beloved disciple's witness, or if John is referring to himself indirectly and in the third person. The difficulty remains with the use of the first person plural 'we know.' It is not unlikely that John is referring to himself and his disciples, or possibly himself and his readers. The final verse reminds us that historical knowledge of Jesus is limited, but we have been given all we need to know in the biblical accounts of His life.

Reflections

The similarity between 21:1-14 and Luke 5:1-11 reminds us that the church is called to 'fish for people'. If the passage is something akin to an enacted parable two points can be made. First, the church must never forget Christ's call to worldwide evangelization (to be 'fishers of men'). Second, if the church is to be successful in actually 'catching men', it must follow the leadership of Christ Jesus. Evangelism and missions that fail to follow Christ's example and teaching will fall flat, represented by the disciples' futility in the passage. Missions and evangelism must be done under the leadership and direction of Jesus if the church is to be faithful to her call.

The latter part of the chapter has much to say to every believer as well. We learn from the exchange of Jesus with Peter that Jesus is most concerned about our love for Him. Earlier He told the disciples, 'If you love me, you will keep my commandments' (14:15, 23). Now He connects love for Him with service, but the point that He drives home is that love must precede true service, and service must never be a substitute for love.

How did Peter do with his second commission? The answer is found in the Book of Acts. What was true of Peter is true to a lesser degree of all of God's people. While we may not be called to a key leadership position in the church, we are called to love Christ by serving His people. To be disconnected from Christ's people is to be disconnected from Christ. To fail or refuse to serve Christ's people is to fail to love Christ.

Finally, Peter's death is a clear rebuke to our own lackadaisical approach to Christian living. He gave up his life, yet we seldom will even give up our sin – pride, anger, ambition, and arrogance. Peter was used of God because he gave his life to Jesus – will we give ours to Him?

STUDY QUESTIONS

1. Why do you think John included chapter 21?

2. How does it fit in with the overall message of the Gospel (cf. 20:30-31)?

3. What do you think this passage teaches us about the scope of missions?

4. What are the implications for a believer from Jesus' encounter with Peter?

Subject Index

Scripture Index

The Focus on the Bible Commentary Series
Old Testament

Genesis: The Beginning of God's Plan of Salvation
– Richard P. Belcher
ISBN 978-1-84550-963-7

Deuteronomy: The Commands of a Covenant God – Allan Harman
ISBN 978-1-84550-268-3

Joshua: No Falling Words – Dale Ralph Davis
ISBN 978-1-84550-137-2

Judges: Such a Great Salvation – Dale Ralph Davis
ISBN 978-1-84550-138-9

Ruth & Esther: God Behind the Seen
– A. Boyd Luter/Barry C. Davis
ISBN 978-1-85792-805-9

1 Samuel: Looking on the Heart – Dale Ralph Davis
ISBN 978-1-85792-516-6

2 Samuel: Out of Every Adversity – Dale Ralph Davis
ISBN 978-1-84550-270-6

1 Kings The Wisdom and the Folly – Dale Ralph Davis
ISBN 978-1-84550-251-5

2 Kings: The Power and the Glory – Dale Ralph Davis
ISBN 978-1-84550-096-2

1 Chronicles: God's Faithfulness to the People of Judah
– Cyril J. Barber
ISBN 978-1-85792-935-5

2 Chronicles: God's Blessing of His Faithful People – Cyril J. Barber
ISBN 978-1-85792-936-2

Psalms 1-89: The Lord Saves – Eric Lane
ISBN 978-1-84550-180-8

Psalms 90-150: The Lord Reigns – Eric Lane
ISBN 978-1-84550-202-7

Proverbs: Everyday Wisdom for Everyone – Eric Lane
ISBN 978-1-84550-267-6

Ecclesiastes: The Philippians of the Old Testament
– William D. Barrick
ISBN 978-1-84550-776-3

Song of Songs: A Biblical-Theological, Allegorical, Christological Interpretation – James M. Hamilton Jr.
ISBN 978-1-78191-396-3

Isaiah: A Covenant to be Kept for the Sake of the Church
– Allan Harman
ISBN 978-1-84550-053-5

Jeremiah and Lamentations: The Death of a Dream, and What Came After – Michael Wilcock
ISBN 978-1-78191-148-8

Daniel: A Tale of Two Cities – Robert Fyall
ISBN 978-1-84550-194-5

Hosea: The Passion of God – Tim Chester
ISBN 978-1-78191-368-0

Joel and Obadiah: Disaster and Deliverance
– Iwan Rhys Jones
ISBN 978-1-78191-602-5

Amos: An Ordinary Man with an Extraoridinary Message
– T. J. Betts
ISBN 978-1-84550-727-5

Jonah, Michah, Nahum, Habakkuk & Zephaniah – John L. Mackay
ISBN 978-1-85792-392-6

Haggai, Zechariah & Malachi: God's Restored People
– John L. Mackay
ISBN 978-1-85792-067-3

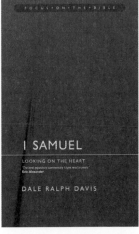

ISBN 978-1-85792-516-6

ISBN 978-1-84550-270-6

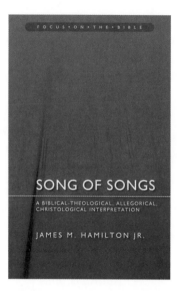

Song of Songs: A Biblical-Theological, Allegorical, Christological Interpretation – James M. Hamilton Jr.
ISBN 978-1-78191-396-3

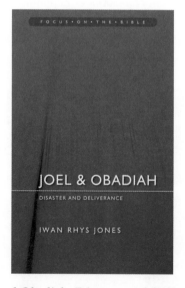

Joel and Obadiah: Disaster and Deliverance
– Iwan Rhys Jones
ISBN 978-1-78191-602-5

The Focus on the Bible Commentary Series

New Testament

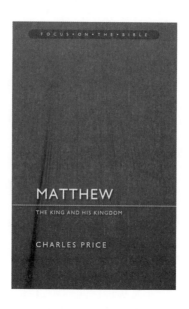

Matthew: The King and His Kingdom – Charles Price
ISBN 978-1-78191-146-4

Acts: Witnesses to Him – Bruce Milne
ISBN 978-1-84550-507-3

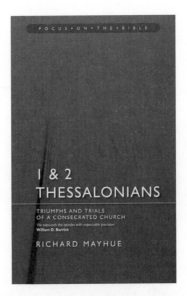

1 & 2 Thessalonians: Triumphs and Trials of a Consecrated Church
– Richard Mayhue
ISBN 978-1-85792-452-7

1 & 2 Peter & Jude: Christian Living in an Age of Suffering
– Paul Gardner
ISBN 978-1-78191-129-7

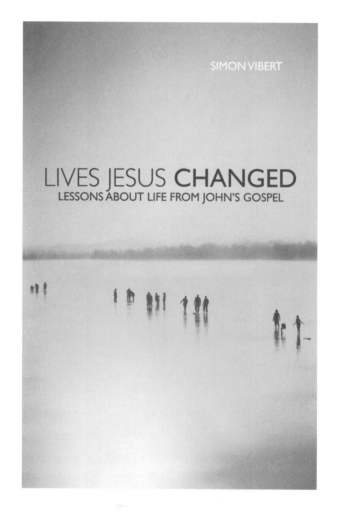

SIMON VIBERT

LIVES JESUS **CHANGED**
LESSONS ABOUT LIFE FROM JOHN'S GOSPEL

ISBN 978-1-84550-543-1

Lives Jesus Changed

SIMON VIBERT

If you look at a family album we will begin to get an idea of the events, which have occurred in the life of that particular family. John's Gospel gives a snapshot of Jesus life and the lives he changed. John's gospel tells the story of Jesus the saviour of the world who came in flesh to forgive sins. Simon Vibert invites us to come and see the lives Jesus changed. But all these characters that we meet are not the one that the people had been waiting for. Jesus was that one but all these characters were 'signposts' that pointed to Jesus so that might cause us to respond. Ideal for individuals or small group studies.

John the evangelist was a consummate chronicler and Simon Vibert's book reflects his genius... Vibert shows us how the form is the vehicle that carries the story forward. In fact we feel close to these people and are drawn into their stories.

Paul Wells

Adjunct dean of the Faculté Jean Calvin in Aix-en-Provence, France

One of the ways in which Matthew, Mark and Luke's Gospels differ from John is that they recount Jesus speaking to crowds, whereas in John, we have many private interviews and conversations. This is the realm that Simon Vibert has marvellously mined in Lives Jesus Changed. Quite rightly the emphasis is not so much on the characters themselves but rather at the Lord Jesus and what He was - and is - able to do in numerous lives. Each chapter is very accessible and heart-warming.

Jonathan Fletcher

Minister, Emmanuel Church, Wimbledon, London

Simon Vibert is Vice Principal and Director of the School of Preaching at Wycliffe Hall, Oxford. Prior to that he was the minister of St. Luke's Church of England, in Southwest London. He studied in the USA, taught at Bible School in Haiti and is Chairman of Fellowship of Word & Spirit in Southwark Diocese. Simon is a preaching facilitator with Lanham Partnership and is married with 3 children.

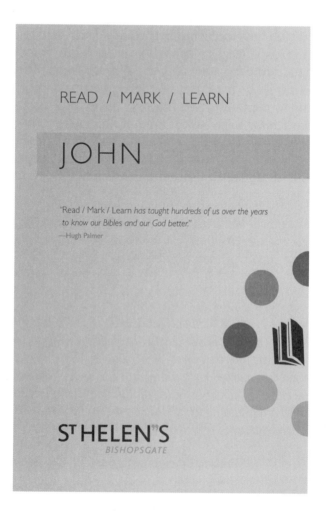

READ / MARK / LEARN

JOHN

"Read / Mark / Learn *has taught hundreds of us over the years to know our Bibles and our God better.*"
—Hugh Palmer

ST HELEN'S
BISHOPSGATE

ISBN 978-1-84550-361-1